T0185977

Communications in Computer and Information Science 1429

Editorial Board Members

Joaquim Filipe ⓘ
  Polytechnic Institute of Setúbal, Setúbal, Portugal

Ashish Ghosh
  Indian Statistical Institute, Kolkata, India

Raquel Oliveira Prates ⓘ
  Federal University of Minas Gerais (UFMG), Belo Horizonte, Brazil

Lizhu Zhou
  Tsinghua University, Beijing, China

More information about this series at http://www.springer.com/series/7899

Johanna Barzen (Ed.)

Service-Oriented Computing

15th Symposium and Summer School, SummerSOC 2021
Virtual Event, September 13–17, 2021
Proceedings

Editor
Johanna Barzen 🆔
University of Stuttgart
Stuttgart, Germany

ISSN 1865-0929 ISSN 1865-0937 (electronic)
Communications in Computer and Information Science
ISBN 978-3-030-87567-1 ISBN 978-3-030-87568-8 (eBook)
https://doi.org/10.1007/978-3-030-87568-8

© Springer Nature Switzerland AG 2021
This work is subject to copyright. All rights are reserved by the Publisher, whether the whole or part of the material is concerned, specifically the rights of translation, reprinting, reuse of illustrations, recitation, broadcasting, reproduction on microfilms or in any other physical way, and transmission or information storage and retrieval, electronic adaptation, computer software, or by similar or dissimilar methodology now known or hereafter developed.
The use of general descriptive names, registered names, trademarks, service marks, etc. in this publication does not imply, even in the absence of a specific statement, that such names are exempt from the relevant protective laws and regulations and therefore free for general use.
The publisher, the authors and the editors are safe to assume that the advice and information in this book are believed to be true and accurate at the date of publication. Neither the publisher nor the authors or the editors give a warranty, expressed or implied, with respect to the material contained herein or for any errors or omissions that may have been made. The publisher remains neutral with regard to jurisdictional claims in published maps and institutional affiliations.

This Springer imprint is published by the registered company Springer Nature Switzerland AG
The registered company address is: Gewerbestrasse 11, 6330 Cham, Switzerland

Preface

The 15th Symposium and Summer School on Service Oriented Computing (Summer-SOC 2021) continued a successful series of summer schools that started in 2007. As the COVID-19 pandemic did not allow travel, SummerSOC 2021 unfortunately was turned into a virtual event. SummerSoC regularly attracts world-class experts in service oriented computing (SOC) to present state-of-the-art research during a week-long program organized in several thematic tracks: IoT, formal methods for SOC, cloud computing, data science, advanced manufacturing, software architecture, digital humanities, quantum computing, and emerging topics. The advanced summer school is regularly attended by top researchers from academia and industry as well as by PhD and graduate students.

During the SummerSOC symposium original research contributions in the areas mentioned above were presented. All accepted contributions were submitted in advance and were subject to a single-blind peer review process. Each paper was reviewed by at least three reviewers. Based on the reviews, the program chairs accepted or rejected contributions. Out of 24 submitted contributions, only 11 were accepted with an acceptance rate of less than 50%. The contributions were extensively discussed after their presentation during the paper session. In addition to the reviewers' comments, the feedback from these discussions was incorporated into the final versions of the papers published in this special issue.

The volume is structured into three parts focusing on (i) quantum computing, (ii) advanced application architecture, and (iii) service-based applications. The first article in the section on quantum computing introduces a connection between Petri nets and quantum systems. The next article provides quantum computing patterns for hybrid quantum algorithms, followed by a vision on quantum service-oriented computing. The final article of the first section focuses on automating the comparison of quantum compilers for quantum circuits; this last contribution received the SummerSOC Young Researcher Award sponsored by ICSOC. The section on advanced application architecture provides four contributions proposing approaches on how to address the adaptivity problem by formalizing poly-/multi-store topology descriptions via blueprints, how to increase failure tolerance in model-driven IoT applications by feedback loops, investigating the use of machine learning techniques in random physical systems, and validating data quality assessment with a smart contract approach. Finally, the first article of the section on service-based applications introduces a model-based methodology for automatically identifying failure causalities in microservice-based applications. The next article provides a Delphi study with industry experts on the importance and impact on software quality of RESTful API design rules. The section is concluded by an article that proposes to switch the refactoring perspective from implementation to integration and studies how refactoring can be applied to the problem domain of agile service API design.

August 2021   Johanna Barzen

Organization

General Chairs

Schahram Dustdar   Technische Universität Wien, Austria
Frank Leymann   Universität Stuttgart, Germany

Organization Committee

Johanna Barzen   Universität Stuttgart, Germany
George Koutras   OpenIT, Greece
Themis Kutsuras   OpenIT, Greece .

Steering Committee

Marco Aiello   Universität Stuttgart, Germany
Schahram Dustdar   Technische Universität Wien, Austria
Christoph Gröger   Bosch, Germany
Frank Hentschel   Universität zu Köln, Germany
Willem-Jan van Heuvel   Eindhoven University of Technology, The Netherlands
Rania Khalaf   IBM, USA
Frank Leymann   Universität Stuttgart, Germany
Kostas Magoutis   University of Crete, Greece
Bernhard Mitschang   Universität Stuttgart, Germany
Dimitris Plexousakis   University of Crete, Greece
Wolfgang Reisig   Humboldt-Universität, Germany
Norbert Ritter   Universität Hamburg, Germany
Jakka Sairamesh   CapsicoHealth Inc. USA
Sanjiva Weerawarana   WSO2, Sri Lanka
Guido Wirtz   Universität Bamberg, Germany
Alfred Zimmermann   Hochschule Reutlingen, Germany

Program Committee

Marco Aiello   Universität Stuttgart, Germany
Johanna Barzen   Universität Stuttgart, Germany
Steffen Becker   Universität Stuttgart, Germany
Wolfgang Blochinger   Hochschule Reutlingen, Germany
Uwe Breitenbücher   Universität Stuttgart, Germany
Antonio Brogi   Università di Pisa, Italy
Guiliano Casale   Imperial College London, UK

Christian Decker	Hochschule Reutlingen, Germany
Stefan Dessloch	TU Kaiserslautern, Germany
Schahram Dustdar	TU Wien, Austria
Sebastian Feld	TU Delft, The Netherlands
Christoph Freytag	Humboldt-Universität, Germany
Frank Hentschel	Universität zu Köln, Germany
Melanie Herschel	Universität Stuttgart, Germany
Willem-Jan van Heuvel	Eindhoven University of Technology, The Netherlands
Christian Kohls	Technische Hochschule Köln, Germany
Eva Kühn	TU Wien, Austria
Ralf Küsters	Universität Stuttgart, Germany
Winfried Lamersdorf	Universität Hamburg, Germany
Frank Leymann	Universität Stuttgart, Germany
Claudia Linnhoff-Popien	Ludwig Maximilians Universität München, Germany
Kostas Magoutis	University of Crete, Greece
Bernhard Mitschang	Universität Stuttgart, Germany
Eric Newcomer	WSO2, Sri Lanka
Daniela Nicklas	Universität Bamberg, Germany
Maria Papadopouli	University of Crete, Greece
Adrian Paschke	Freie Universität Berlin, Germany
Cesare Pautasso	University of Lugano, Switzerland
Srinath Perera	WSO2, Sri Lanka
René Reiners	Fraunhofer FIT, Germany
Wolfgang Reisig	Humboldt-Universität, Germany
Norbert Ritter	Universität Hamburg, Germany
Jakka Sairamesh	CapsicoHealth Inc, USA
Ulf Schreier	Hochschule Furtwangen, Germany
Heiko Schuldt	Universität Basel, Switzerland
Stefan Schulte	TU Wien, Austria
Holger Schwarz	Universität Stuttgart, Germany
Craig Sheridan	University of Edinburgh, UK
Stefan Tai	TU Berlin, Germany
Damian Tamburri	Eindhoven University of Technology, The Netherlands
Massimo Villari	Università degli Studi di Messina, Italy
Stefan Wagner	Universität Stuttgart, Germany
Sanjiva Weerawarana	WSO2, Sri Lanka
Manuel Wimmer	WSO2, Sri Lanka
Guido Wirtz	Johannes Kepler University Linz, Austria
Uwe Zdun	Universität Wien, Austria
Alfred Zimmermann	Hochschule Reutlingen, Germany
Olaf Zimmermann	Hochschule für Technik Rapperswil, Switzerland

Additional Reviewers

Martin Beisel
Darya Martyniuk
George Stamatiou
Daniel Vietz
Vladimir Yussupov

Contents

Quantum Computing

How to Bake Quantum into Your Pet Petri Nets and Have Your Net Theory Too

Heinz W. Schmidt[(⊠)] [iD]

School of Computing Technologies, RMIT University, Melbourne, Australia
heinz.schmidt@icloud.com

Abstract. Petri nets have found widespread use among many application domains, not least due to their human-friendly graphical syntax for the composition of interacting distributed and asynchronous processes and services, based in partial-order dependencies and concurrent executions. Petri nets also come with abstract semantics, and mathematical methods for compositional synthesis, structural checks and behavioural analysis. These have led to the use of various kinds of nets for real-time, distributed and parallel programming languages, software and services systems, with a view to their interfaces and interaction protocols. These affordances make Petri nets invaluable for distributed software architecture approaches focused on components, their mutual dependencies and environment-facing interactions. Quantum computing – and in particular quantum software engineering – is in its infancy and could benefit from the accumulated insights of software architecture research and of net theory, its methods, and its applications.

In this paper, we establish a connection between Petri nets and quantum systems, such that net theory and the component architecture of nets may help in the synthesis and analysis of abstract software models and their interface protocols in hybrid classical-and-quantum programming languages and services systems. We leverage some insights from net formalisms for software specification for a versatile recipe to bake quantum into extant Petri net flavours, and prove universality and compositionality of Petri nets for quantum programming.

Keywords: Component software · Compositionality · Petri nets · Software architecture · Quantum Petri nets · Quantum software engineering · Quantum computing · Model-checking and simulation · Stochastic Petri nets

1 Introduction

Petri nets (PNs) have found widespread use among many application domains. Their graphical syntax is tailored for systems exhibiting concurrency, parallelism and often wide distribution. Their use across different levels and scales from

© Springer Nature Switzerland AG 2021
J. Barzen (Ed.): SummerSOC 2021, CCIS 1429, pp. 3–33, 2021.
https://doi.org/10.1007/978-3-030-87568-8_1

high-level software systems requirements through low-level chip architecture to chemical reactions has assisted their far-flung applications and made PN diagrams a lingua franca for expressing concurrency directly in its interaction with causal partial ordering and mutual exclusion [23,25]. Petri nets empower systems and services analysts, architects and developers alike to engage in informal dialogues with each other and with users, over more or less formal, but accessible, diagrams, about diverse and complex systems issues including extra-functional properties such as liveness, reliability and performance.

Petri nets also come with an abstract semantics, and mathematical methods for composition (gluing nets together in different ways) and for structural and behavioural analysis using the system and services architecture, i.e., its components, their interrelation and interaction with their external environment. The *unmarked net structure* itself is amenable to analysis and transformation, independent of a specific initialisation in a *system net* with a selected initial marking. The structure represents the behaviour rules for all possible initial markings; the system net all runs connected with the initial marking and possible in that net structure. The preparation of the initial state remains outside the model. Net behaviour is observer-independent: a *run* of the net consists of partially ordered occurrences of events tracing, or simulating, the Petri net token game, in which tokens are redistributed from one reachable marking to another. Each marking represents an *alternative world* or *configuration*. The events of a run may be *sequential*, when one depends causally on the result of another, or *concurrent and spatially distributed*, when they are mutually independent. A set of runs may also reflect *choices*, which may non-deterministically or probabilistically evolve to different markings. All possible strict sequential event orders that respect their partial order in a run are *conceivable observations* of the given run, whether placed on a timeline or not. Moreover, the system net behaviour can be analysed and transformed both in terms of an algebra of matrices and the marked net structure itself. Thus, an initial marking of the net system provides resource constraints on top of those set by the net structure. This empowers modellers to determine many crucial characteristics of a time-less synchronisation defined solely by the causal dependency and concurrency of underlying net structure. Different logics have been used for model-checking in terms of system Petri nets and their behaviour. Industry-strength model-checkers exist for years capable of handling hundreds of millions of states (cf. e.g., [2,11]), often using special on-the-fly methods for dealing with the 100s of millions of states without storing transition matrices. The semantics of PNs has led to their use as formal models for real-time, distributed and parallel programming languages, for software systems and services. These affordances make Petri nets invaluable for distributed software and services architecture approaches focused on components, their mutual dependencies and environment-facing interactions.

Quantum computing – and in particular quantum software engineering – is in its infancy and could benefit from the accumulated insights of software architecture research and of net theory, their methods, and their applications. Quantum cryptography is already a viable business; so are niche applications of a number of quantum computing cloud services accessing the first real quantum computers by IBM and Google with a moderate number of qubits [7,27]. Microsoft and others aim to accelerate the development of quantum software with breakthroughs expected in the application of quantum computers to modelling and simulation of real quantum systems that are currently beyond the reach of supercomputers. These include quantum chemistry and pharmaceutics, advanced materials, quantum neurophysiology and others. Distributed quantum computing is making rapid advances. Research in optical networks and photonics has made the quantum internet [15] feasible. Experimental physics have also demonstrated teleportation of coherent quantum states experimentally, over many tens of kilometres and from a ground station on earth to a satellite in orbit [22]. Networked quantum computing is poised to revolutionise distributed computing and lead to orders of magnitude increases in network speeds and bandwidth.

However, advances in distributed algorithms and software architecture for hybrid, i.e., classical-quantum and hardware-software, systems are far from mainstream software engineering. Currently the field of quantum software engineering requires a blend of physics, applied mathematics and theoretical computer science knowledge. Its models and methods are inaccessible to most practitioners and academics in distributed systems analysis, architectural design, software development and testing. An exposition of quantum principles in reasonably widely applied diagrammatic software models and programming language constructs, like those related to Petri nets, has appeal. For research, teaching and practice, especially in parallel and distributed quantum software engineering, PNs could potentially make a significant difference to practitioners, if quantum were accessible for different kinds of Petri nets.

Based on this motivation, the *main contribution* of this paper establishes a connection between Petri nets and abstract quantum systems. We take *entanglement* as *the characteristic trait of quantum* systems and weave it into several kinds of Petri nets orthogonally to all their existing structuring capabilities for causal, cyclic, concurrent and nondetermistic processes. The main result shows that Quantum Petri nets (QPNs) can represent any universal gate set, in fact any circuit in the circuit model of abstract quantum computation. We also prove novel compositionality results.

Structure. The paper starts with an informal introduction to Quantum Petri Nets (QPNs) aiming to minimise any vector space knowledge. We then give a formal definition with the theoretical results, followed by showing how variations in the underlying classical nets can be kept separate from quantum characteristics, yet uniquely extend to QPNs. In a section on related and future work we contrast the novel approach with others, and sketch future research avenues. (Proofs and other technical material are provided as supplementary material on the web at https://arxiv.org/abs/2106.03539.)

2   A Gentle Introduction to Quantum Petri Nets

Before we introduce QPNs formally and connect them with the mathematics of quantum information processing, we briefly look at some simple examples to guide our choices in the design of these models. Beside addressing PN researchers, this introduction is written with a community of net practitioners, software developers and applied informaticians in mind. Many in this community will only be fleetingly familiar with the mathematics of quantum information processing, if at all. Therefore, this section is an attempt to explain the basic principles only in terms of nets and their reachability, wherever possible. We try to tie principles such as superposition, entanglement, tunnelling and teleportation directly to the action of token flow in nets well-known to many in this community. In the words of Petri himself, we aim to "raise the entertainment value from negative to zero" [21] – at least for this gentle introduction. Where they are needed, net-theoretic terminology and notation follow that of Reisig [9] widely used in teaching Petri nets to undergraduate students and practitioners alike. Readers feeling at home in both the "mathematical engine room" of net theory and quantum information theory, may glance at the figures of this section, select relevant text explaining the examples and move straight on to the formalisation of QPNs.

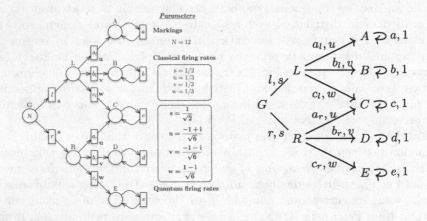

Fig. 1. *Quantum interference in a simplified particle system model of the double-slit experiment. Left:* For any positive integer N, the Place-Transition net (PTN) carries N tokens on place G only, as its initial marking. Every transition can fire at least once. That means, the net is live (L_1-live). Moreover, one of the transitions a through e will eventually keep firing (there is no dead marking). When weighting its transitions with classical rates, the PTN becomes a Stochastic Petri net (SPN) of the bullet scattering. With quantum rates, it is a Quantum PTN (QPTN) representing a photon scattering in a simplified double-slit experiment model. Rates not shown default to 1. *Right:* The weighted reachability relations for N = 1 are shown as a reachability graph. With edge weights, it becomes the weighted reachability graph of the SPN or QPTN to the left. All PTN states remain reachable in the SPN. For the SPN, markings in A, B, D and E are equiprobable at $1/6$. C attracts tokens from both slits, hence with twice the probability, $1/3$. For the QPN however, the probability of reaching C from G^N (here $N = 12$) is zero, as the complex rates cancel each other. Markings in A, B, D and E are equiprobable.

In a nutshell, given a classical PN, the corresponding QPN associates *complex-number rates with transition firings, including with their inseparable firing as an ensemble of mutually concurrent transitions.*

2.1 Transition Firing with Amplitudes

The system net of Fig. 1 uses N tokens (N being a positive integer) and classical rates to model the outcome of firing bullets through two slits. Or it uses quantum rates for modelling photon scattering through the two slits. With classical rates, the resulting Stochastic Petri Net (SPN) describes a gun loaded with N bullets (in G). With transitions l and r, the gun randomly sends a bullet through either the left (L) or right (R) slit. For each slit, a scattering (a, b or c) occurs to three of five possible detectors (A through E). The location of a single bullet can then be found always, by firing the respective transition a through e. For these final transitions, the number of transition firings per time unit can measure the number of bullets reaching the respective place, if $N > 1$. The probability of a single bullet of N hitting place A, B, D or E, respectively, is $su = sv = 1/6$, i.e., the product of transitions weights on the respective path from G. C is reachable either by the firing sequence lc_l or ra_r, i.e., with probability $sw + su = 1/2 \times 1/3 + 1/2 \times 1/3 = 1/3$. The token game played on the system Place-Transition net (PTN) and SPN (to the left) and its reachability graph (RG) or weighted RG (to the right) reflect the same reachability relation. As the sum of non-zero probabilities is non-zero for any SPN, all reachable states have non-zero probability, however small—assuming that transitions have non-zero probability in the first place. In our example, like in the underlying PTN, all transitions $a-e$, including c, are enabled at least in some marking. The system is, what is called in net theory, L_1-live. Moreover, there is no reachable dead marking, as every token will eventually arrive in one of the detector places and the corresponding transition will then keep firing. Like for its SPN sibling, the quantum firing rates of the Quantum PTN (QPTN) to the left weight its firings and hence its token game. This QPTN abstracts from a simple quantum-physical double-slit experiment. Photons are beamed through two slits and are eventually detected. In the real experiment, unsurprisingly the light shows an interference pattern confirming its wave character for very large numbers of photons (N) and any number of runs of the same setup. However surprisingly to physicists about a century ago, for repeated measurements of single photons (here modelled by $N = 1$) the same wave pattern appears in the probabilities of photons arriving in those detector positions, given a sufficiently large number of test runs. The above system QPTN explains a simple cancellation by complex-number rates. Amplitude probabilities exclude C from any marking for all $N \geq 1$. No token will ever be detected in C. Many details pertaining to a real physical quantum system are abstracted from our model: for example, in reality, photons bounce back and force. While complex rates cancel, all tokens make their way to one of the remaining four detectors with equal probability.

For a quantum firing rate, one uses a complex number $c = a + bi$ and follows the paths of the net token game, forming products and sums, in a similar way

to that for the SPN above. In this paper, we do not wish to go into mathematical physics and wave interpretations of complex rates. Suffice to say, that
complex numbers allow compact characterisations of real classical mechanical
waves and also of complex waves appearing in quantum mechanics. A complex
number is also called *amplitude*. Its modulus $|c| = |\sqrt{a^2 + b^2}|$ measures its real
magnitude, its modulus squared $|c|^2 = a^2 + b^2$ a real probability, possibly after
some normalisation in the context of other complex numbers. So in the exam-
ple, we have, $su = \frac{-1+i}{\sqrt{2}\sqrt{6}}$, $sv = \frac{-1-i}{\sqrt{2}\sqrt{6}}$, and $sw = \frac{1-i}{\sqrt{2}\sqrt{6}}$. Since amplitudes can
cancel, $|sw + su|^2 = 0$. No token can reach C from G^N. Moreover, that is the
case, however many experiments are run, and however large $N \in \mathbb{N}$ is chosen
to begin with. Hence transition c is dead and the QPTN is not live for any N.
On the other hand, a short calculation shows that A, B, D and E are equiprobable. We normalise each their four amplitudes with their sum total magnitude
$|m| = |su| + 2|sv| + |sw| = |\sqrt{4}/\sqrt{6}|$. Place A, for instance, is therefore reached
with probability $(|su|/|m|)^2 = |su|^2/|m|^2 = \frac{1}{6}/\frac{4}{6} = 1/4$.

2.2 Superposition States and Measurements over Nets

Let $\mathbb{M}_0$ denote the *reachability set*, i.e., the set of reachable markings, of the
underlying PN with initial marking M_0. For example, in Fig. 1, $\mathbb{M}_0$ is the set of
nodes in the RG on the right. A *superposition state a* (*superposition* for short) is
a function $\mathbb{M}_0 \xrightarrow{a} \mathbb{C}$ that assigns a complex number to each marking in $\mathbb{M}_0$, i.e.,
to each node of the reachability graph of the net. The set of all superpositions
of the reachability set $\mathbb{M}_0$ is also denoted as $\mathbb{A}_0$ and called the *span of the QPN*.
We call $a(m)$ the *probability amplitude* of marking (node) $m \in \mathbb{M}_0$ in a and write
a_m instead of $a(m)$ for brevity. We also denote a algebraically as a weighted sum
of its markings, each placed in a special bracket: $a_1|m_1\rangle + \cdots + a_n|m_n\rangle$, omitting
terms with weight 0. For convenience in examples, we avoid the brackets, when
there is no risk of confusion. The trivial superposition $|m\rangle$ (i.e., $a_m = 1$ and
other $a_{m'} = 0$) represents a single marking. We liberally use familiar algebraic
manipulation of superpositions (and defer the formal treatment to Sect. 3).

The state of a quantum system is not directly observable. Observation requires
a measurement of some sort. A superposition expresses Heisenberg's uncertainty
principle inherent in quantum systems. Only once measured, the subsystem will
be in a certain classical state. Physicists speak of the *collapse* of the wave function. Measurement in a real test setup requires a physical instrument, which is
ultimately a quantum system itself, interfering with the system under test (commonly abbreviated SUT in software engineering). For example, a software-defined
nanorobotic system may consist of a software-controlled laser measuring and con-
trolling some nanorobotic material in superposition. Light beams sent from the
laser change the energy levels and conductivity of particles making up that material. They affect the material properties and shape of the nanorobotic system.
Any test effect before the ultimate collapse can be regarded as a transition in the
SUT from the superposition a prior to the test to another superposition b immediately before the ultimate collapse. That transition is typically forgetful and hence

irreversible, because it abstracts from many characteristics of the system not of interest. The ultimate collapse remains unpredictable.

For QPNs, the result of the ultimate collapse is a marking m. That measurement and collapse may be restricted to a part of the system only, not entangled (see below) with the rest of the system. Then collapse may be restricted to the subsystem state. So, having modelled the test setup in terms of its effect on the SUT by a transition from a to b, the modeller can now inspect the amplitude of a marking m in b (in the model) to determine the probability of that outcome (in the actual system) as $|b_m|^2$, if b is *normal*[1]. A superposition a is defined as normal if $a = a/|a|$, where $|a|$ is the real-valued norm of the superpositon defined by $|a| = \sqrt{\sum_m |a_m|^2}$.

2.3 Entangled Transitions and States

Quantum-mechanically, entanglement requires superposition of *multiple interacting subsystems*. The German term "Verschränkung" and its translation to "entanglement" were coined by physicist Erwin Schrödinger in a 1935 letter to Einstein and soon thereafter used in seminal papers. Schrödinger writes, *two or more separate systems enter into temporary physical interaction due to known forces between them* and can only be described as one inseparable ensemble. Then *after a time of mutual influence the systems separate again*. He argues, that entanglement is *not one but rather the characteristic trait of quantum mechanics* [26]. For example, two or more independent molecules may each be in a superposition of conformations, when "swinging" on a double-bond hinge or "rotating" on a single-bond pivot. These conformations may be frequency-coupled between the molecules, due to the surrounding electronic structure, i.e. the distribution

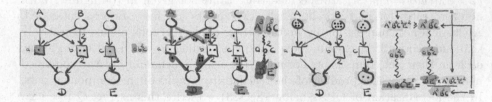

Fig. 2. *Concurrence enabling and firing. Left:* The concurrence ab^2c includes two occurrences of b and one each of a and c. *Middle Left:* The flow weights define the input and output markings of any concurrence, here A^3B^5C and D^5E^3, respectively. *Middle Right:* Is ab^2c enabled in the given marking $A^4B^6C^3E^2$? And what is the effect of firing it? *Right:* ab^2c is indeed enabled, since the required input marking satisfies $A^3B^5C \le A^4B^6C^3E^2$ (as multisets). This means, the given marking makes all transition occurrences of ab^2c mutually concurrent, i.e., conflict-free under this marking. Firing the concurrence ab^2c in this marking as a single indivisible and joint step reaches the marking ABC^2E^5, atomically.

---

[1] Faithful modelling may require operations on quantum systems at any scale and hence result in superpositions at any scale. This may require re-normalisation.

of a number of electrons they share and the wave-shaped uncertainty of their observable position. In QPNs, entanglement couples[2] multiple occurrences of otherwise concurrent transitions in space-time. We therefore call such a joint firing of mutually concurrent transitions a *concurrence*[3]. Formally, a concurrence is a multiset t of enabled and mutually independent transitions, i.e., $t \in \mathbb{N}^T$ (the set of multisets over T). We think of them as firing together with some given amplitude. Like the transition structure of nets is the dual of its place structure, concurrences can be regarded as the dual of markings. However, like single transitions, concurrences define indistinguishable atomic marking updates and must not be confused with historic attempts in net theory to separate the beginning and the ending of transitions. As an abstract example of a concurrence, consider the concurrence ab^2c in Fig. 2 (Left). The shown marking $A^4B^6C^3E^2$ in Fig. 2 (Middle Right) has sufficient tokens for an interference-free firing of any pair of subconcurrences partitioning and covering the given concurrence. Hence it can also fire in an atomic *single step*. This example also shows that concurrences do not have to be maximal. Thus, for QPNs, concurrences can be entangled by rating the inseparability of any of their substeps. In fact, it is possible to acausally force their atomic firing by rating the individual transition firings with amplitude 0, while using amplitude 1 for the joint firing. This is a kind of soft mutual excitement. Inversely, the joint firing could be rated much lower than the individual firing, as a kind of soft mutual inhibition. A *marking-dependent rate function* r is a function $\mathbb{M}_0 \times \mathbb{N}^T \xrightarrow{r} \mathbb{C}$ assigning complex numbers to concurrences. We refer to $r(m,t)$ by $r_m(t)$, for brevity, and use $r_m(t) = 1$ as the default. For example, in Fig. 3 (Left), there are four possible concurrences between the two classical bit PTNs P and Q. Here each concurrence consists of two transitions highlighted by a coloured line. As usual, rates not shown explicitly default to 1. In the example, two rates $r1 = r_{00}(uu) = r_{11}(dd)$ and $r2 = r_{01}(ud) = r_{10}(du)$ are specified (rate table not given in the figure). With non-zero rates for $r1, r2$ or both, the two qubits are more or less entangled. A classical net composition by juxtaposition of their graphs means figuratively that independent players can move tokens according to the usual token game, each on their net component. Formally, the usual reachability of the combined nets is the Kronecker product of the reachability graphs of the component nets. In the formalisation of QPNs below (Sect. 3) we write this as $P \otimes Q$ (see e.g., [6,10] and advanced books on graph theory and matrices). Classical net architecture design usually discourages disconnected nets, unless there are further constraints to two juxtaposed components, such as gluing the nets in transitions, for example $P_u = Q_u$ and $P_d = Q_d$ (contracting the red lines). This forces the respective players into mutually dependent moves – players holding hands, so to speak, in their now locally and causally synchronised token game. The contracted net becomes behaviourally equivalent to a single classical bit: the RG of

---

[2] We use the term space-time coupling to avoid the term 'synchronisation' which is loaded with temporal meaning, etymologically the old-Greek 'khronos' means time and the prefix 'sun' together.

[3] Concurrences are to transitions what markings are to places.

the constrained net is isomorphic to the RG of each single player. Juxtaposition with transition identification loses the individual transition firings. In contrast, a *QPN can fire all transitions of a concurrence together, individually, or anything in between* controlled by the rate function: a complex kind of soft gluing or 'coalescing' of separate (cyclic) behaviours into ensembles.

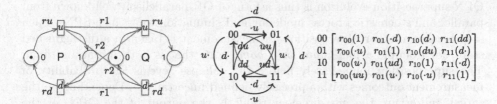

Fig. 3. *Complex firing rates turn a pair of bits into a pair of qubits. Left:* A QPN system with underlying PTN of two unconnected bits, P and Q, in black. Initially both bits are 0. The possible PTN transitions, in each, flip the respective bit up (u) or down (d). All conceivable combinations of states are reachable in the composite net of the pair. Pairs of mutually concurrent transitions are highlighted by coloured lines. Rates $r1$ and $r2$ entangle P and Q; rates ru and rd control single transitions; rates default to 1. *Middle:* The reachability graph of the PTN to the left is shown in black. A marking P_iQ_j is abbreviated by juxtaposition ij, for short (e.g., 01 for P_0Q_1). Likewise, the reachability edges are labeled with juxtaposed transition symbols, for short, filling in $\cdot$ for no action (NOP) on the respective subnet (e.g., $\cdot u$ for Q_u). The coloured reachability edges add concurrences, i.e. co-occurrences of transition multisets (e.g., uu) controlled by entanglement. This extended RG is the QPN RG. *Right:* The weighted adjacency matrix A of the QPN RG to the left represents the QPN rate function r. Rows and columns are indexed 00 through 11. For every reachability step (edge) $m \xrightarrow{t} m'$, we have $A_{m',m} = r_m(t)$. NOP is represented by the unit multiset $t = 1$. NOP self-loops are not shown in the QPN RG to the left.

Formally, an *entangled superposition* (state) is defined as a superposition that cannot be expressed as a product of the two component superpositions [26]. In Fig. 3, for instance, $\frac{1}{\sqrt{2}}(|01\rangle + |10\rangle)$ is an entangled state. In contrast, the superposition $\frac{1}{2}(i|00\rangle - i|01\rangle - |10\rangle + |11\rangle) = \frac{1}{2}(i|P_0Q_0\rangle - i|P_0Q_1\rangle - |P_1Q_0\rangle + |P_1Q_1\rangle) = \frac{1}{2}(|P_0\rangle + i|P_1\rangle) \times (i|Q_0\rangle - i|Q_1\rangle)$ is a product of superpositions of the P and Q qubit taken by themselves. Therefore this superposition is not entangled. The so-called Bell states[4] of a qubit pair are the four entangled superpositions of the reachability set of Fig. 3 (Middle): $\frac{1}{\sqrt{2}}(|00\rangle \pm |11\rangle)$ and $\frac{1}{\sqrt{2}}(|01\rangle \pm |10\rangle)$. To stay in $\frac{1}{\sqrt{2}}(|00\rangle \pm |11\rangle)$, for instance, uu and dd have to be rated with probability 1 (or a complex equivalent) with u and d rated 0. Informally, rating the individual transitions in the coupling both with amplitude 0 means that the intermediate markings 01 and 10 attract an amplitude of 0 as result of firing the concurrence in a single step.

---

[4] Named after physicist John S. Bell. These states are maximally entangled.

2.4   Superposition Evolution and Complex Token Game

*Complex rates for single transitions and for concurrences allow a QPN to evolve
the state from superposition to superposition with entanglement.* An evolution
process starts from a *initial state*: any superposition is a valid initial state. The
QPN process executes in parallel for all superposed markings and all possible
concurrences enabled in any of them, incl. the empty multiset, aka NOP process.
QPN superposition evolution is thus a form of OR-parallelism, well-known from
parallel and stochastic process modeling and simulation tools, incl. SPNs. Each
step reaches another superposition. A measurement is taken in a distinguished
state, for example a *final state*, or a *home state* that is both initial and final.
The superposition immediately before the collapse reveals the probability of
measurement outcomes with a precisely defined uncertainty[5]. Depending on the
target and setup, the measurement result is the output of the QPN, or the
sampling provided by its successive runs, which may also be embedded in a
discrete real-time control loop.

Recall like in stochastic variants of Petri nets, QPN rates are *marking-
dependent*. In the RG of an SPN, this permits a modeller to assign different rates
$r_m(t) \neq r_{m'}(t)$ to different enabling markings for the same transition ($m \xrightarrow{t}$,
vs. $m' \xrightarrow{t}$). For QPNs, the step t may be a concurrence. Rating a concurrence
with a single transition ($|t| = 1$) is trivial and classical. Rating the unit multiset
($|t| = 0$), i.e., the NOP process, caters for a *resting* rate. For example something
may change elsewhere in space-time and result in redistribution of amplitudes, in
particular for entanglements. Any concurrence and its entanglement can now be
fully grasped in terms of transition firings in the net. For example, consider the
RG (black and coloured) in Fig. 3. Assume we want to compute the amplitude of
marking $|11\rangle$ after a direct reachability step starting from a given superposition
a. Given the uncertainty expressed in a, there are many steps of length 1, that
reach $|11\rangle$, i.e. the target node 11 in the RG on the right of the figure. To com-
pute the required amplitude (here a_{11}), one forms the weighted sum over these
edges with their source node (marking) amplitudes as the respective weight, plus
the weighted resting rate.

$$
\begin{aligned}
a_{00} &:= a_{00} \times r_{00}(1) & + a_{01} \times r_{01}(\cdot d) & + a_{10} \times r_{10}(d\cdot) & + a_{11} \times r_{11}(dd) \\
a_{01} &:= a_{00} \times r_{00}(\cdot u) & + a_{01} \times r_{01}(1) & + a_{10} \times r_{10}(du) & + a_{11} \times r_{11}(d\cdot) \\
a_{10} &:= a_{00} \times r_{00}(u\cdot) & + a_{01} \times r_{01}(ud) & + a_{10} \times r_{10}(1) & + a_{11} \times r_{11}(\cdot d) \\
a_{11} &:= a_{00} \times r_{00}(uu) & + a_{01} \times r_{01}(u\cdot) & + a_{10} \times r_{10}(\cdot u) & + a_{11} \times r_{11}(1)
\end{aligned}
\tag{1}
$$

Since node 11 is reachable only by making a move (a step in one of the first
three terms listed) or by resting (fourth term), the normalisation of the rates
in Eq. 1 (line 4) results in the sum of their moduli squared equaling 1, provided
that a is normalised to begin with. Philosophically, the required probability sum
of 1 (after normalising and converting amplitudes to probabilities) expresses
this principle[6]: *whether something moves or nothing happens, the system is in a*

---

[5] The precision of the mathematics underpinning quantum mechanical predictions is
unrivaled and differs from classical stochastic models.

[6] In a blend of Einstein and Aristotle.

defined state. In other words, a measurement will collapse the state to a defined outcome.

For each marking amplitude a_m, a corresponding equation in Eq. 1 captures the direct reachability relation reaching marking m. Note that according to Eq. 1 the amplitudes of the next superposition are exactly the result of multiplying row 11 of the adjacency matrix A (cf. Fig. 3) with a as a vector of marking amplitudes in the order 00 through 11. Step sequences of different lengths (lengths of paths in RG) and width (cardinality of concurrences) represent partially ordered runs. The net structure of a QPN and various behaviourally equivalent transformations on the classical underlying net [4] may serve transformations of the QPN with different complexity and performance characteristics, yet resulting in the same final measurement up to an error Δ.

Note, that the rate function does not change the reachability of the underlying classical net. Therefore, QPNs do not add to the classical state space explosion already attributable to concurrency and stochasticity. For example, SPNs already calculate with stochastic uncertainty in their parallel simulations. However, QPNs add concurrence edges to their reachability graph filling the equivalent rate matrix with finely differentiated rates. A secondary and lesser complication arises from the use of complex numbers as rates. Each complex number requires two reals and hence doubles the space and possibly access time compared to SPN implementations. More importantly, adding classical probabilities increases them and multiplying them decreases them. Therefore, rates for classical stochastic nets may converge over increasing numbers of steps, allowing a modelling tool to prune the number of OR-parallel branches. In contrast, complex rates may cancel each other, yet oscillate forever, with no or little chance of reducing the number of processes to follow.

2.5   Rate Function Composition and Acausal Computation

For today's quantum computers, quantum circuit diagrams [18] are a universal abstract representation of any quantum computational function, like a universal assembler language, to which quantum programming languages are compiled. QPNs can express any such function (see Sect. 3). Below, we show by example (using Figs. 3 and 4), how quantum circuit diagrams translate to QPNs. For technical details see Sect. 3.

In circuit diagrams, the controlled-not gate, aka CNOT, assigns amplitudes so as to flip qubit Q if and only if qubit P is 1, with the rate function CNot induced by the steps of the underlying net of the qubit pair P and Q. The corresponding QPN amplitude definition (**defqp**) declares CNot as a rate function on the qubits P and Q, induced by the steps of the underlying net. The default amplitude is 0 ('@ 0' follows the rate function prototype). The CNot definition body follows the **with** keyword and defines marking-dependent rules overriding the default for firing steps. With $P.0$ marked the resting amplitude is 1 ('**rest** @ 1'), i.e., regardless of the marking of Q. This means $CNot_{00}(1) = CNot_{01}(1) = 1$. With $P.1$ marked, the system is forced to fire one step to a different marking as the resting rate is 0 by default for the remaining markings. In a superposition,

	defqp (Qubit P,Q).CNot @ 0 with	defqp (Qubit P).Had @ $\frac{1}{\sqrt{2}}$ with
	P.0 rest @ 1	P.1 rest @ $-\frac{1}{\sqrt{2}}$.
	| P.1 (Q.u | Q.d) @ 1 .	

Fig. 4. *Quantum circuits and rate functions. Left:* A quantum circuit diagram with two qubits (horizontal lines, say P at top, Q at bottom) and two gates (operating on lines left to right). The first gate, a so-called CNOT gate, does nothing when $P = 0$. For $P = 1$ it flips the superposition of Q. The second gate, a so-called Hadamard gate maps $|0\rangle \mapsto \frac{1}{\sqrt{2}}(|0\rangle + |1\rangle)$ and $|1\rangle \mapsto \frac{1}{\sqrt{2}}(|0\rangle - |1\rangle)$. *Middle:* The amplitude definition of CNOT as rate function *CNot* over the QPN in Fig. 3. *Right:* Hadamard gate as rate function Had over single qubit P in Fig. 3. The combined circuit can be written as (P,Q).CNot; P.Had over the 2-qubit net.

the enabling markings have different amplitudes, but for each marking there is only one enabled transition: $10 \xrightarrow{Q.u}$ and $11 \xrightarrow{Q.d}$. Thus with $P.1$ the rate is $CNot_{10}(.u) = CNot_{11}(.d) = 1$, thus performing the respective flip with probability 1. Using parentheses, the two transition amplitude rules are contracted here into one rule for $P.1$.

Similarly, the so-called Hadamard gate, which operates on the single qubit, here P in Fig. 3, is given by the rate function Had at amplitude $1/\sqrt{2}$ for all steps bar $H_1(1) = -1/\sqrt{2}$.

Each rate function on one or more qubits corresponds to a primitive or composite gate of quantum computing circuits on those qubits. QPNs are not limited to nets representing bits, however. Hence, more generally, each rate function corresponds to a combined causal-and-acausal function of the QPN, in which amplitudes regulate casuality, concurrency and choice.

2.6 Teleportation Protocols and Tunnelling

Due to the particle-wave character of quantum systems, their behaviour includes simultaneous (same point in time) but non-locally entangled states and transitions over large spatial distances, local (same point in space) but acausally superposed states over temporal distance, and blends thereof in bounded space-time regions. Quantum-state teleportation experiments have confirmed qubit entanglement over large distances. For example, qubit P could be located on Earth while qubit Q is on a satellite in orbit. If the entangled state $\frac{1}{\sqrt{2}}(|00\rangle + |11\rangle)$ were distributed with P in space and Q on Earth and a measurement in space resulted in the outcome of P_0 (and thus a collapse of that state to $P_0 Q_0 = 00$), then instantaneously it can be known that the qubit Q on Earth is in state Q_0. Yet the outcome remains uncertain until a measurement is taken with Q or the result is signalled (classically) from space to Earth. An analogous argument holds for the alternative outcome P_1. Furthermore, symmetrically, the measurement could be taken on Earth with the same result. Superposition with entanglement does not only work like a perfect quantum oracle. It also enables rapid consumption of distributed measurement outcomes. Moreover, any eavesdropping on entangled qubits results in the collapse of the superposition, which can be immediately noticed by the distributed parties. Therefore, quantum protocols are also poised to offer unparalleled security and safety. It should be noted, however, that the acausal entanglement is not signalling shared information between remote locations. Teleporting a state from space to Earth, means that it is lost in space. However, teleportation can be used in combination with classical message signalling protocols over such distances to leverage the quantum advantage in protocol security and processing speed. Using the examples above we have the tools to understand the following teleportation protocol, which abstractly captures the common structure of a number of real teleportation protocols that have been conducted over different distances (tunnelling under the Donube in Germany, offshore to onshore US, Tibet to space satellite and others, cf., e.g. [29]). In this variant of the protocol, Alice and Bob each share one half of an entangled qubit pair (A and B say), in the Bell state $\frac{1}{\sqrt{2}}(|00\rangle + |11\rangle)$, which results from evolving $|00\rangle$ with $(A, B).Bell$ in our QPTN. They both have agreed on the entanglement but neither has knowledge of the specific Bell state or its amplitudes. Alice aims to teleport a third qubit C to Bob. The state of C – also unknown to Alice and Bob – can be represented as the superposition of markings $c|0\rangle + d|1\rangle$. Now juxtapose the QPTNs in the order C, A and B with our convention for marking abbreviations 000 through 111. Alice is located in the space station, Bob on Earth. The entanglement of A and B is prepared in a third place before the experiment using the `Bell` function above. Next the separate qubits are sent to Alice and Bob taking care not to break the entanglement. This completes the preparation of the initial three-qubit superposition $\frac{1}{\sqrt{2}}(c|000\rangle + c|011\rangle + d|100\rangle + d|111\rangle)$. Now:

1. Alice uses `(C,A).CNot; C.Had` (Fig. 4) transferring the entanglement from A and B to A and C. This results in $\frac{1}{2}(c(|000\rangle + |011\rangle + |100\rangle + |111\rangle) + d(|010\rangle + |001\rangle - |110\rangle - |101\rangle))$ which can be refactored $\frac{1}{2}(|00\rangle(c|0\rangle + d|1\rangle) + |01\rangle(c|1\rangle + d|0\rangle) + |10\rangle(c|0\rangle - d|1\rangle) + |11\rangle(c|1\rangle - d|0\rangle))$ to show Bob's qubit as a function of any possible marking of Alice's qubit pair.
2. Next Alice measures her qubits (C, A) and finds them in one of the four underlying markings, 00, 01, 10 or 11 shown above, and leaving the amplitudes of C hidden in Bob's formerly entangled qubit. Alice sends the two classical bits of that measured marking to Bob.
3. To reveal C, Bob applies one of four functions, depending on the message received and arrives in superposition $c|0\rangle + d|1\rangle$ for C. Note that Alice has lost the initial state of C in the process.

We view tunnelling as a massive entangling with collective teleportation. For example, a long sequence of juxtaposed QPNs of identical system nets can represent a tunnel architecture, with only moderate causal connections between adjacent QPNs. Now the instances of the same transition across different positions can be entangled and teleportation achieved from one end of the tunnel to the other. Causal interconnections in the architecture may reinforce entanglement over the length of the tunnel. Concurrences over instances t_i of the same transition are powers t^n (ignoring the position). Firing rates for these powers may be expressed in terms of the exponent n in one net.

The question arises, how is a software designer supposed to come up with QPN rate functions for larger and more complex nets? Fortunately, as we will see in later sections, QPNs are compositional. Hence one specifies the rate function of a small intelligible net or refactors and fine-tunes that of on existing net. Then one 'simply' composes QPN architectures, resulting in the composite rate function, too. Future research may also adapt machine learning to match rate functions to training data and select the fittest fast behavioural response in intelligent real-time sensing and control.

3   Quantum Petri Nets with Variation Points

QPNs have standard Petri nets as underlying classical nets. To avoid ambiguity of similar terminology and notation in nets and quantum computing, we reconcile basic notation first for nets and their matrices. This will also provide variation points for others to "bake in quantum characteristics" to their pet net interpretation, using the machinery laid out in this paper. The fundamental variation points are markings, concurrences and direct reachability. At higher levels there are further variation points in diagram notation and net inscriptions.

Variation points are a familiar concept in software architecture, analysis and design, where they serve the separation of the architectural framework from the more variable architectural elements. For example in the Model-View-Controller framework, a reoccurring pattern of software architecture, the aim is to allow modifications of the view, while minimally, or not at all, affecting the model and controller part of the software. The same goes for changes to the data model or the user and software control of the model. Plugin architectures and feature combinations are further examples. There are many more variation concepts. All have in common that parts of the software are parametrised and varied functionally and as independently as possible.

3.1   Superpositions of Multisets

We begin with a formal account of multisets which are used for markings, concurrences and superpositions in QPNs. Given a set A, a multiset over A is a mapping $s : A \to \mathbb{N}$. We also write $s \in \mathbb{N}^A$ for brevity and abbreviate $s(a)$ by s_a ($a \in A$). Let $s, s' \in \mathbb{N}^A$ be two multisets.

The monomial representation of multisets used throughout this paper is one of many common representations of multisets in mathematics, for example, in the representation of the prime factorization of an integer, as a multiset of prime numbers on the one hand, and the corresponding exponent vector $ev(s)$ indexed in the order of prime numbers, on the other. In the monomial representation of $s \in \mathbb{N}^A$, the elements $a \in s$ are raised to their respective integer multiplicity s_a as their exponent. Multisets are then formed by multiplication (or concatenation) for brevity. For example ab^2c is short for $abbc$ and represents the multiset $\{a \mapsto$

$1, b \mapsto 2, c \mapsto 1\}$. A superposition v of multisets is a function $\mathbb{N}^A \xrightarrow{v} K$ mapping multisets s_i to coefficients c_i in a field K, such as the integers $\mathbb{Z}$, rationals $\mathbb{Q}$, reals $\mathbb{R}$, Gaussian rationals $\mathbb{Q}[i]$ or complex numbers $\mathbb{C}$. v is also written as the polynomial $v = c_1 s_1 + \cdots + c_i s_i + \cdots$ with $c_i = v(s_i) \neq 0$, i.e. listing only the non-zero terms. Multiplication and addition of monomials and polynomials work with the usual algebraic laws, treating net elements as variable symbols in multivariate polynomials.

In net theory and the simulation of net behaviour, the vector $ev(s)$ of exponents is often used for efficiently representing a corresponding multiset s. Then multiplication ss' can be equivalently represented as $ev(s) + ev(s')$, consistent with $a^{n+m} = a^n a^m$. We define the partial order $s < s'$ by comparing the exponents $s_a < s'_a$ (for all $a \in A$) and $s \leq s'$ iff $s < s'$ or $s = s'$. For the monomial as a product, $s \leq s'$ means s divides s' and can be cancelled in the division $\frac{s'}{s}$. Consequently, $ev(s') - ev(s) + ev(s'')$, as used for transition firings, shows as $\frac{s}{s'} s''$ and simplifies to a monomial again. Set operations extend to multisets as does some algebraic terminology we need on occasion: The degree $deg(s)$ is the largest exponent of s, and the cardinality (aka total degree) $|s|$ the sum of the exponents. We write $s = 1$ iff $deg(s) = 0$. s is called a proper subset of s' iff $s < s'$, and a subset iff $s \leq s'$. Membership $a \in s$ is defined by $s_a > 0$. The intersection (aka greatest common divisor) $s \cap s'$ is the element-wise minimum of the exponents in s and s'. The union (aka smallest common multiple) $s \cup s'$ is the corresponding maximum. The set difference $s \backslash s'$ is defined by element-wise subtraction of exponents, if the result is non-negative and otherwise 0. If f is a function $A \xrightarrow{f} \mathbb{N}^B$ from a set to a multiset, then f can be lifted naturally to a function $\mathbb{N}^A \xrightarrow{f} \mathbb{N}^B$, s.t., for all $s \in \mathbb{N}^A$ we have: $f(s)_b = s_a \times f(a)_b$ for all $a \in A$ and $b \in B$. This was illustrated in Fig. 2.

3.2 Classical Petri Nets

Next, we define Petri nets parametrised at two variation points. Various extant net classes can then be derived as variations and restrictions, incl. their quantum variants. Firstly, a generator G is a function $Set \xrightarrow{G} Set$, such that $G[P]$ and $G[T]$ are disjoint, when P (the place set) and T (the transition set) are. This captures a range of net extensions. Secondly, a Boolean function well-formedness, short WF, on $G[N]$, $\mathbb{N}^{G[N]}$ and $\mathbb{N}^{G[N]} \times \mathbb{N}^{G[N]}$ captures constraints appearing in the net literature under different names, incl. guards and inhibitors. We define $\mathbb{P}$ and $\mathbb{T}$ as the maximal subsets of $G[P]$ and $G[T]$ with WF($\mathbb{P}$) = **true** and WF($\mathbb{T}$) = **true**, respectively. $G[N]$ is called the set of generated net elements. For $m \in \mathbb{N}^{\mathbb{P}}$ and $t \in \mathbb{N}^{\mathbb{T}}$, we interpret WF($m, t$) as m may enable t. Also we require strictness of WF on multisets and pairs, i.e., WF(m) = **false** implies WF(mm') = **false**, WF(m, m') = **false** and WF(m', m) = **false**. Informally, a composite cannot be well-formed, if one of its components is ill-formed. It follows from strictness, that WF(1) = **true**.

Definition 1 (Net structure). A Petri net structure $\mathbf{N} = (P, T, F)$ (short net) with generator G and well-formedness WF is a structure where P and T

are disjoint sets, called places *and* transitions. F, *which is called* flow, *is a pair of functions* $\mathbb{N}^\mathbb{P} \xleftarrow{F^-} \mathbb{T} \xrightarrow{F^+} \mathbb{N}^\mathbb{P}$. $N = P \cup T$ *is also called the set of* net elements *and* $\mathbb{P} \cup \mathbb{T}$ *the set of* generated net elements. *We call* $F^-(t)$ *the* input *and* $F^+(t)$ *the* output *of* t *and the set of elements* $p \in F^-(t)$ *the* preset *of* t *denoted by* $^\bullet t$. *Analogously, the elements of* $F^+(t)$ *form its* postset *and are denoted* $t^\bullet$. *We require of* F *that* $|^\bullet t| + |t^\bullet| > 0$.

For $G[N] = N$ and WF= **true**, we get PTNs. Coloured Petri nets and algebraic nets pair places with data of some sort in $G[P]$ (see Sect. 4.3).

Convention 1. *For the rest of the paper, let* **N** *be the PN structure with the above components. In the well-known incidence matrix representation of a PTN, F^- and F^+ are represented as $P \times T$-indexed matrices called the* input *and* output incidence matrix, *respectively (c.f., e.g., [19, 23]). This generalises to corresponding $G[P] \times G[T]$-indexed matrices for the net structures above with a generator G.*

Definition 2 (Enabling and firing). *Let* $m, m' \in \mathbb{N}^\mathbb{P}$ *and* $t \in \mathbb{N}^\mathbb{T}$. *Then m is called a* marking *and* t *a* concurrence *of* **N**. *Now, if $F^-(t) \le m$ and $WF(m,t)$, then t is said to be* enabled *in m. This is abbreviated by $m \xrightarrow{t}$. If $ev(m') = ev(m) - ev(F^-(t)) + ev(F^+(t))$, then we say m' is* concurrently *(or* asynchronously*) reachable from m by firing t. This is abbreviated by $m \xrightarrow{t}_c m'$. We write $m \longrightarrow_c m'$ if there is a concurrence t, s.t. $m \xrightarrow{t}_c m'$. This binary relation on markings is called* direct concurrence reachability. *Its transitive closure $\longrightarrow_c^+$ is called* concurrence reachability. *With the restriction $|t| = 1$, we abbreviate $m \xrightarrow{t}_c m'$ to $m \xrightarrow{t}_1 m'$ and $m \longrightarrow_c m'$ to $m \longrightarrow_1 m'$. The binary relation $m \longrightarrow_1 m'$ is called* direct single-transition reachability *and its transitive closure $\longrightarrow_1^+$* single-transition reachability. *Moreover, if $m \xrightarrow{t}_c m'$, we call $(m \backslash m', m' \backslash m)$ the* effect *of t. We omit the subscripts c and 1, if there is no risk of confusion in the given context.*

Note that the effect of t ignores the intersection of its input and output. Importantly, enabling, firing effect and reachability are defined purely in terms of net structure and WF. Note that $\longrightarrow_c$ is reflexive by definition, given that 1 is a concurrence.

Definition 3 (Loop-free, reversible, pure and simple). *The net* **N** *is* loop-free, *iff $F^-(t) \ne F^+(t)$ (for all $t \in \mathbb{T}$);* reversible, *iff for all $t \in \mathbb{T}$ there is a $t' \in \mathbb{T}$, s.t., $F^-(t) = F^+(t')$ and $F^+(t) = F^-(t')$;* pure, *iff $^\bullet t \cap t^\bullet = \emptyset$ (for all $t \in \mathbb{T}$); and* simple, *iff for any $t, t' \in \mathbb{T}$: $F^-(t) = F^-(t')$ and $F^+(t) = F^+(t')$ implies $t = t'$.*

A loop is thus a transition whose input equals its output, making its effect trivial. Purity means, its inputs and outputs do not share common factors (intersection) in any multiplicity. Simplicity means, the input-output pair uniquely defines the transition. Purity implies loop-freedom. Simplicity does not exclude impurity or loop-freedom. For example, the net in Fig. 1 is simple, but has loops and is impure, while the net in Fig. 3 is simple, pure and loop-free. The definition of purity and simplicity can also be used to define a respective equivalence in order to *purify* or *simplify* the net, respectively by forming the quotient, after also removing loops in the case of purification. The resulting net is pure or simple, respectively, by construction.

Definition 4 (System net, reachability set and graph). $S = (N, M_0)$ *is called a* system net *with* initial marking $M_0 \in \mathbb{N}^{\mathbb{P}}$. *The* reachability set $\mathbb{M}_0$ *is defined as the set of all markings reachable from M_0 by single-transition reachability. The* reachability graph $G_S = (V, E)$ *is the multigraph[7] with $V = \mathbb{M}_0$ and $E = \{(m, t, m') | m \xrightarrow{t}_1 m', t \in \mathbb{T} \text{ and } m, m' \in \mathbb{M}_0\}$. S is called* safe *iff $\deg(m) \leq 1$ for all $m \in \mathbb{M}_0$ and* reduced *iff for all $t \in \mathbb{T}$, there are markings $m, m' \in \mathbb{M}_0$ with $m \xrightarrow{t} m'$.*

It is straightforward to verify that the underlying system net of the 2-qubit QPTN of Fig. 3 is loop-free, reversible, pure, simple, safe and reduced.

Definition 5 (Equivalent shape and behaviour). *Let $S = (N, M_0)$ and $S' = (N', M_0')$ be two system PNs. Then S and S' are called* shape-equivalent *under a bijection f between their place sets $\mathbb{P} \overset{f}{\rightleftharpoons} \mathbb{P}'$, if $M_0 \cong M_0'$ and $\mathbb{M}_0 \cong \mathbb{M}_0'$ under the congruence uniquely induced by f on $\mathbb{N}^{\mathbb{P}}$. They are called* behaviour-equivalent *if they are shape-equivalent under f and f moreover extends to a bijection $\mathbb{T} \overset{f}{\rightleftharpoons} \mathbb{T}'$, s.t. their reachability graphs are isomorphic under $f\colon G_S \cong G_{S'}$.*

Shape-equivalent system PNs operate on isomorphic markings but possibly with different transitions and concurrences. With equivalent behaviour, the nets can simulate each other as their direct reachability relations mirror each other under the bijection f between their net elements. Behaviour equivalence implies that f is an isomorphism on their reachability graphs and preserves the direct concurrence reachability. The reverse is not true, because a reachability graph isomorphism may not preserve the enabling of concurrent transitions. For simplicity, henceforth we identify places, markings and reachability set in two nets of equivalent shape, without mentioning f.

3.3 Baking Quantum into Petri Net Theory

Next, we formalise QPNs and look at the matrix calculus and linear algebra operators they induce based on their underlying nets.

Definition 6 (Quantum Petri net). *Let $S = (N, M_0)$ be a system PN, then $Q = (S, r)$ is a* Quantum Petri net *(short QPN) where r is a function $\mathbb{M}_0 \times \mathbb{N}^{\mathbb{T}} \xrightarrow{r} \mathbb{C}$. We write $r_m(t)$ for $r(m, t)$. A* superposition state *(short super-position) of Q is any $|\mathbb{M}_0|$-dimensional complex vector v.*

---

[7] In a multigraph a single pair of edges (u, v) may have multiple parallel edges, here represented as triples (u, k, v). A graph with a single unique edge for each pair of connected vertices is called simple in graph theory.

Thus, the underlying net spans an $|\mathbb{M}_0|$-dimensional complex Hilbert space of marking superpositions. The canonical basis vectors are $\mathbf{b}_m (m \in \mathbb{M}_0)$ with all entries 0 except a single 1 at index m. We conveniently abbreviate $\mathbf{b}_m$ by $|m\rangle$. Any superposition v can be written as the linear combination $\sum_m v_m |m\rangle$ of basis vectors. v is also written as $|v\rangle$ to recall it is a column vector. The inner product of the Hilbert space is $\langle u|v\rangle$, which multiplies the row vector $\langle u|$, which is the conjugate transpose of $|u\rangle$, with the column vector $|v\rangle$. The inner product lends a geometry to this complex vector space, with the real-valued length $|u| = \langle u|u\rangle$. The distance of two vectors is $||u\rangle - |v\rangle|$ and the angle between them is $\alpha = arccos \frac{\langle u|v\rangle}{|u| \times |v|}$.

Definition 7 (Rate graph). *Let* $\mathbf{Q}$ *be a QPN as above (Definition 6). The rate graph of* $\mathbf{Q}$ *is the multigraph* $G_Q = (V, E)$ *with* $V = \mathbb{M}_0$ *and* $E = \{(m, t, m')|m \xrightarrow{t}_c m', t \in \mathbb{N}^{\mathrm{T}}$ *and* $m, m' \in \mathbb{M}_0\}$. $E_{m,m'}$ *denotes the set of edges between* m *and* m' *and we often simply write* $m \xrightarrow{t}_c m'$ *instead of* $(m, t, m') \in E_{m,m'}$ *given the correspondence between edges and the direct concurrence reachability.*

Note that the rate graph of a QPN is defined purely in terms of the underlying system PN, as its concurrence reachability graph. This defines the domain of the rate function, in the sense that any direct concurrence reachability $m \xrightarrow{t}_c m'$ has a unique edge in the rate graph, for which $r_m(t)$ defines the amplitude, and vice versa. Also note, that $|\mathbb{M}_0| = \infty$ is possible in more than one way. Firstly, the generator G may create infinite nets, i.e., $|G[N]| = \infty$. Secondly, even for a very small finite net, the reachability set may be very large (or even infinite). This generative power is well-known for nets and used, for instance, in SPNs, where it is combined with structural (net-level) methods and behavioural (reachability graph or matrix) methods. However, some numerical net-theoretic methods for concurrent and stochastic processes require working directly with the reachability graph and therefore, more often than not, we ask whether a given system PN is bounded[8] and therefore $\mathbb{M}_0$ is finite. This is solved for the classical underlying PN. We also say a QPN has property X if its underlying system PN has property X. For example $\mathbf{Q}$ is simple if $\mathbf{S}$ is simple and shape-equivalent with another QPN if their underlying system PNs are. Any n-qubit QPN that juxtaposes n qubits is loop-free, reversible, pure, simple, safe and reduced (cf. e.g., Fig. 3). Therefore its rate graph is a simple graph[9]. All these are decidable in $\mathbf{S}$.

Definition 8 (Rate matrix). *Let* $\mathbf{Q}$ *be a QPN with* $G_Q = (V, E)$ *and* $|V| = n$. *Then its rate matrix* R_Q *is defined as the* n-*dimensional square matrix, satisfying:* $R_Q[m', m] = \sum_{t, m \xrightarrow{t}_c m'} r_m(t)$. *The normal rate matrix is defined by normalising the row vectors of* R_Q.

---

[8] A system PN is called bounded if there is a bound $b \in \mathbb{N}$ with $deg(m) < b$ for all reachable markings. It is bounded iff its reachability set is finite.

[9] Ignoring self-loops associated with $r_m(1)$ edges.

Let R be a normal rate matrix of a QPN. Then it can be interpreted on the underlying system PN **S** as follows. $Rx = y$ evolves any superposition x of markings of **S** in a single-step quantum-parallel evolution to a marking superposition y (cf., e.g., Eq. 1). Since every n^2 matrix with complex entries is an operator in the n-dimensional complex Hilbert vector space, the following sentence is a consequence of the above definition.

Corollary 1 (QPN rate matrices are Hilbert space operators). *Let* $\mathbf{Q} = (\mathbf{S}, r)$ *be a QPN. Then the rate matrix* R_Q *and its normal rate matrix are both operators of the complex Hilbert space* $\mathcal{H}^n$, *with dimension* $n = |\mathbb{M}_0|$ *and state vectors* $a \in \mathbb{A}_0$. *If the net is reversible, let* $t^{-1} \in \mathbb{T}$ *be the reverse transition for every* $t \in \mathbb{T}$. *If the rate function* r *is conjugate symmetric, i.e., for every* $m \xrightarrow{t} m'$, $r_{m'}(t^{-1}) = r_m(t)^*$, *then the normal rate matrix is unitary.*

Universality. Next, we wish to show that QPNs are a universal computation model in the sense of the quantum circuit model for quantum computation. Firstly, we show that the operator matrix of any gate defines a QPN. Secondly, we represent a specific universal gate set in terms of QPNs. Thirdly, we demonstrate the compositional algebraic nature of QPNs for the construction and analysis of hybrid causal and acausal quantum-parallel processes (cf. proofs in the online appendix).

Theorem 1 (Universality of QPNs). *Any quantum gate circuit defines a QPN* **Q** *with* R_Q *the operator matrix of the circuit.*

Theorem 2 (Clifford+T QPNs). *The universal Clifford+T gate set below of 2-qubit and 1-qubit circuit matrices has a straightforward representation as QPNs:*

$$CNOT = \begin{bmatrix} 1 & 0 & 0 & 0 \\ 0 & 1 & 0 & 0 \\ 0 & 0 & 0 & 1 \\ 0 & 0 & 1 & 0 \end{bmatrix} \quad H = \frac{1}{\sqrt{2}} \begin{bmatrix} 1 & 1 \\ 1 & -1 \end{bmatrix} \quad S = \begin{bmatrix} 1 & 0 \\ 0 & i \end{bmatrix} \quad T = \begin{bmatrix} 1 & 0 \\ 0 & e^{i\pi/4} \end{bmatrix} \quad (2)$$

For the benefit of interpreting the above universality results, we briefly recall the circuit model of quantum computation and its notion of universal gate set, in order to make this paper somewhat self-contained. For a detailed treatment, the reader is referred to [18]. Circuit diagrams are made from qubits (lines oriented from left to right) and logic gates (typically drawn as boxes or connectors crossing lines vertically). Gates operate on some of the qubits only (cf. e.g., Fig. 4). For a gate, the number of input lines equals that of its outputs. The function of each logic gate on its n qubits is a complex $2^n \times 2^n$ matrix on the corresponding Hilbert subspace $\mathcal{H}^{2^n}$ spanned by the 2^n canonical basis vectors, i.e., vectors everywhere 0 except for a single position that is 1. The operation of two gates G after F is applied graphically in series from left to right, on the *same* n qubit lines. It is defined by the matrix-matrix multiplication GF of the corresponding operator matrices. Top to bottom juxtaposition of two gates (incl. NOP as a special case, see below) represents parallel composition, defined by the tensor of the corresponding matrices. The NOP (no operation) gate is simply represented by continuing the n qubit lines it operates on, i.e., without showing the NOP box. Its function is the corresponding 2^n-squared identity matrix. This leaves the states of these qubits unchanged. Therefore, NOP can be inserted were needed, for example in extending a n-qubit gate to a larger number of qubits using the tensor product with the corresponding identity matrix.

A number of finite gate sets (typically very small sets) have been identified as universal, i.e., capable of representing any quantum computation. The Clifford+T gate set above (Theorem 2) has been proven to have this property. However, any finite circuit diagram is equivalent to a finite square operator matrix, when, in general, continuous-space-time quantum computations may involve infinite-dimensional Hilbert spaces, i.e., superposition vectors with an infinite number of positions. Therefore, a gate set is defined as universal more subtly, viz., as follows. If an arbitrarily long but finite sequence of circuits entirely built from this gate set can approximate any quantum computation to any required precision. While this means working with limits, it is not an issue for finite-dimensional Hilbert spaces, which are always *complete*, i.e., have limits for any converging Cauchy sequence, such as those resulting from arbitrarily long state evolutions from an initial superposition, and converging ever closer to some limit. Completeness guarantees that such limits exist as a superposition in the system.

Hierarchical Component Architecture. Petri net theory offers a rich set of compositional constructions for the causal, parallel and hierarchical structuring of the underlying system nets of QPNs. For example, foldings are net morphisms that can partition the place set $\mathbb{P}$ lumping together all elements of a single partition into a macro-state and consistently re-interpreting markings and transitions, altogether arriving at a smaller net and generally smaller reachability graph with lower-dimensional matrices. Beyond net compositionality, the relational nature of reachability and the functional character of rates, from single steps to entire QPNs and their rate graphs, lend linear algebra properties to the resulting rate matrices, naturally. However, the linear algebraic compositionality of the target space is present in the QPNs themselves already, as the following compositionality theorem shows. To our knowledge, the generality of this compositionality result is novel and somewhat surprising, although research in stochastic Petri nets has used Kronecker algebra [6,10], however with constraints.

Theorem 3 (Compositionality of QPNs). *The class of QPNs is closed under the following operations with QPNs* $\mathbf{Q} = (\mathbf{S}, r)$, $\mathbf{Q}' = (\mathbf{S}', r')$, *and complex numbers* $c, c' \in \mathbb{C}$:

zero: $\mathbf{0}_Q$, *is the QPN over any system PN, with zero rate function defined as* $r_m(t) = 0$ *for all reachable markings* m *and concurrences* t *with* $m \xrightarrow{t}_c m'$. R_{0_Q}. *It follows, that* R_Q *is the all-0 matrix.*

unit: $\mathbf{1}_Q$, is the QPN over any system PN, with the unit rate function defined as $r_m(1) = 1$ and $r_m(t) = 0$ $(t \neq 1)$ for all reachable markings m and concurrences with $m \xrightarrow{t}_c m'$. It follows, that R_{1_Q} is the identity matrix.

scaling: $c\mathbf{Q} = (\mathbf{S}, c \times r)$, with $(c \times r)_m(t) = c \times r_m(t)$. It follows that $R_{cQ} = c \times R_Q$.

product: $\mathbf{Q}\mathbf{Q}' = (\mathbf{S}'', r'')$ is called the monoidal product (aka concatenation) and defined as follows, if $\mathbf{Q}$ and $\mathbf{Q}'$ are shape equivalent. $\mathbf{Q}\mathbf{Q}'$ has the shape of its components. This means the QPNs have identical places, markings and reachability set (up to isomorphism). We require: for all $m, m', m'' \in \mathbb{M}_0$: $E''_{m,m''} = E_{m,m'} \times E'_{m',mm''}$, where E, E' and E'' are the respective rate graph edge sets. I.e., for every pair of concurrence edges $m \xrightarrow{t}_c m'$ in $E_{m,m'}$ and $m' \xrightarrow{t'}_c m''$ in $E'_{m',m''}$ we have the contracted edge $m \xrightarrow{(t,t')}_c m''$ in $E''_{m,m''}$ and vice versa, with the rate of the contracted edge $r''_m(t,t') = r_m(t) \times r_{m'}(t')$. Finally, we define $\mathbb{T}''$ as contraction of singleton concurrences t and t' in the respective component, using the contracted concurrence pairs (t, t'), $(t, 1)$ and $(1, t')$ with appropriate F^- and F^+ according to the firing sequence tt'. It follows that $R_{QQ'} = R_{Q'}R_Q$.

sum: $\mathbf{Q} + \mathbf{Q}' = (\mathbf{S}'', r'')$ is called the sum and defined as follows, if $\mathbf{Q}$ and $\mathbf{Q}'$ are shape equivalent and all $t \in \mathbb{T} \cap \mathbb{T}'$ satisfy $F^-(t) = F'^-(t)$ and $F^+(t) = F'^+(t)$. $\mathbf{Q} + \mathbf{Q}'$ has the shape of its components. We require $E''_{m,m'} = E_{m,m'} \cup E'_{m,m'}$ for all $m, m' \in \mathbb{M}_0$, where E, E' and E'' are the respective rate graph edge sets. The rate function r'' of the sum is defined s.t. $r''_m(t) = r_m(t)$ for $(m, t, m') \in E_{m,m'} \setminus E'_{m,m'}$, $r''_m(t) = r'_m(t)$ for $(m, t, m') \in E'_{m,m'} \setminus E_{m,m'}$, $r''_m(t) = r_m(t) + r'_m(t)$ for $(m, t, m') \in E'_{m,m'} \cap E_{m,m'}$, and $r''_m(t) = 0$ otherwise. Finally, we define $\mathbb{T}''$ as singleton concurrences with $m \xrightarrow{t}_c m'$ in E'' with their uniquely defined respective input and output markings. It follows that $R_{Q+Q'} = R_Q + R_{Q'}$.

Kronecker product: $\mathbf{Q} \otimes \mathbf{Q}'$ is the disjoint juxtaposition (aka tensor product) of the two QPNs – their isolated parallel composition – in this order. The resulting rate graph satisfies $G_{Q \otimes Q'} = G_Q \otimes G_{Q'}$ with the usual graph-theoretic Kronecker product of graphs. It follows that the resulting rate matrix satisfies, $R_{Q \otimes Q'} = R_Q \otimes R_{Q'}$.

Kronecker sum: $\mathbf{Q} \oplus \mathbf{Q}'$ is defined as $\mathbf{Q} \otimes \mathbf{1}_{Q'} + \mathbf{1}_Q \otimes \mathbf{Q}'$. It follows that the resulting rate matrix $R_{Q \oplus Q'}$ equals the Kronecker sum of the component rate matrices $R_{Q \oplus Q'} = R_Q \oplus R_{Q'}$

The above compositionality lends linearity poperties to quantum Petri net compositions themselves, including hierarchical composition of marked cyclic nets, which are among the hallmarks of classical net architecture.

For example, considering Fig. 4, the above theorem implies that the 2-qubit QPNs with the following two rate functions are equivalent: `(P,Q).CNot; P.Had` and `(P,Q).CNot.(Had ⊗ 1)`.

Because stochastic rates are 'just' special real-valued rate functions, this result also offers new forms of compositionality to SPNs and similar net classes. In a nutshell, QPN addition is associative and commutative with zero $\mathbf{0}$.

While generally non-commutative, monoidal concatenation, the net equivalent of matrix multiplication, is associative with unit 1 and distributive over addition. Disjoint juxtaposition, with the usual interpretation of concurrent transition firing of isolated subnets, is the free parallel composition. Juxtaposition is associative, but the order matters for the forward reachability and the matrix index sets. Juxtaposition results in the Kronecker product of the rate graphs (graph-theoretically) and of the rate matrices.

As a consequence of the above, we arrive at the following interpretation. If we apply the rate matrix R of a QPN to a definite marking $|m\rangle$, i.e., one of the canonical basis vectors, we obtain the vector $v = R|m\rangle$ identical to the m-th column of R. If $v_{m'} > 0$, then m' is reachable from m in the underlying net with amplitude $v_{m'}$. If $v_{m'} \neq 0$, then m' is either unreachable in the underlying system from m in a single step (transition or concurrence). Or else, this underlying reachability step is rated 0 by the rate function of the QPN generating R. So, we can simply read the rated concurrence reachability off the rate matrix.

An n-step evolution of a quantum system can be obtained by matrix-matrix multiplication. For QPNs the rate matrices work in similar way. However rate matrices are forgetful, in that they do not include the concurrence structure inherent in multisets of places and transitions.

In contrast, the product of QPNs is not forgetful of the concurrency structure. Each path with non-zero amplitude in the rate graph allows us to reconstruct a run of the QPN (a kind of PTN occurrence net) of a length defined by the path and a width defined by the maximal cardinality of its concurrence steps. The product QQ' reflects the OR-parallel quantum execution combinatorially joining up steps and runs through intermediate markings. An n-step superposition evolution of a QPN Q can then be identified with the direct concurrence reachability in its monoidal power Q^n (of the same shape as Q). Similarly, the QPN sum $Q^{(1 \leq n)} := \sum_{1 \leq i \leq n} Q^i$ characterises such an evolution of at least 1 and up to $n \geq 1$ steps; $Q^0 = 1_Q$ is the identity matrix; and $Q^{(0 \leq n)} := 1_Q + Q^{(1 \leq n)}$ the evolution of 0 up to $n \geq 1$ steps[10]. Considering the collective OR-parallelism of QPNs superposition evolutions as superposed runs, we note that these do not have to follow in lock step. Any mix of possible lengths can be expressed using sums, products and powers of QPNs, as if unwinding the (possibly cyclic) QPNs according to their hierarchical composition.

It should be noted that the *concurrences* underlying the rate graphs and rate matrices of QPNs, and hence the various interpretations above *are independent of a global time and hence independent of a specific observer*. The multiple transitions in a concurrence may fire entirely asynchronously. But they can also be entangled in a joint – rhythmical and resonant – firing as a function of the causal net structure, the QPN rates and specific complex amplitudes in initial superposition. Because of this, QPNs unify not only classical and quantum computation but also abstract from various time models associated with the corresponding net systems, opening them up for various interpretations, incl. continuous time,

---

[10] Cf. the similarity to products and sums of adjacency matrices of graphs – determining the existence of runs of specified lengths.

discrete time, partial-order event occurrences, stochastic event occurrences etc. Of course, when modeling real physical systems rather than abstract quantum algorithms, any interpretation must be consistent with the quantum mechanical behaviour, ultimately in terms of very specific Hilbert spaces and their operator matrices, whether the generator is a QPN or a quantum circuit diagram.

4   How to Bake Your Pet Net Class with Quantum Flavour

In the literature, many Petri net classes have been defined as extensions of elementary and of place-transition nets. Another approach, taken here, is to parameterise Petri nets and look at specific actual parameters, variation points and restrictions in the spirit of software architecture families and product lines [5, 13, 30].

For example, we simply define a *place-transition net* structure (short PTN) as a net structure (see Definition 1) with $G[N] = N$ and WF= **true**, and, an *elementary Petri net*, EPN for short, as a PTN with $deg(F^-(t)) = deg(F^+(t)) = 1$ for all $t \in T$. A QPN with the corresponding restriction is naturally called Quantum PTN (QPTN) and Quantum EPN (QEPN), respectively.

QPNs that are based, in this way, on our formalisation (Sect. 3) above with specific parameters for the G, WF and other variation points, then also induce a well-defined quantum interpretation by virtue of their underlying PN variant generating the relevant reachability relations. Most importantly, the theory (i.e., initially the theorems above) is valid and the bridge to quantum information theory and quantum computation, that we established above, applies to any of those variants.

We briefly sketch a few variations related to extant Petri net classes. This demonstration also aims to enable the reader to apply similar constructions to their own pet Petri net class, without compromising the quantum interpretation of the QPNs that arise from them as their pet underlying PN class.

4.1   Quantum Logical Guards

Many PN extensions associate guards with transitions. A guard is typically a Boolean expression inscribed to, or associated with, a transition. It may have free variables that may be bound to the number of tokens in one or more places related to the transition, or to the token values in coloured nets. Sometimes free variables may be bound to constants, i.e., user-defined parameters, or to variable values in an extended notion of marking, e.g., the values of one or more clocks to represent asynchronous time with several local clocks. Any free variables can be absorbed in the generator G and result in transition schemes $t[x_1, \ldots, x_n]$, with concrete instances $t[v_1, \ldots, v_n]$ for some actual values v_i admissible for the free variables. $\mathrm{WF}(t[v_1, \ldots, v_n]) = $ **true** then expresses syntactic well-formedness or semantic well-definedness of such transition instances in $\mathbb{T}$. When a guard is false for a given well-formed transition instance $t \in \mathbb{T}$ and marking m, the transition is disabled even if $F^-(t) \leq m$. This is represented here by $\mathrm{WF}(m,t) = \textbf{false}$. According to Definition 2 this implies that the transition is not enabled and hence a corresponding reachability relation is not present in the reachability graph. Clearly the remaining definitions and theorems for QPNs remain well-founded and valid, respectively.

4.2   Quantum Petri Nets with Inhibitors and Phase Transitions

Figure 5 shows a QPN with initial marking of $A^K G$, here with constant $K = 6$. All rates are positive reals and parametrised by a constant R. Considering the restriction of rate functions to positive real values and the variation of normalisation to a division by the sum of absolute values (L1-norm) instead of the square root of the moduli squared of the relevant amplitudes, we arrive at Generalized SPNs (GSPNs) as a special case of QPNs. However, there are a few further constructs in GSPNs we need to consider, such as for instance, the inhibitor arc from place E and pointing to transition e. This disables e when the marking of E is greater or equal to the arc weight, here 1. For this purpose, the formal definition of GSPNs includes an inhibition function H similar in type to F^-, here modelled as $\mathbb{T} \xrightarrow{H} \mathbb{N}^\mathbb{P}$. The inhibition action can thus be captured in our formalism by $\mathrm{WF}(m,t) = \textbf{false}$ if $H(t) \leq m$. Immediate transitions, depicted in

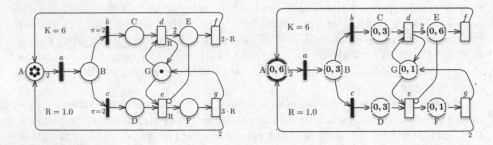

Fig. 5. *GSPNs are a restricted class of QPNs with positive real rates and other restrictions. Left:* The underlying PTN illustrates inhibition and immediate transitions with priorities. Transition e has an incoming *inhibitor arc* from place E, graphically represented by a circle head. *Immediate transitions* are indicated by solid black bars and have associated *priorities* ($\pi > 0$) with default 1. *Rated transitions* are drawn as open boxes and have lowest priority 0. *Right:* Analysis of the underlying system PTN on the left in the GreatSPN toolkit shows that the system is bounded (with bounds shown in places), and (not shown here) that the system has two S-invariants (S-semiflow eigenvectors) and two T-invariants (T-semiflow eigenvectors) allowing further reduction using a basis of eigenvectors in the matrix representation of the underlying net.

Fig. 5 by solid black bars, have an explicit priority π associated to them in the net, which defaults to 1 if not specified. When any immediate transitions is enabled, only the immediate transitions of highest priority are enabled. This can be modeled by WF similar to the above conditions, given that all these GSPN firing constraints are expressed in terms of the enabling marking. With successive firings of immediate transitions and acyclic dependencies (which are required for GSPNs) priority levels inductively decrease until only *timed* transitions, of default priority 0, are enabled. If there is a conflict, a probability distribution (encoded in the rate restrictions for such transitions) resolves that said conflict and chooses one of the conflicting immediate transitions. Any marking that enables an immediate transition is considered *vanishing* and therefore not part of the reachability set proper that generates the reachability. Typically, one constructs a reachability graph with immediate transitions and then reduces it by contracting all paths consisting of only vanishing markings. This can be done coherently in respect of rates by several PN modelling and simulation tools. We omit the details of the relevant algorithms here and refer to the literature (cf. e.g., [3]). The resulting reduced reachability set can then form the basis for our QPN theory.

Note that GSPNs with the above rate restrictions and those other variations are now a special restricted class of QPNs. In addition, Quantum GSPNs (QGSPNs) with complex-valued rate functions arise from the above transliteration of inhibitors, immediate transitions and priorities.

Historically GSPNs cater to the need of modellers to capture significant differences in real rates, especially splitting transitions into those that complete important functions after some duration and those that are orders of magnitude shorter – effectively timeless. Hence immediate transitions are important in this type of net and likely in QPN applications. In practice moreover, for real-time systems modelling, the latter have priorities associated. Amparore et al. write in [3], "*a change of state occurs not only because there has been a completion of an activity which takes time, but also because there has been a change of some logical conditions, which may depend on the current state in a rather intricate manner.*" Physical systems often exhibit rapid phase transitions and engineered systems rapid mode transitions as a response to critical sensory input or reaching critical reactivity levels etc. Modelling these different types of transitions fully on the basis of Hilbert operators for QPNs, or CTMCs in the case of GSPNs, makes their numerical analysis very complex and sometimes infeasible. Like with real-time systems, we expect that for real-space-time quantum systems, such structuring mechanism will empower modellers similarly, to represent the causal and acausal architecture of quantum systems using both logical and physical dependencies.

4.3   Data-Rich Higher-Level Quantum Petri Nets

Many high-level nets have been studied and a variety of net classes adds data to enrich markings. Among these are Predicate-Transition nets, various kinds of algebraic nets and Coloured Petri nets. A marking in such a net is generally a multiset of data items for each place. Different net classes add type-checked data types, tuples and various other bells and whistles. We capture such extensions by the generator G, which pairs the place set P and data set D and forms $P \times D$ with projections to the respective place and data item. Marking $p \in P$ by multiset $a_1^{n_1} \cdots a_n^{k_n}$ in such a net translates, for our nets, to $(p, a_1)^{n_1} \cdots (p, a_n)^{k_n}$. Similar to the above use of WF, the well-formedness function eliminates ill-formed data pairing with places, or adds further restrictions on markings such as excluding out-of-bound multiplicities and potentially errors.

Likewise, transitions are paired with all the data that can reach them via flow arcs inscribed with data and multiplicity expressions using variables. We can use transition schemes similar to the encoding of guards in WF. Thus G generates a data-rich set of net elements, the flow F between them is generated from the arc inscriptions. F^- and F^+ remain input and output multisets like before, for all well-formed and legitimate combinations in the higher-level net. And finally guards on the transitions are transcribed to WF as already shown above.

Algebraic specification of partial functions and predicates mimicking Horn clause logic specification uses a similar construction and has been applied to nets. For example, Predicate-Event nets use many-sorted algebraic specification over nets to generate an ordinary net structure and its markings modulo theory [16,17,24] and enriching net interface descriptions with the power of abstract data types and modules. Analysis methods and executable nets are implemented there based on term rewriting and a compiled functional language. In a partial algebra specification, the free generation and the definedness constraints (here encapsulated[11] in G and WF) use weak and strong equality in a system of conditional equations. Weak equality satisfies: $t \doteq t'$ iff t defined, t' defined and $t = t'$. Therefore, we have that $t \doteq t$ iff t is defined. This makes such an equation also useful in a conclusions of a conditional equation, to express conditions for definedness. For strong equality $\equiv$ we have that: $t \equiv t'$ iff (t defined or t' defined) implies $t \doteq t'$. That is to say, if one side of the equation is defined, the other must be defined and the two must be equal.

5   Related and Future Work

Ojala's group [20] used Coloured Petri nets for the analysis of a certain class of quantum cellular automata designs, by example. They achieve a considerable state space reduction compared to the cellular automata. They do not make full use of the asynchronous nature of Petri nets, nor arrive at the kind of universality that characterises QPNs. They model the control structure of the cellular automaton explicitly as a classical PN with complex values as token colours and do not aim at a universal representation of quantum computations. Their encoding achieves a considerable reduction in the state space compared to that of the equivalent quantum cellular automaton. This work was one of the motivations for our approach, in the hope that causal modelling, immediate transitions and other well-known constructions from classical Petri nets can provide a hybrid classical-quantum design with such gains despite offering universality and quantum-only QPNs in the pure quantum case.

Much work exists on classical hybrid and fluid nets, in which causal structuring and stochasticity is mixed with real and integer markings of places [8,12].

---

[11] And leaving open how this variation point is actualised.

Especially their connection with GSPNs has helped us envisage a general approach to superposition and entanglement with its difference to classical stochasticity. For reasons of brevity, we have omitted detailing hybrid quantum nets, in this paper. Suffice it to mention, that one can always partition the set of places into a finite number of place kinds carrying different kinds of tokens, including Boolean, integer, complex integer ($\mathbb{Z}[i]$), real or complex values. Then transitions are classified to form actions on these, including on mixtures of these kinds. This path has been well trodden in Petri net theory and a number of connections can be drawn to QPNs, although, to our knowledge, quantum has never before been combined directly with these nets.

Future work may be fruitful in

1. *graphical calculi* combining QPNs with circuit diagrams such as the ZX calculus [28]. There are well-known theorems relating partial-order semantics of Petri nets with hierarchical message sequence charts and rational algebraic theories of partially ordered event structures, which may benefit quantum calculi. Dually, the circuit diagrams of QPNs may lend themselves for the execution of QPNs on real quantum computers. QPNs and perhaps nets more generally may benefit from the complexity and execution time advantages of quantum computing.
2. *machine learning and optimisation* of quantum protocols leveraging both the quantum computing speed advantage and advances in classical hardware for machine learning has received much attention recently. Novel approaches such as quantum and classical co-design [14] may be especially applicable to our approach so fundamentally intertwining the two aspects.
3. *asynchronous quantum automata* have not received much attention. Petri nets have been studied for decades as asynchronous automata for formal languages, both generating and accepting. A rich set of theorems exists on their decidability and expressive power in comparison to other automata and formal language approaches. A corresponding analysis of quantum automata is still in its infancy. QPNs may assist revisiting these from the perspective of the underlying PNs, their composition and their soft gluing or 'coalescing' using shades of entanglement.
4. *open quantum interaction protocols* at the interface of classical and quantum components of QPN systems. Much current focus in quantum hardware is naturally on closed quantum systems. Measurements are typically final, collapse the system as a whole and require the restart of the entire system. With their hybrid causal and acausal structure, QPNs enable a true hybrid between open and closed systems, where the network architecture can increase coherence from the collapse due to partial measurement.

6   Conclusion

This paper introduced a novel diagrammatic model for quantum information processing, Quantum Petri nets (QPNs). It adds to the rich theory of Petri nets new results that are far from straightforward, including the universality of QPNs for quantum computation and their architectural compositionality that reaches from the well-known classical net structure to the operator matrices of Hilbert vector spaces. To our knowledge, these results are *novel and original*. While compositionality is expected for the rate matrices generated by these nets, the matrices are forgetful of the net structure. However, the compositionality we explore here is already inherent in the net structure of the highly parallel quantum processes. QPNs therefore lend themselves for a formal component-based software architecture with well-defined entanglement, teleportation and tunnelling across component boundaries beside the traditional interface protocols, for which nets have been studied in theory and practice. QPNs and their theory are based on the formalism of Petri nets which dates back well before the notion of quantum computation was formulated, to Petri's 1962 PhD thesis, which itself was developed with reference to principles of relativity and quantum uncertainty [25]. Over the many decades since, nets have become a widely used and standardized notation for concurrent processes in parallel and distributed software modelling and other process-rich domains with several directly and indirectly associated ISO and DIN standards. QPNs are reconnecting with Petri's original motivation for his nets. Abramsky wrote in [1]:

Petri's thinking was explicitly influenced by physics. To a large extent, and by design, net theory can be seen as a kind of discrete physics: lines are time-like causal flows, cuts are space-like regions, process unfoldings of a marked net are like the solution trajectories of a differential equation. This acquires new significance today, when the consequences of the idea that information is physical are being explored in the rapidly developing field of quantum informatics.

The paper demonstrated that a separation of concerns can be achieved between the classical concurrency structures, typical for Petri nets, and the specific quantum character of entanglement. This separation allows modellers to apply Petri net methods and tools to QPNs and leverage them for quantum information processing. Moreover, likely novel results in either field may accelerate advances in the other through a joint focus on the orthogonal connection that QPNs show is possible for the two fields of concurrent and quantum information processes. To this end, this paper included a number of related and future research problems.

Modern *systems architecture requires a dialog* between hardware and software platform designers, compiler writers, software library engineers and application software developers, whether for a highly integrated multi-core tablet and single-user workstation, or a high-performance supercomputer. The same will undoubtedly be required of future hybrid quantum and classical systems architectures for networked distributed quantum systems accessible via cloud services. Such services architectures are currently nascent in commercial offerings. Petri nets have served this dialog in classical distributed systems as a visual user-friendly and at the same time mathematically strong tool alongside other strong representations as a *lingua franca crossing fields of expertise*. As part of the formal treatment of quantum processes in the framework of net theory, the paper therefore identified architectural variation points in its formal and informal constructions. We used insights from our prior research in software architecture design and verification. We sketched how the resulting architectural variability can be applied from elementary Petri nets to Generalized Stochastic Petri nets with or without colours. A variety of QPN models, their compositionality and architectures may then be utilised across several classes of Petri nets.

The paper started by a gentle introduction to quantum computation with QPNs to appeal to the 'rest of us': software engineers, practitioners and computer scientists less familiar with the technical details of quantum mechanics and their vector spaces than with diagrammatic models for software programs and their computational processes, in particular state-machine based concurrent processes such as espoused in Petri nets and UML architecture diagrams and dynamic models. The aim was not only to introduce QPNs, but also to recognise and demonstrate – before diving into the requisite formalisation – that a *quantum software engineering narrative is needed and possible*, with minimal knowledge of complex numbers, some basic familiarity with high-school algebra, and almost no knowledge of vector spaces, at least at the introductory level. The hope is that this diagrammatic approach, or perhaps its combination with other suitable and familiar software models and programming language constructs, may provide a more gradual entrance ramp to the highway of quantum computing, that is bound to become a fast multi-lane freeway. Current on-ramps offer a mix of physics, applied mathematics and theoretical computer science terminology yet to be standardised and require a steep learning curve.

Through the architectural compositionality results for QPNs presented in this paper, one might hope, that hybrid classical and quantum software design can be based on a diagram-plus-program approach, with verification in graphs and nets, yet ease of design following principles of modularity, information hiding and separation of concerns. These hallmarks of software engineering may empower domain experts and a future open-source quantum software development community to leverage both classical methods and advances in quantum computing.

References

1. Abramsky, S.: What are the fundamental structures of concurrency? Electron. Notes Theoret. Comput. Sci. **162**, 37–41 (2006). https://doi.org/10.1016/j.entcs. 2005.12.075
2. Amparore, E., Donatelli, S.: Efficient model checking of the stochastic logic CSLTA. Perform. Eval. **123–124**, 1–34 (2018). https://doi.org/10.1016/j.peva.2018.03.002
3. Amparore, E.G., Balbo, G., Beccuti, M., Donatelli, S., Franceschinis, G.: 30 years of GreatSPN. In: Fiondella, L., Puliafito, A. (eds.) Principles of Performance and Reliability Modeling and Evaluation. SSRE, pp. 227–254. Springer, Cham (2016). https://doi.org/10.1007/978-3-319-30599-8_9
4. Berthomieu, B., Le Botlan, D., Dal Zilio, S.: Petri Net reductions for counting markings. In: Gallardo, M.M., Merino, P. (eds.) SPIN 2018. LNCS, vol. 10869, pp. 65–84. Springer, Cham (2018). https://doi.org/10.1007/978-3-319-94111-0_4

5. Bosch, J., Bosch-Sijtsema, P.: From integration to composition: On the impact of software product lines, global development and ecosystems. J. Syst. Softw. **83**(1), 67–76 (2010). https://doi.org/10.1016/j.jss.2009.06.051
6. Campos, J., Donatelli, S., Silva, M.: Structured solution of asynchronously communicating stochastic modules. IEEE Trans. Software Eng. **25**(2), 147–165 (1999). https://doi.org/10.1109/32.761442
7. Castelvecchi, D.: IBM's quantum cloud computer goes commercial. Nature (London) **543**(7644), 159 (2017)
8. Ciardo, G., Muppala, J.K., Trivedi, K.S.: SPNP: stochastic Petri net package. PNPM **89**, 142–151 (1989)
9. Desel, J., Reisig, W.: The concepts of Petri nets. Softw. Syst. Model. **14**(2), 669–683 (2015)
10. Donatelli, S.: Kronecker algebra and (stochastic) Petri nets: is it worth the effort? In: Colom, J.-M., Koutny, M. (eds.) ICATPN 2001. LNCS, vol. 2075, pp. 1–18. Springer, Heidelberg (2001). https://doi.org/10.1007/3-540-45740-2_1
11. Heiner, M., Rohr, C., Schwarick, M.: MARCIE – model checking and reachability analysis done efficiently. In: Colom, J.-M., Desel, J. (eds.) Application and Theory of Petri Nets and Concurrency. PETRI NETS 2013. LNCS, vol. 7927, pp. 389–399. Springer, Heidelberg (2013). https://doi.org/10.1007/978-3-642-38697-8_21
12. Horton, G., Kulkarni, V.G., Nicol, D.M., Trivedi, K.S.: Fluid stochastic Petri nets: theory, applications, and solution techniques. Eur. J. Oper. Res. **105**(1), 184–201 (1998). https://doi.org/10.1016/S0377-2217(97)00028-3
13. Jazayeri, M., Ran, A., van der Linden, F.: Software Architecture for Product Families: Principles and Practice. Addison-Wesley, Reading (2000)
14. Jiang, W., Xiong, J., Shi, Y.: A co-design framework of neural networks and quantum circuits towards quantum advantage. Nat. Commun. **12**(1), 669–683 (2021)
15. Kimble, H.J.: The quantum internet. Nature (London) **453**(7198), 1023–1030 (2008)
16. Krämer, B.: Stepwise construction of non-sequential software systems using a net-based specification language. In: Rozenberg, G. (ed.) Advances in Petri Nets 1984. LNCS, vol. 188, pp. 307–330. Springer, Heidelberg (1985). https://doi.org/10.1007/3-540-15204-0_18
17. Krämer, B., Schmidt, H.W.: Types and modules for net specifications. In: Voss, K., Genrich, H.J., Rozenberg, G. (eds.) Concurrency and Nets, pp. 269–286. Springer, Heidelberg (1987). https://doi.org/10.1007/978-3-642-72822-8_19
18. Miszczak, J.: High-Level Structures for Quantum Computing: High Level Structures for Quantum Computing. Morgan & Claypool Publishers, San Rafael (2012)
19. Murata, T.: Petri nets: properties, analysis and applications. Proc. IEEE **77**(4), 541–80 (1989)
20. Ojala, L., Penttinen, O.-M., Parviainen, E.: Modeling and analysis of Margolus quantum cellular automata using net-theoretical methods. In: Cortadella, J., Reisig, W. (eds.) ICATPN 2004. LNCS, vol. 3099, pp. 331–350. Springer, Heidelberg (2004). https://doi.org/10.1007/978-3-540-27793-4_19
21. Petri, C.A.: Introduction to general net theory. In: Brauer, W. (ed.) Net Theory and Applications: Proceedings of the Advanced Course on General Net Theory, Processes and Systems (Hamburg, 1979). LNCS, vol. 84, pp. 1–20. Springer, Berlin (1980)
22. Popkin, G.: China's quantum satellite achieves spooky action at a distance. Sci. Mag. (2017). https://doi.org/10.1126/science.aan6972

23. Reisig, W.: Petri Nets: An Introduction. EATCS Monographs on Theoretical Computer Science, Springer, Berlin (1985). https://doi.org/10.1007/978-3-642-69968-9

24. Schmidt, H.W.: Prototyping and analysis of non-sequential systems using predicate-event nets. J. Syst. Softw. **15**(1), 43–62 (1991). https://doi.org/10.1016/0164-1212(91)90076-I

25. Schmidt, H.W.: Petri Nets: the next 50 years—an invitation and interpretative translation. In: Reisig, W., Rozenberg, G. (eds.) Carl Adam Petri: Ideas, Personality, Impact, pp. 45–66. Springer, Cham (2019). https://doi.org/10.1007/978-3-319-96154-5_7

26. Schrödinger, E.: Discussion of probability relations between separated systems. Math. Proc. Cambridge Philos. Soc. **31**(4), 555–563 (1935). https://doi.org/10.1017/S0305004100013554

27. Steffen, M., DiVincenzo, D.P., Chow, J.M., Theis, T.N., Ketchen, M.B.: Quantum computing: an IBM perspective. IBM J. Res. Dev. **55**(5), 13:1-13:11 (2011). https://doi.org/10.1147/JRD.2011.2165678

28. van de Wetering, J.: ZX-calculus for the working quantum computer scientist. Online, Cornell University, USA (2020). arxiv:2012.13966

29. Yanofsky, N.S., Mannucci, M.A.: Quantum Computing for Computer Scientists. Cambridge University Press, Cambridge (2008)

30. Yusuf, I., Schmidt, H.: Parameterised architectural patterns for providing cloud service fault tolerance with accurate costings. In: Proceedings of CBSE 2013, pp. 121–130. ACM (2013). https://doi.org/10.1145/2465449.2465467

Patterns for Hybrid Quantum Algorithms

Manuela Weigold[(⊠)][iD], Johanna Barzen[iD], Frank Leymann[iD],
and Daniel Vietz[iD]

Institute of Architecture of Application Systems, University of Stuttgart,
Universitätsstrasse 38, Stuttgart, Germany
{manuela.weigold,johanna.barzen,frank.leymann,
daniel.vietz}@iaas.uni-stuttgart.de

Abstract. Quantum computers have the potential to solve certain problems faster than classical computers. However, the computations that can be executed on current quantum devices are still limited. Hybrid algorithms split the computational tasks between classical and quantum computers circumventing some of these limitations. Therefore, they are regarded as promising candidates for useful applications in the near future. But especially for novices in quantum computing, it is hard to identify why a particular splitting strategy is proposed by an algorithm. In this work, we describe the best practices for splitting strategies as patterns to foster a common understanding of hybrid algorithms.

Keywords: Quantum computing · Patterns · Hybrid algorithms

1 Introduction

Quantum computers are no longer a purely theoretical concept – a first generation of quantum computers is already available to the public [1,2]. These devices differ considerably from classical computers as their central unit of information is not a classical bit (which can be in a state of either zero or one), but a quantum bit (qubit). Because they are based on qubits, quantum computers are expected to solve certain problems faster than their classical counterparts [3,4]. Famous examples for quantum algorithms that promise a theoretical linear or exponential speedup are Shor's algorithm [5] for factoring prime numbers or the HHL algorithm [6] for solving linear equations.

However, as current devices still have severe hardware limitations, they are also referred to as *Noisy Intermediate Scale Quantum (NISQ)* devices [7]. Measured by their number of qubits, these devices are of intermediate size (they contain up to a few hundred qubits). Their noisy qubits are only stable for a limited amount of time. Due to their short lifespan, the number of operations that can be executed on a NISQ device is limited. As a consequence, the required operations of many quantum algorithms exceed those of NISQ devices, or they can only be executed for small problems. For example, recent experiments were able to demonstrate Shor's algorithm [5] for factoring small numbers such as 15

© Springer Nature Switzerland AG 2021
J. Barzen (Ed.): SummerSOC 2021, CCIS 1429, pp. 34–51, 2021.
https://doi.org/10.1007/978-3-030-87568-8_2

or 21 [8]. Given the current state of hardware, Shor's algorithm is one of many algorithms which will not be of much practical use in the near future.

Nevertheless, even with these limitations, first practical applications of quantum computers are expected [7]. Since the size of quantum computations is limited, it has been suggested to use classical computers to overcome the limitations of NISQ devices [9]. Thus, hybrid algorithms strategically split the computational tasks between classical and quantum computers. In the quantum computing literature, an abundance of hybrid algorithms have been proposed and new algorithms appear frequently. However, especially for novices in the field it is often not clear what hybrid algorithm have in common or why they split the computational tasks in a particular manner. This raises the following questions: What are common splitting strategies of hybrid algorithms? What are the benefits and drawbacks of a splitting strategy, and in which contexts are they useful?

To answer these questions, we identify best practices for a *quantum-classical split* and describe them as patterns. In many domains, patterns are an established concept for the documentation of proven solutions for frequently reoccurring problems. Each of our patterns captures the abstract idea behind various quantum algorithms and its relations to other patterns. They are targeted at readers that are already familiar with the basics of quantum computing, such as qubits or quantum circuits. Together, the patterns form a common knowledge base through which different approaches (i) can be understood, and (ii) can be applied in combination to solve a broader problem.

The remainder of this work is structured as follows: we first give an overview of patterns for quantum algorithms of previous works [10,11] and describe fundamentals of hybrid algorithms in Sect. 2. Then, we present the six new patterns for hybrid algorithms in Sect. 3. Related work is described in Sect. 4. Finally, a conclusion and overview of future work is given in Sect. 5.

2 Patterns for Quantum Algorithms

In this section, we introduce fundamentals and patterns for quantum algorithms. First, the structure of hybrid algorithms is described and an overview of existing [10–12] and new patterns is given (Sect. 2.1). This is followed by Sect. 2.2 that introduces our pattern format and method for pattern authoring.

2.1 Overview of Patterns for Quantum Algorithms

Figure 1 illustrates the basic structure of hybrid algorithms. The first step on a classical computer is *pre-processing*. A simple example for a pre-processing task is the normalization of input data, however, more complex tasks are also possible. On a quantum computer, the first step is always to *prepare an initial state* of a qubit register. Note that this step can also be used to load data which is usually done by encoding it into the initial state. The resulting state can also be entangled which is one characteristic of quantum states described by patterns of the quantum states category. Additionally, data encoding patterns in the upper

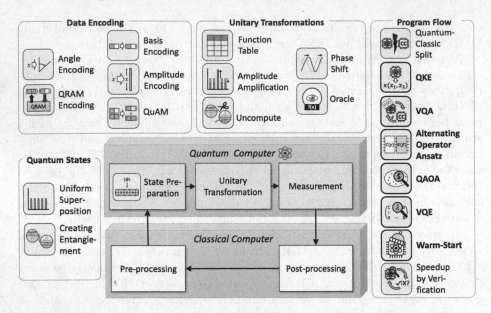

Fig. 1. Overview of previous and new patterns (in bold), adapted from [10].

left of the figure describe in more detail how this can be realized for a particular encoding. In the next step, the quantum computer performs *unitary transformations*. Patterns of the same category describe common transformations, for example, the application of a PHASE SHIFT to mark a particular amplitude. Finally, all or a subset of the qubits are *measured*. The measurement results are *post-processed* on a classical computer. Depending on the overall goal, the algorithm terminates or iterates. Patterns of the category program flow (including the new patterns) describe higher-level strategies for quantum algorithms.

2.2   Pattern Format and Method

For the structure of our patterns, we used a pattern format of previous work [10,11]. A pattern is introduced by a *Name* and represented graphically as an *Icon*. A pattern name can also be inspired by the name of a prominent algorithm that applies the pattern. Other names under which this pattern may be known are listed as an *Alias*. This is followed by the *Context* of a pattern, which includes a description of the problem. Next, its *Forces* are described that must be considered when solving the problem. Then, the *Solution* is described and often visualized by a *Sketch*. The consequences are described as the *Result* of the solutions. Finally, *Related Patterns* and *Known Uses* are listed.

To identify the patterns, we analyzed the structure of hybrid algorithms documented in the quantum computing literature. If we found various occurrences of a splitting approach (for example, in publications introducing quantum algorithms or in implementations of algorithms) which is also regarded as promising in the literature, we authored a pattern. As quantum computing hardware is still in an early stage, we do not require concrete implementations as known uses of the patterns. Instead, we focus on finding and describing re-occurring solutions in quantum algorithms.

3 Patterns for Hybrid Algorithms

In this section, we present patterns for hybrid algorithms. In previous work [12], we already introduced the QUANTUM-CLASSIC SPLIT pattern which motivates that the computational workload is split between quantum and classical resources. As illustrated in Fig. 2, the new patterns further refine this pattern by introducing best practices for realizing a QUANTUM-CLASSIC SPLIT. Thus, the problem, context, and solution of each refining pattern are further specialized towards a concrete use case [13]. As hybrid algorithms are often not invented from scratch but extend previously known splitting strategies, we identified several other refinement relations as shown in Fig. 2. In the following, the most abstract QUANTUM-CLASSIC SPLIT [12] pattern is introduced first via a brief summary and a list of its forces. Note that these are also the forces of all refining patterns. We then present the new patterns, starting with QUANTUM KERNEL ESTIMATOR (Sect. 3.2). This is followed by VARIATIONAL QUANTUM ALGORITHM (Sect. 3.3) and its further refining patterns (Sects. 3.4 to 3.6). Finally, the WARM START (Sect. 3.7) pattern is presented. An excerpt of the patterns can be found at http://quantumcomputingpatterns.org.

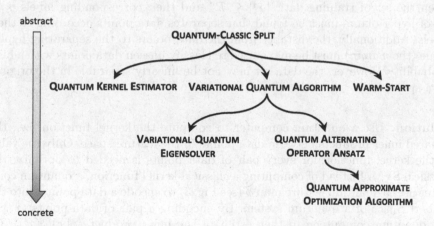

Fig. 2. Overview of all patterns presented in this section. A black arrow indicates that a pattern is further refined by another pattern.

3.1 QUANTUM-CLASSIC SPLIT

Summary: Solve a given problem using classical as well as quantum resources (also referred to as *hybrid approach*). Depending on the problem, the computational tasks are split between quantum and classical resources.

Forces. A good split of the computational tasks balances the following forces:

(i) Quantum computations are limited: NISQ devices contain a limited number of qubits that are not fully connected. The number of operations which can be executed within the decoherence time of the qubits is also limited [7]. Since the devices are not fully connected, additional operations may be needed to realize operations on multiple qubits [14].

(ii) It is often not possible to divide quantum computations into smaller parts as for example a superposition of inputs needs to be processed at once.

3.2 QUANTUM KERNEL ESTIMATOR (QKE)

Use the quantum computer as a kernel estimator for a classical SVM

Context. A classification task must be solved by a support vector machine: given the set of training data $\{x_i\} \subseteq \mathcal{R}^d$ and their corresponding labels y_i, a set of hyper-planes must be found that separates data points according to their labels. Additionally, the distance from the data points to the separating hyperplane (the *margin*) must be maximized to classify unseen data points with a high probability. However, the data set may not be linearly separable in the original data space.

Solution. Use a quantum computer to compute the kernel function, i.e., the squared inner products between data points in the feature space. Only the value of the kernel function for every pair of data points is needed to optimize the classical SVM. Instead of computing a classical kernel function, a quantum computer uses a quantum feature map ϕ (see Fig. 3) to encode a data point x into the Hilbert Space of a quantum system. By encoding a pair of data-points (x, x'), the quantum computer can then estimate the inner product $\langle\phi(x)|\phi(x')\rangle$, for example by using the SWAP test routine [15]. Based on the inner product, the kernel function $K(x, x') = |\langle\phi(x)|\phi(x')\rangle|^2$ can be computed for the data pair and used for the training of the classical SVM.

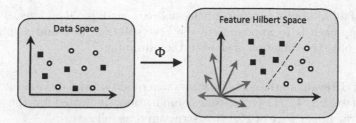

Fig. 3. The quantum feature map ϕ encodes data-points into the Hilbert Space.

Result. The training and classification of the classical support vector machine is efficient if the inner products between data points in the feature space can be evaluated efficiently. Therefore, this setup allows to use feature mappings that cannot be computed efficiently on a classical computer. However, it remains an open research question how a suitable quantum feature map can be chosen.

Related Patterns. This pattern refines QUANTUM-CLASSIC SPLIT.

Known Uses. In the original paper of the algorithm [16], the authors also demonstrated it in a proof-of-principle experiment on two qubits. Independently, Schuld et al. [15] published the same algorithm and additionally introduced a feature map for continuous-variable quantum systems. Since then, an additional proof-of-principle experiment followed which demonstrated that photonic qubits can be used for this particular task [17]. The approach was also extended in [18]. We implemented this pattern in the QHAna[1] project [19], and also provided a user interface for the selection of different feature maps.

3.3 VARIATIONAL QUANTUM ALGORITHM (VQA)

 Optimize the parameters of a quantum circuit on a classical computer

Context. For a given problem, the solution space and, thus, all potential solutions are known. The overall goal is to find the best solution or a solution that is sufficiently good for the task at hand. Since each solution can be evaluated by an objective function, different solutions can be compared with respect to their costs. The objective function C must be *faithful*, i.e., the minimum of C corresponds to the best solution [20]. Ideally, it is also *operationally meaningful* such that smaller values indicate better solutions [20]. However, as the solution space grows exponentially with the problem size, it is difficult to identify the best solution. Consequently, a brute force approach, i.e., calculating the objective

---

[1] https://github.com/UST-QuAntiL/qhana.

function of all solutions, is often only feasible for small problem sizes. Therefore, another approach is to approximate the best solution, i.e., find a solution for which the objective function is close to the minimum.

Solution. To evaluate the cost of a solution, a quantum and a classical computer are used (see Fig. 4). The quantum computation (indicated by the quantum circuit in the upper part of Fig. 4) is structured as follows:

First, an initial state $|\psi_{in}(x)\rangle$ is prepared which may also depend on a set of input data x. Then, an ansatz circuit $U(\theta)$ is applied to the initial state producing the output state $|\psi_{out}(x,\theta)\rangle$. An ansatz is a unitary operation that is varied by a set of parameters θ. An often-used example of an ansatz is a rotation operation on multiple qubits where the angle depends on θ.

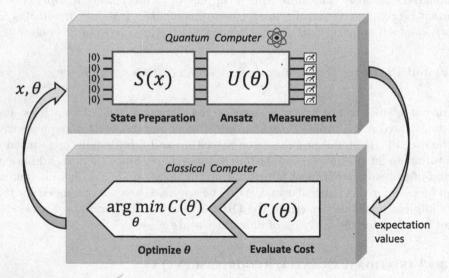

Fig. 4. Quantum-classical setup in which the quantum computation depends on a set of parameters θ updated by an optimization routine running on a classical computer.

Based on the measured expectation values, the value of the objective function for the chosen parameter θ is computed by the classical computer:

$$C(\theta) = \sum_i f_i(\langle O_i \rangle_{|\psi_{out}(x,\theta)\rangle}) \tag{1}$$

where O_i is the observable associated with the i-th measurement, $\langle O_i \rangle_{|\psi_{out}(x,\theta)\rangle}$ is the expectation value for this measurement, and f is a function that associates the expectation values with an overall cost. If the termination condition is fulfilled, e.g., if $C(\theta)$ is sufficiently low, the algorithm terminates. Otherwise, an updated parameter can be obtained by either an optimization technique [20] for a new iteration.

Result. A major drawback of this approach is that it is not trivial to choose a suitable function f, the observables for the measurements, and a good ansatz. How fast the solution converges depends on the objective function as well as the chosen optimization strategy. In particular, *barren plateaus* which are regions of the objective function with a small norm of the gradient can slow down this process even further [20] or even worse may result in non-convergence of the overall algorithm. Since the classical computer performs the optimization, classical computations can also contribute significantly to the overall runtime complexity.

Related Patterns. This pattern refines QUANTUM-CLASSIC SPLIT [12] and uses STATE PREPARATION [12].

Known Uses. There are plenty of known uses for this pattern. For example, variational quantum algorithms for quantum classifiers [21], quantum neural networks [22], a quantum support vector machine [15,16], and an alternative to Shor's algorithm for factoring prime numbers [23] exist.

3.4   VARIATIONAL QUANTUM EIGENSOLVER (VQE)

 Approximate the lowest eigenvalue of a matrix

Alias. Quantum Variational Eigensolver (QVE) [21]

Context. The goal is to find the lowest eigenvalue λ of a hermitian matrix H. The hardware requirements for Quantum phase estimation (QPE) are beyond those of NISQ devices, and thus, an approach for NISQ devices is needed.

Solution. Write H as a linear combination of Pauli strings:

$$H = \sum_\alpha h_\alpha P_\alpha \tag{2}$$

Following the structure of VARIATIONAL QUANTUM ALGORITHM, prepare trial states by using a suitable ansatz. For example, the unitary coupled cluster ansatz [24] or a hardware-efficient ansatz [20] can be used. Then, the objective function is the sum of the expectation values of the Pauli strings:

$$C(\theta) = \langle\psi(\theta)|H|\psi(\theta)\rangle = \sum_\alpha h_\alpha \langle\psi(\theta)|P_\alpha|\psi(\theta)\rangle \tag{3}$$

By the variational principle, the expectation value is always greater or equal to the smallest eigenvalue of H. Optimize and update the parameters as described in VARIATIONAL QUANTUM ALGORITHM.

Result. Analogously to VARIATIONAL QUANTUM ALGORITHM, the result, and performance of this approach depend on the objective function, the choice of the ansatz as well as the optimization strategy. The lowest eigenvalue is approximated and can be used to find other eigenvalues (see known uses). This is especially useful for dimension reduction based on principal component analysis (PCA) which requires all eigenvalues of the matrix.

Related Patterns. This pattern refines VARIATIONAL QUANTUM ALGORITHM.

Known Uses. Based on the original algorithm [25] of Peruzzo et al., an approach for finding all eigenvalues of a given matrix was proposed [26]. In quantum chemistry, this algorithm is especially useful for finding ground states of chemical systems and has been applied to various systems [27]. The recently founded Quantum Technology and Application Consortium (QUTAC)[2] identified this algorithm as a possible solution for various industry applications [28].

3.5   ALTERNATING OPERATOR ANSATZ (AOA)

 Approximate the solution of an optimization problem

Context. A given combinatorial optimization problem must be solved that consists of n binary variables and m clauses which each depend on a subset of the variables. A solution is specified as a bit string $z = z_1 \ldots z_n$ that assigns each binary variable z_i to either 0 or 1. The domain is the set of all feasible solutions. Typically a larger configuration space (e.g., all possible bit strings z of length n) is constrained to a subset [29]. The objective function $C(z)$ for a solution is the number of clauses fulfilled by its bit string z:

$$C(z) = \sum_{j=1}^{m} C_j(z) \text{ where } C_\alpha(z) = \begin{cases} 1, & \text{if } C_\alpha \text{ is fulfilled by z} \\ 0, & \text{otherwise} \end{cases} \quad (4)$$

Evaluating the objective function for a certain solution is not computationally intensive, but identifying the best solution, i.e., finding the solution which minimizes or maximizes the objective function, is. To circumvent this difficulty, heuristic approaches can be used in order to find a solution whose value of the objective function is close to the maximum or minimum of the objective function.

Solution. Like in VQA, an initial state $|s\rangle$ is created (see Fig. 5) and an ansatz is constructed based on a *phase-separating operator* $U(C, \gamma)$ and a *mixing operator* $U(B, \beta)$ which depend on the parameter sets γ and β.

---

[2] https://www.qutac.de/.

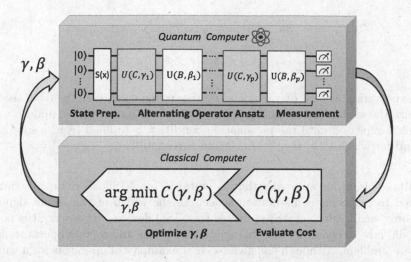

Fig. 5. Quantum alternating operator ansatz.

The initial state $|s\rangle$ is assumed to be created in constant depth, which in general is not possible for some quantum states. For example, $|s\rangle$ can be a state that represents one single solution. Alternatively, a superposition of suitable solutions can be created.

The separating phase operator encodes the objective function and changes the phase of a computational basis state $|y\rangle$ according to $C(y)$:

$$U(C,\gamma)|y\rangle = f(y)|y\rangle \qquad (5)$$

For example, $U(C,\gamma)$ can be defined such that a phase shift is applied to $|y\rangle$ for every fulfilled clause. The mixing operator $U(B,\beta)$ changes the amplitudes of the solutions. In particular, it must be possible to transition from any solution to every other solution, i.e., for every pair $(|x\rangle, |y\rangle)$ of computational basis states within the problem domain there exist some parameter β^* for which $U(B,\beta^*)$ provides a transition between them. Therefore, this operator depends on the structure of the domain.

The solution creates on a quantum computer the initial state $|s\rangle$ and applies unitaries drawn from $C(\gamma)$ and $B(\beta)$ in alternation. This results in the following state:

$$|\gamma,\beta\rangle = U(B,\beta_p)U(C,\gamma_p)\ldots U(B,\beta_1)U(C,\gamma_1)|s\rangle \qquad (6)$$

where γ,β can be initialized randomly at first and $p \in \mathbb{N}$ is a hyper-parameter. Measurement then results in a single solution z for which $C(z)$ can be evaluated. By sampling, the expectation value for γ,β can be determined. Because $|\gamma,\beta\rangle$ is a linear combination of computational basis states, its expectation value is always smaller or equal to the objective function for the best solution z':

$$\langle C \rangle_{|\gamma,\beta\rangle} = \langle \gamma, \beta | C | \gamma, \beta \rangle = \left\langle \sum x_z | z \rangle \middle| \sum x_z f(z) | z \rangle \right\rangle \qquad (7)$$

$$= \sum |x_z|^2 f(z) \leq \sum |x_z|^2 f(z') = f(z') = C_{max} \qquad (8)$$

The expectation values of variations of the parameters can then be used to optimize the angles for optimizing the objective function and thus, update γ and β. This is repeated until the termination condition is fulfilled (e.g., a solution z is found for which $C(z)$ is above a certain threshold).

Result. This is an approach that is suitable for NISQ devices and can be adapted to a specific configuration space. As the width of the circuit depends on p, only small values of p are suitable for NISQ devices. However, it is not at all trivial how to construct suitable separating phase and mixing operators for a concrete problem. Although [29] gives several examples of operators for a variety of problems, further research regarding the design of these operators is needed. Analogously to VQA, the choice of the operators (which define the ansatz), the objective function, and the chosen optimization strategy influence how fast the solution converges.

Related Patterns. This pattern refines VQA (the varied parameters are β and γ) and can be combined with WARM START. Solutions are represented in BASIS ENCODING [10]. The phase separating operator uses a PHASE SHIFT [12] to mark suitable solutions based on their objective function.

Variations. Besides using computational basis states to represent solutions, also other encodings such as one-hot encoding are possible.

Known Uses. In the original paper [29] that introduces this algorithm, the authors give plenty of examples of how their approach can be applied to a variety of optimization problems and emphasize that is suitable for a broader range of applications. The approach has been used in [30,31].

3.6   QUANTUM APPROXIMATE OPTIMIZATION ALGORITHM (QAOA)

 Approximate the solution of an optimization problem

Context. Similar to AOA, an optimization problem must be solved (see Context of AOA for a detailed description) and thus, an objective function is given. In contrast to AOA, the domain of possible solutions is not constrained, and therefore, every bit string $z = z_1 \dots z_n$ is a possible solution of the problem.

Solution. Figure 6 illustrates the *Quantum Approximate Optimization Algorithm (QAOA)* [32] that follows the structure described in AOA. $|s\rangle$ is prepared as the UNIFORM SUPERPOSITION [12] that represents all possible solutions in

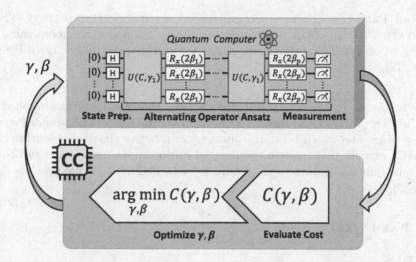

Fig. 6. Overview of QAOA.

BASIS ENCODING [10]. For example, $|0\ldots0\rangle$ represents the solution where all variables are assigned to 0, $|0\ldots01\rangle$ represents $z = 00\ldots01$, etc.

The two operators $U(C, \gamma)$ and $U(B, \beta)$ are defined as follows:

$$U(C, \gamma) = e^{i\gamma C} = \prod_{\alpha=1}^{m} e^{-i\gamma C_\alpha}; \ U(B, \beta) = e^{-i\beta B} = \prod_{j=1}^{n} e^{-i\beta\sigma_x^j} \tag{9}$$

For every clause, $U(C, \gamma)$ applies a phase shift $e^{-i\gamma}$ to every computational basis state that fulfills it. As this only marks but does not affect the amplitude of the solutions, $U(B, \gamma)$ is needed to "mix" their amplitudes. This is realized as a rotation around the X-axis with an angle of 2β ($R_x(2\beta)$).

Following the structure described in AOA, $|\gamma, \beta\rangle$ is prepared. Measuring all qubits then results in a single solution (the bit string z), for which the objective function can be evaluated. The parameters β and γ are first chosen at random and then iteratively updated until the termination condition is fulfilled.

Result. This approach is regarded as a promising approach to solve optimization problems on NISQ devices since the required circuit depth is shallow (at most $mp + p$ [32]).

For $p \to \infty$ and suitable small values for γ, β, it approximates the best solution.[3] However, the performance of QAOA depends on the optimization strategy for the angles β, γ and the objective function.

Related Patterns. This pattern creates a UNIFORM SUPERPOSITION [12] in the STATE PREPARATION [12] of the algorithm. Solutions are represented in BASIS ENCODING. This pattern refines AOA, and thus, also makes use of PHASE SHIFT [12].

Known Uses. In the initial publication [32], the algorithm was applied to MaxCut. The authors also showed a quantum advantage for the *bounded occurrence problem* [34] which led to the discovery of a better classical algorithm [35]. QUTAC[4] expects that numerous industrial optimization use cases may benefit from quantum computing in the future for which QAOA is one possible approach [28].

3.7   WARM START

 Fine-tune an optimization algorithm by warm starting it

Context. A solution to an optimization problem (see AOA for a detailed description) must be found. Assuming that the *Unique Game Conjecture* (UGC) is true, there is a theoretical upper bound for the approximation ratio of efficient classical methods, i.e., they can only guarantee to approximate the best solution to a certain degree. Since the UGC does not hold for algorithms that exploit entanglement, corresponding quantum algorithms can approximate beyond these bounds.

Solution. Use a classical method to find an approximate solution of the problem. Often, an approximated solution to the original problem can be found solving a simpler, related problem, e.g., for which some of the constraints of the original problem are relaxed.

Result. Warm starting results in a good initial starting solution (near the optimum) which is then used as the start-point for the optimization of the original problem. However, the classical optimization for the related problem also contributes to the overall runtime complexity.

---

[3] [32] proves this by showing how this algorithm relates to the adiabatic algorithm [33], which also inspired the ansatz of the algorithm.

[4] https://www.qutac.de/.

Related Patterns. This pattern can be specialized for QAOA or VQE.

Known Uses. For the MaxCut [36] problem and quadratic optimization problems [37] the warm start of a QAOA was proposed and improved the performance of the optimization. The approach followed in [38] can also be seen as an example for warm starting VQE [37].

4   Related Work

In this work, we use the concept of patterns as introduced by Alexander et al. [39]. The new patterns presented complement quantum computing patterns of previous work [10–12]. Out of the 15 previous patterns, 13 patterns focus on quantum computations (see Sect. 2), whereas all new hybrid patterns comprise quantum as well as classical computations. To our best knowledge, there exist no other patterns for quantum computing that conform to the notion of patterns of Alexander et al. [39].

Since the appearance of the first quantum algorithms, numerous algorithms have followed. The most extensive catalog of quantum algorithms known to us is presented at *Quantum Algorithm Zoo*[5] which summarizes algorithms of three categories. An high-level overview of current quantum machine learning algorithms can be found in [40]. The authors also identified whether Grover's search algorithm [41] (a special case of our AMPLITUDE AMPLIFICATION pattern [12]) was used as subroutine. Since VQE [25] and QAOA [32] are the most prominent variational algorithms, they have been described on a higher level [19,40,42,43] and a more technical level [44,45] in various other works. In contrast to this work, none of the works describes these proven solutions as interconnected patterns which build on each other to solve larger problems.

In the literature, the term "hybrid quantum-classical algorithms" is sometimes used as a synonym [45,46] for variational algorithms neglecting hybrid algorithms that are not variational. In this work, we consider hybrid algorithms to include all algorithms consisting of both quantum and classical computations. This for example also includes the hybrid quantum linear equation algorithm [47] or Shor's algorithm [5]. The challenges listed in the VARIATIONAL QUANTUM ALGORITHM pattern are active research areas, such as choosing a suitable ansatz [46] or optimization strategy. An extensive overview of challenges and applications of variational algorithms can be found in [20].

Lloyd [48] proved the universality of the quantum approximate optimization algorithm, i.e., any unitary operator (thus, any quantum algorithm) can in principle be approximated. In [49], the theoretical connections between variational algorithms (which use the structure in our QUANTUM VARIATIONAL ALGORITHM pattern) and kernel-based methods (for which our QKE pattern is the standard example) are explored. The author concludes that especially in the near future, kernel-based methods are an appealing alternative to variational

---

[5] https://quantumalgorithmzoo.org/.

methods. These theoretical results can be regarded as further evidence why the patterns identified by us are proven solutions.

5   Conclusion and Future Work

Especially in interdisciplinary collaborations for building software systems for quantum algorithms, a common understanding of interactions between quantum and classical computers is needed [50]. This work introduced six patterns for hybrid algorithms which refine the QUANTUM-CLASSIC SPLIT pattern of our previous work [12]. We also describe the relations between them, which reflect that hybrid algorithms often extend previous approaches and are therefore similar in their structure. All of the newly presented patterns try to limit computations on NISQ devices as much as possible. Note that we do not claim that this list of patterns for hybrid algorithms is exhaustive. For example, it should be further investigated if following a divide-and-conquer approach to split up computational tasks until they are suitable for a NISQ device also qualifies as another hybrid pattern. As the hardware improves it may be possible to divide the computational load differently in the future.

The patterns extend our collection of patterns of previous work [10–12]. In the future, we plan to collect more patterns and further known uses of our patterns within the PlanQK[6] platform. As quantum computing is still in an early stage and hardware improvements constantly open up new possibilities, the patterns presented and their potential applications should be re-evaluated. Following best practices for pattern writing [51], therefore, we plan to revisit and re-evaluate the quality and validity of patterns within the community.

Acknowledgment. This work was partially funded by the BMWi projects *PlanQK (01MK20005N)* as well as the project SEQUOIA funded by the Baden-Wuerttemberg Ministry of the Economy, Labour and Housing. We would also like to thank Felix Truger and Martin Beisel for various discussions about hybrid algorithms.

References

1. IBM makes quantum computing available on IBM cloud to accelerate innovation. https://www-03.ibm.com/press/us/en/pressrelease/49661.wss. (2016)
2. LaRose, R.: Overview and comparison of gate level quantum software platforms. Quantum **3**, 130 (2019)
3. Horodecki, R., Horodecki, P., Horodecki, M., Horodecki, K.: Quantum entanglement. Rev. Mod. Phy. **81**(2), 865 (2009)
4. Nielsen, M.A., Chuang, I.L.: Quantum Computation and Quantum Information. Cambridge University Press, Cambridge and New York (2010)
5. Shor, P.W.: Algorithms for quantum computation: discrete logarithms and factoring. In: Proceedings 35th Annual Symposium on Foundations of Computer Science, pp. 124–134, IEEE (1994)

---

[6] http://planqk.de/.

6. Harrow, A.W., Hassidim, A., Lloyd, S.: Quantum algorithm for linear systems of equations. Phys. Rev. Lett. **103**(15), 150502 (2009)
7. Preskill, J.: Quantum computing in the NISQ era and beyond. Quantum **2**, 79 (2018)
8. Amico, M., Saleem, Z.H., Kumph, M.: Experimental study of shor's factoring algorithm using the IBM q experience. Phys. Rev. A **100**(1), (2019)
9. Perdomo-Ortiz, A., Benedetti, M., Realpe-Gómez, J., Biswas, R.: Opportunities and challenges for quantum-assisted machine learning in near-term quantum computers. Quant. Sci. Technol. **3**(3), 030502 (2018)
10. Weigold, M., Barzen, J., Leymann, F., Salm, M.: Data encoding patterns for quantum computing. In: Proceedings of the 27th Conference on Pattern Languages of Programs. The Hillside Group (2021, to appear)
11. Weigold, M., Barzen, J., Leymann, F., Salm, M.: Expanding data encoding patterns for quantum algorithms. In: 2021 IEEE 18th International Conference on Software Architecture Companion (ICSA-C). pp. 95–101. IEEE, March 2021. https://ieeexplore.ieee.org/document/9425837/
12. Leymann, F.: Towards a pattern language for quantum algorithms. In: Feld, S., Linnhoff-Popien, C. (eds.) QTOP 2019. LNCS, vol. 11413, pp. 218–230. Springer, Cham (2019). https://doi.org/10.1007/978-3-030-14082-3_19
13. Falkenthal, M., et al.: Leveraging pattern application via pattern refinement. In: Proceedings of the International Conference on Pursuit of Pattern Languages for Societal Change (PURPLSOC 2015). epubli, June 2015
14. Leymann, F., Barzen, J.: The bitter truth about gate-based quantum algorithms in the NISQ era. Quant. Sci. Technol. **5**, 1–28 (2020). https://doi.org/10.1088/2058-9565/abae7d
15. Schuld, M., Killoran, N.: Quantum machine learning in feature hilbert spaces. Phys. Rev. Lett. **122**(4), 040504 (2019)
16. Havlíček, V., Córcoles, A.D., Temme, K., Harrow, A.W., Kandala, A., Chow, J.M., Gambetta, J.M.: Supervised learning with quantum-enhanced feature spaces. Nature **567**(7747), 209–212 (2019)
17. Bartkiewicz, K., Gneiting, C., Černoch, A., Jiráková, K., Lemr, K., Nori, F.: Experimental kernel-based quantum machine learning in finite feature space. Sci. Rep. **10**(1), 12356 (2020)
18. Ghobadi, R., Oberoi, R.S., Zahedinejhad, E.: The power of one qubit in machine learning. arXiv preprint arXiv:1905.01390 (2009)
19. Barzen, J.: From digital humanities to quantum humanities: Potentials and applications. arXiv preprint arXiv:2103.11825 (2021)
20. Cerezo, M., et al.: Variational quantum algorithms. arXiv preprint arXiv:2012.09265v1(2020)
21. Mitarai, K., Negoro, M., Kitagawa, M., Fujii, K.:Quantum circuit learning. Phy. Rev. A **98**(3) (2018)
22. Farhi, E., Neven, H.: Classification with quantum neural networks on near term processors. arXiv preprint arXiv:1802.06002(2018)
23. Anschuetz, E.N., Olson, J.R., Aspuru-Guzik, A., Cao, Y.: Variational quantum factoring. arXiv preprint arXiv:1808.08927 (2008)
24. Taube, A.G., Bartlett, R.J.: New perspectives on unitary coupled-cluster theory. Int. J. Quant. Chem. **106**(15), 3393–3401 (2006). https://onlinelibrary.wiley.com/doi/abs/10.1002/qua.21198
25. Peruzzo, A., et al.: A variational eigenvalue solver on a photonic quantum processor. Nat. Commun. **5**(1), 4213 (2014)

26. Higgott, O., Wang, D., Brierley, S.: Variational quantum computation of excited states. Quantum **3**, 156 (2019. https://doi.org/10.22331/q-2019-07-01-156

27. Cao, Y., et al.: Quantum chemistry in the age of quantum computing. Chem. Rev. **119**(19), 10 856–10 915 (2019)

28. Industry quantum computing applications - qutac application group. https://www.qutac.de/wp-content/uploads/2021/07/QUTAC_Paper.pdf (2021)

29. Hadfield, S., Wang, Z., O'Gorman, B., Rieffel, E.G., Venturelli, D., Biswas, R.: From the quantum approximate optimization algorithm to a quantum alternating operator ansatz. Algorithms **12**(2), (2019). https://www.mdpi.com/1999-4893/12/2/34

30. Wang, Z., Rubin, N.C., Dominy, J.M., Rieffel, E.G.: xy mixers: analytical and numerical results for the quantum alternating operator ansatz. Phys. Rev. A **101**, 012320 (2020). https://link.aps.org/doi/10.1103/PhysRevA.101.012320

31. Fingerhuth, M., Babej, T., Ing, C.: A quantum alternating operator ansatz with hard and soft constraints for lattice protein folding. arXiv preprint arXiv:1810.13411(2018)

32. Farhi, E., Goldstone, J., Gutmann, S.: A quantum approximate optimization algorithm. http://arxiv.org/pdf/1411.4028v1

33. Farhi, E., Goldstone, J., Gutmann, E., Sipser, M.: Quantum computation by adiabatic evolution. arXiv preprint arXiv:quant-ph/0001106 (2000)

34. Farhi, E., Goldstone, J., Gutmann, C.: A quantum approximate optimization algorithm applied to a bounded occurrence constraint problem. arXiv preprint arXiv:1412.6062(2015)

35. Barak, B., et al.: Beating the random assignment on constraint satisfaction problems of bounded degree. CoRR, vol. abs/1505.03424 (2015). http://arxiv.org/abs/1505.03424

36. Tate, R., Farhadi, M., Herold, C., Mohler, E., Gupta, S.: Bridging classical and quantum with sdp initialized warm-starts for qaoa. arXiv preprint arXiv:2010.14021(2020)

37. Egger, D.J., Marecek, J., Woerner, S.: Warm-starting quantum optimization. Xiv preprint arXiv:quant-ph/0001106(2020)

38. Barkoutsos, P.K., et al.: Quantum algorithms for electronic structure calculations: particle-hole hamiltonian and optimized wave-function expansions. Phys. Rev. A **98**(2) (2018)

39. Alexander, C., Ishikawa, S., Silverstein, M.: A Pattern Language: Towns, Buildings Construction. Oxford University Press, Oxford (1977)

40. Ramezani, S.B., Sommers, A., Manchukonda, H.K., Rahimi, S., Amirlatifi, A.: Machine learning algorithms in quantum computing: a survey. In: International Joint Conference on Neural Networks (IJCNN), vol. 2020, pp. 1–8 (2020)

41. Grover, L.M.: A fast quantum mechanical algorithm for database search. In: Proceedings of the Twenty-Eighth Annual ACM Symposium on Theory of Computing (STOC 1996) (1996)

42. Schuld, M., Petruccione, F.: Supervised Learning with Quantum Computers, Springer International Publishing, Quantum Science and Technology (2018). https://doi.org/10.1007/978-3-319-96424-9

43. National Academies of Sciences: Engineering and Medicine, Quantum Computing: Progress and Prospects. The National Academies Press, Washington, DC (2019)

44. Moll, N.: Quantum optimization using variational algorithms on near-term quantum devices. Quant. Sci. Technol. **3**(3), 030503 (2018). https://iopscience.iop.org/article/10.1088/2058-9565/aab822/meta

45. McClean, J.R., Romero, J., Babbush, R., Aspuru-Guzik, A.: The theory of variational hybrid quantum-classical algorithms. New J. Phys. **18**(2), 023023 (2016). https://doi.org/10.1088/1367-2630/18/2/023023
46. Sim, S., Johnson, P.D., Aspuru-Guzik, A.: Expressibility and entangling capability of parameterized quantum circuits for hybrid quantum-classical algorithms. Adv. Quant. Technol. **2**(12), 1900070 (2019)
47. Lee, Y., Joo, J., Lee, S.: Hybrid quantum linear equation algorithm and its experimental test on IBN quantum experience. Sci. Rep. **9**(1), 4778 (2019)
48. Lloyd, S.: Quantum approximate optimization is computationally universal. arXiv preprint arXiv:1812.11075 (2018)
49. Schuld, M.: Quantum machine learning models are kernel methods. arXiv preprint arXiv:2101.11020 (2021)
50. Weder, B., Barzen, J., Leymann, F., Salm, S., Vietz, D.: The quantum software lifecycle. In: Proceedings of the 1st ACM SIGSOFT International Workshop on Architectures and Paradigms for Engineering Quantum Software (APEQS 2020). ACM, Workshop, pp. 2–9, November 2020. https://doi.org/10.1145/3412451.3428497
51. Fehling, C., Barzen, J., Breitenbücher, U., Leymann, F.: A Process for pattern identification, authoring, and application. In: Proceedings of the 19th European Conference on Pattern Languages of Programs (EuroPLoP 2014), ACM, January 2014

QSOC: Quantum Service-Oriented Computing

Indika Kumara[1,2(✉)], Willem-Jan Van Den Heuvel[1,2],
and Damian A. Tamburri[1,3]

[1] Jheronimus Academy of Data Science, Sint Janssingel 92,
5211 DA 's-Hertogenbosch, Netherlands
[2] Tilburg University, Warandelaan 2, 5037 AB Tilburg, Netherlands
{i.p.k.weerasinghadewage,w.j.a.m.vdnHeuvel}@tilburguniversity.edu,
d.a.tamburri@tue.nl
[3] Eindhoven University of Technology, 5612 AZ Eindhoven, Netherlands

Abstract. Quantum computing is quickly turning from a promise to reality, witnessing the launch of several cloud-based services that provide access to quantum resources, simulators, runtimes, and programming tools, all through the cloud. Unfortunately, however, existing solutions typically implicitly assume intimate knowledge about quantum computing concepts and operators. This vision paper introduces Quantum Service-Oriented Computing (QSOC), a model for building applications using a well-balanced mix of classical and quantum (hybrid) computing approaches. We propose a model-driven methodology that allows application developers, classical service developers, and quantum programmers to build hybrid enterprise applications collaboratively. As a result, quantum programmers and service developers can develop and publish quantum and classical components. At the same time, the application developers can discover, compose, configure and compose pre-built components to build and operate enterprise applications without intimate knowledge on the underlying quantum infrastructure, advocating knowledge reuse and separation of concerns.

Keywords: Quantum computing · Services · SOA · MDA ·
Model-driven engineering · Reference architecture

1 Introduction

Quantum computing holds the potential to boost memory exponentially larger than its apparent physical size, treat an exponentially large set of inputs in parallel while marking a leap forward in computing capacity in close to Hilbert space [24]. Cloud services are being heralded as the key computing technology to unlock the massive computing power touted by quantum computing [17].

European Commission grant no. 825480 (H2020), SODALITE.

© Springer Nature Switzerland AG 2021
J. Barzen (Ed.): SummerSOC 2021, CCIS 1429, pp. 52–63, 2021.
https://doi.org/10.1007/978-3-030-87568-8_3

Prominent industry vendors have already started to offer cloud-enabled quantum computing infrastructures, witnessing launching Quantum Computing as a Service (QCaaS) models, such IBM's Quantum Experience, Microsoft's Azure Quantum, and Amazon's Braket. Moreover, several SDKs are offered by vendors such as IBM (QisKit) and Microsoft Quantum Development Kit (QDK) to support developing quantum applications. In this way, programmers may focus on application-level problem-solving and coding without concerning hardware-specific details while developing their quantum programs [20].

Quantum computing seems to be of a specific value-add in industry verticals such as healthcare, financial services, and supply chains [2]. For example, quantum computing may help fuel the speed significantly and harness the effectiveness of detecting potential fraud and anomalies in astronomic amounts of financial transactions at a national or even global scale. For these reasons, according to *ResearchAndMarkets.com*[1], the market for quantum computing is believed to rise as significant as $6 billion by 2023.

The basic fabric of quantum computing constitutes qubits with fascinating yet "quirky" principles like entanglement and superposition strongly interconnected, multi-state quantum particles in a quantum system. Qubits allow the quantum computers to not only simulate non-deterministic physical quantum systems but also analyze a large amount of numerical data and run simulations with exponential and polynomial speedups, and so on that have not been possible before with conventional computing infrastructures [5,8,11].

However, this compelling promise of quantum computing is not delivered yet. Indeed, the current quantum infrastructures suffer from various severe shortcoming [20,24,25]. Firstly, quantum algorithms are, in practice, only more efficient for certain classes of problems, notably problems that can be solved for bounded error, quantum, polynomial time (BQP). Secondly, quantum computers are (still) vulnerable to the lightest disturbances, causing decoherence. Thirdly, quantum applications embrace a single-application-single-model approach, implying they assume a one-to-one mapping to a stand-alone quantum computing infrastructure, making them notoriously hard to port.

Another more recent trend commences relaxing the single-application-single-model paradigm, departing from the stand-alone assumption of quantum applications. Hybrid models have been suggested where quantum and traditional computing infrastructures co-exist, allocating parts of the application to noise quantum devices and other less demanding components to conventional computing infrastructures, reducing the risk of unstable and unreliable applications [20]. In general, a hybrid quantum application consists of quantum algorithms and classical programs, data to be processed, workflows orchestrating quantum tasks and classical tasks, and resource provisioning models [17].

The above developments pose severe challenges to enterprise application developers to be able to effectively exploit the capacity of quantum computing hardware and the algorithms and SDKs tied to them, while at the other hand

---

[1] https://www.researchandmarkets.com/reports/4845826/quantum-computing-global-market-trajectory-and.

delivering industry-strength applications. We believe it is fair to assume that designers and developers often lack the knowledge and capabilities to perform the low-level plumbing activities assumed by quantum computing infrastructures. They would have to go through a steep learning curve of pulses, circuits, Hamiltonian parameters, and complex algorithms.

Workflow-oriented approaches such as [27] certainly provide an essential building block to enable the orchestration of classical applications and quantum circuits. Unfortunately, however, they are limited in their capacity to systematically reuse modularized and parameterized knowledge along with a structured lifecycle model. In addition, they are typically application context agnostic and do not explicitly consider quality and resource constraints. What would require is methodologies and tools to design, develop, deploy, monitor, and manage applications that may be (partially) executed on quantum infrastructure without much concern of the underpinning details of quantum mechanics. At the same time, the enterprise applications must be dynamically amendable and dependable and thus able to deal with (unexpected) changes in the underlying quantum hardware infrastructure.

In this vision paper, we propose QSOC (Quantum Service-Oriented Computing), which combines the concepts from model-driven engineering and SOA (Service-Oriented Architecture) to address the above-mentioned challenges of hybrid quantum application development. QSOC includes a layered reference architecture to support the realization of hybrid applications as a set of loosely coupled, coexisting classical and quantum services (Sect. 2). QSOC also provides a methodology that enables quantum programming experts and enterprise application developers to collaboratively build and manage heterogeneous hybrid applications (Sect. 3). Finally, we also present a roadmap that consists of short-term and long-term research goals for realizing the proposed reference architecture and methodology (Sect. 4).

2   Quantum Service-Oriented Architecture

Inspired by the classical layered SOA [22], we propose a layered reference architecture for QSOC, namely QSOA (Quantum Service-Oriented Architecture). It provides an architectural framework for building applications exploiting a collection of reusable functional units (services) with well-defined interfaces and implemented using a well-balanced mix of classical and quantum (hybrid) computing approaches. Figure 1 depicts the overall stratified QSOA architecture, which consists of the following six layers, starting from conceptual problem domain to the physical compute infrastructure: business and data domains, business processes and data pipelines, middleware services, component services, service realizations, and computing infrastructures.

2.1   Business and Data Domains

The topmost layer of QSOA captures the results of the problem domain analysis. To develop the QSOA applications (the technical solutions) that are in syn-

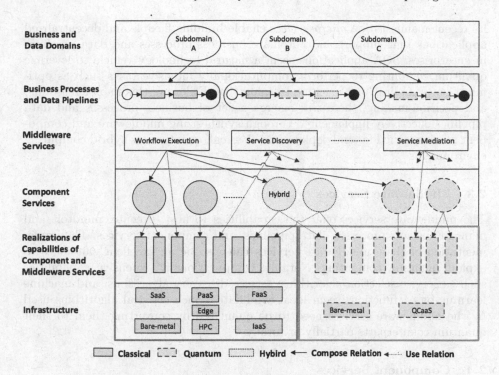

Fig. 1. Quantum service-oriented architecture

ergy with the business problem domain, we advocate the Domain-Driven Design (DDD) [9]. The DDD first partitions the problem domain into the process- or data-oriented sub-domains. For example, we can split an online auction business domain into sub-domains such as auction, seller, listing, dispute resolution, and membership. When analyzing the problem domain, it is crucial to identify those segments of the business domains where quantum computing adds value, for example, in terms of performance, cost, adding to its competitive advantage.

Enterprise data can be partitioned into *operational data* and *analytical data*. Operational data is used to run the day-to-day operations of the business. Analytical data presents a temporal and aggregated view of the facts of the business over time, derived from operational data, and enables making data-driven business decisions. Typically this data is of special importance to decision-makers at the tactic and strategic level. The DDD can be applied to segment the analytical data space into data domains aligned with the business domains (namely, the *data mesh* [6] approach).

2.2 Business Processes and Data Pipelines

Business processes produce and consume operational data, while data pipelines, including ML (machine learning) pipelines and classical ETL (extract, transform, load) pipelines, typically ingest and generate analytical data. SOA and its recent manifestation *microservices* enable building flexible and decentralized applications that support and automate business processes and data pipelines in enterprises. SOA applications seem a natural technology vehicle to leverage quantum computing to perform computationally intensive tasks such as optimization, sampling, and machine learning [10]. Following this line of reasoning and decision-making, there will emerge a set of business processes and data pipelines effectively implemented through synthesizing middleware and component services coded for and deployed on classical, quantum, or hybrid computing environments.

2.3   Middleware Services

The middleware services offer the capabilities to host, execute, monitor, and manage business processes, data pipelines, and component services. The implementation of these middleware services can also be an excellent candidate to exploit quantum computing. Notably, computationally expensive capabilities such as service selection algorithms, service discovery algorithms, and machine learning-based functions seem ideal candidates. Such classical algorithms used by the middleware services need to be quantized by converting them to their quantum counterparts partially or totally.

2.4   Component Services

In DDD, the concept in the solution domain that corresponds to a sub-domain constitutes the *bounded context (BC)*, which is simply the boundary within a sub-domain where a particular domain model applies. Each BC includes its domain model and discrete solution artifacts such as business processes, services, models, and requirements. A systematic approach to carving out solution artifacts from a BC is to apply tactical DDD patterns, especially for identifying services with natural, clean boundaries. Additional "auxiliary"/"secondary" artifacts (e.g., speed-layer services) may be needed for achieving the non-functional requirements of the domain. Quantum computing can also be considered as a strategy for supporting such non-functional requirements as performance, scalability, and energy efficiency [25]. For example, by quantizing some classical algorithms used in service implementations, the performance of such algorithms can be improved [1,18].

Once the primary and secondary class services have been pinpointed and defined in clean, separate service definitions, the next step is to decide which services are to be implemented using classical computing, quantum computing, and hybrid computing. Typically, business processes encompass (primary) business services and (secondary) utility services such as services implementing calculations and data processing algorithms. Such utility services and the computationally intensive data processing services in the data pipelines can be suitable candidates to be implemented using hybrid or quantum computing. For instance, a drone delivery process may be instrumented with a routing service to calculate the flight course for good deliveries. This service can be implemented using quantum computing as computing the optimal route is computationally expensive. In a typical classification ML pipeline, most data pre-processing and feature engineering tasks can be implemented using classical programs, and the tasks such as computing eigenvalues of the covariance matrix and determining clusters can be implemented using quantum algorithms [17].

2.5 Infrastructure

QSOC applications and middlewares are deployed over multiple, well-managed infrastructures, including cloud, edge, HPC, and quantum. Portability and adaptability will be crucial to support seamless and dynamic switching between different types of infrastructures as they or their usage contexts evolve. The appropriate mechanisms need to be developed to help the efficient migration of application components across multiple infrastructures at runtime. On the other hand, the infrastructure heterogeneity can make it challenging to design, deploy, test, and manage applications [25]. Infrastructure as code (IaC) approaches [13,29] and heterogeneous resource orchestration approaches [7,15] can help to address such challenges.

3 Model-Driven Quantum SOA Application Engineering Methodology

This section introduces a model-driven QSOA methodology (MD-QSOA) that facilitates the enterprise application developers and quantum experts to design, compose, deploy, execute, and manage the heterogeneous QSOA applications in a portable way while sharing and reusing design and implementation artifacts. The methodology is designed to guide DevOps teams to implement and evolve the next generation of hybrid enterprise applications in a well-structured, repeatable and transparent manner.

Our approach is firmly grounded on model-driven engineering [3] and has been inspired by our previous works on classical and cloud service engineering [21,23]. Notably, the QSOA methodology has benefited from ongoing works on heterogeneous application engineering [7,15]. Figure 2 provides an overview of the proposed approach for engineering QSOA applications.

The methodology has been designed on the assumption that the quantum applications are to be packaged as containerized services embracing the Quantum Algorithm/Application as a Service (QaaS) model [17]. Moreover, we advocate the development of the QSOA artifacts (e.g., classical services, workflows, and quantum programs) as *customizable* artifacts [12,14] so that the end-users can dynamically assemble and (re)use the variants of the artifacts.

3.1 Developing Blueprints

The critical element of our model-driven methodology constitutes reusable knowledge models, called *blueprints*. We identify two main categories of

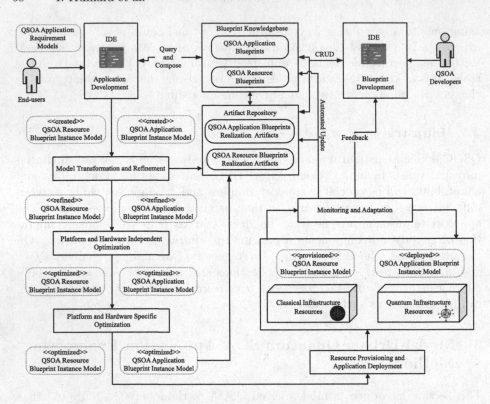

Fig. 2. Model-driven QSOA application engineering methodology

blueprints: application blueprints and resource blueprints. The application blueprints are akin to computation-independent model (CIM) and platform-independent models semantically compartmentalizing meta-data on various aspects of a QSOA application, for example, requirements, service contracts, high-level process models, and deployment architecture models. The resource blueprints capture meta-data on operational-, performance-, and capacity requirements of infrastructure resources (e.g., cloud, edge, HPC, and quantum nodes) and the external services.

Artifact Repository stores versioned-controlled realizations of blueprints, for example, source codes for services and quantum algorithm codes, Docker files and images, and IaC (Infrastructure as code) scripts. *Blueprint Knowledgebase* consists of versioned-controlled ontologies or knowledge graphs of abstract blueprints to support discovery, matchmaking, reuse, composition, validation, and optimization of concrete blueprints [26]. To implement the *Blueprint Knowledgebase*, the existing ontologies can be adopted, for example, IaC ontologies [7] and service ontologies [19]. Ontologies enable representing both structural and semantics relationships of blueprints in an unambiguous manner, promoting reusability and interoperability. The existing automated ontology reasoning tools can be leveraged to implement the decision support required by the IDE and other components, for example, context-aware assistance of users at design-time (IDE), detection of the violation of best practices or the usage of bad practices, blueprint models enrichment taking into account domain knowledge (model transformers), and finding substitutable resources or services (the runtime adaptation support). In the SODALITE project [7,15,16], we have implemented similar capabilities for hybrid applications that use the cloud, HPC, and edge resources.

IDE and *Domain Specific Language (DSL)* can be used by application developers and quantum programming experts to create, manipulate, and use blueprints. The Quantum (resource and algorithm) experts can model their infrastructure resources, the platforms, and the applications using blueprints and store the models in the *Blueprint Knowledgebase*. In addition, they can add the implementations of algorithms and services into the *Artifact Repository* and store the metadata necessary to discover, validate and use the implementation artifacts.

3.2   Composing and Instantiating Blueprints

Reusable and composable blueprints enable adopting the low-code approach [4] for the quantum application development, where the end-users develop the applications through a graphical user interface, reusing and configuring pre-built components. End-users can assemble and configure their QSOC application accurately and quickly by making use of the context-aware intelligent assistance provided by the IDE powered by the *Blueprint Knowledgebase*. In this way, assisted mixing-and-maxing and optimization of requirements against resources allow faster and improved construction of application models by optimized selection and configuration of the resources and platforms to host the application components.

The blueprint instance models produced by the IDE represent the platform-independent knowledge models, for example, service contracts, business processes, policies, and deployment architecture models in the abstract. Such models need to be further refined and transformed into executable platform-specific models and codes yet hardware-agnostic models/codes. For example, the deployment architecture models can be transformed into IaC programs such as TOSCA and Ansible [7,29]. The service variants can be generated from the service implementation artifacts retrieved from the *Artifact Repository* using the service contracts. The model transformation and refinement process can utilize the reasoning capabilities of the *Blueprint Knowledgebase*.

The refined blueprint instance models may not be optimal and can have security vulnerabilities, performance anti-patterns, code smells, and so on. Such issues should be detected and corrected. There exist a vast body of knowledge on quality assurance of program codes and software designs. Both classical and quantum algorithms can be optimized to achieve the best performance on a target environment [7,28]. In the case of code artifacts, they can be built with the optimized compiler flags and libraries for a target environment, and the application parameters can also be auto-tuned [7]. Domain (optimization) experts can use the *Blueprint Knowledgebase* to define the information about optimization options. The application optimizer can use such domain knowledge to select the correct options to map application configurations to the target hardware, build the optimized variants of the services, and encapsulate the variants as containers.

3.3 Deploying and Managing Instantiated Blueprints

The refined, composed, and optimized blueprint instance models for the application include the executable and deployable artifacts, for example, deployment models as IaC scripts, services as containers, and processes as executable workflows. To deploy the applications, the IaC scripts can be executed using an orchestrator [15,29]. Different infrastructure providers exist, and they generally offer the REST APIs to create and manage the resources in their infrastructures. These REST APIs hide the underlying low-level resource orchestrators and aid in achieving interoperability of heterogeneous infrastructures. The orchestrator can be implemented as a meta-orchestrator that coordinates low-level resource orchestrators by directly executing REST APIs or IaC scripts [15].

The deployed application and the infrastructures can be continuously monitored by collecting various resource and application metrics to assure the satisfaction of the application's service level objectives (SLOs). The monitored data can also be used to determine sub-optimal use of resources, faults, abnormal behaviors, and so on. This feedback loop allows for corrective, adaptive, and preemptive actions to be performed, for example, auto-scaling resources, selecting different service variants. In addition, this may involve moving application components from classical computers to cloud/HPC clusters to different types of quantum devices at runtime.

4 Conclusion and Research Directions

Quantum computing is now quickly becoming a reality, and enterprises need to make sure their enterprise applications to be quantum-ready to offer unprecedented and non-linear services in a way that could not be provided before, keeping, or gaining a competitive edge.

In this vision paper, we coin the concept of quantum service-oriented computing (QSOC). In particular, we have introduced a reference architecture for the quantum SOA model adopting the proven, industry-strength layered SOA model. In addition, we presented a novel model-driven methodology for realizing QSOA applications that makes it easier for enterprises to build portable and adaptive QSOA applications.

Indeed, the results presented in this article are core research in nature. The paper is meant as a foundation for the manifold of future research with a high academic and industrial relevance and impact. We propose three research directions for further exploring and realizing the vision of QSOC and MD-QSOC.

Firstly, we intend to further flesh out each layer of the QSOA model, improving our understanding of which issues are best solved by classical, quantum, and/or hybrid algorithms. Indeed, empirical studies and action-design methodologies for mapping computing models to problems considering multiple criteria are necessary. Moreover, the migration of classical and legacy algorithms/services to quantum and hybrid models also needs to be investigated as a logical continuation of our earlier works in SOC.

Secondly, we plan to develop and validate the concepts, theories, and techniques underpinning the model-driven methodology for engineering and managing QSOA applications. The blueprint models, customizable QSOA artifacts, IDE and DSLs, model transformation and refinement processes, semantic knowledgebase and decision support, platform/hardware-independent/specific optimizations, orchestration, monitoring, and run-time adaptation will have numerous research challenges. Understanding and resolving such research challenges would be crucial for the successful longer-term adoption of quantum computing within enterprises to support their business processes and analytical data pipelines.

Thirdly, and lastly, we intend to set up short-cyclic, "learning-by-doing" industrial experimentation with the MD-QSOA and the tools developed in the first- and second research lines, deriving patterns, improving the decision-model underpinning the methodology, and improving our understanding and theoretical implications of the QSOA applications.

Acknowledgements. This paper has been supported by the European Union' Horizon 2020 research and innovation programme under grant agreement no. 825480, SODALITE.

References

1. Aïmeur, E., Brassard, G., Gambs, S.: Quantum speed-up for unsupervised learning. Mach. Learn. **90**(2), 261–287 (2013)
2. Bova, F., Goldfarb, A., Melko, R.G.: Commercial applications of quantum computing. EPJ Quant. Technol. **8**(1), 1–13 (2021). https://doi.org/10.1140/epjqt/s40507-021-00091-1
3. Brambilla, M., Cabot, J., Wimmer, M.: Model-Driven Software Engineering in Practice, 2nd edn. Morgan and Claypool Publishers, San Rafael (2017)
4. Cabot, J.: Positioning of the low-code movement within the field of model-driven engineering. In: Proceedings of the 23rd ACM/IEEE International Conference on Model Driven Engineering Languages and Systems: Companion Proceedings (MODELS 2020), Association for Computing Machinery, New York (2020). https://doi.org/10.1145/3417990.3420210
5. Cao, Y., et al.: Quantum chemistry in the age of quantum computing. Chem. Rev. **119**(19), 10856–10915 (2019). https://doi.org/10.1021/acs.chemrev.8b00803
6. Dehghani, Z.: Data mesh principles and logical architecture, December 2020. https://martinfowler.com/articles/data-mesh-principles.html
7. Di Nitto, E., et al.: An approach to support automated deployment of applications on heterogeneous cloud-hpc infrastructures. In: 2020 22nd International Symposium on Symbolic and Numeric Algorithms for Scientific Computing (SYNASC), pp. 133–140 (2020)

8. Emani, P.S., et al.: Quantum computing at the frontiers of biological sciences. Nat. Methods **18**(7), 701–709 (2021). https://doi.org/10.1038/s41592-020-01004-3

9. Evans, E., Evans, E.J.: Domain-Driven Design: Tackling Complexity in the Heart of Software. Addison-Wesley Professional, Boston (2004)

10. Gabor, T., et al.: The holy grail of quantum artificial intelligence: major challenges in accelerating the machine learning pipeline. In: Proceedings of the IEEE/ACM 42nd International Conference on Software Engineering Workshops (ICSEW 2020), pp. 456–461. Association for Computing Machinery, New York (2020). https://doi.org/10.1145/3387940.3391469

11. Givi, P., Daley, A.J., Mavriplis, D., Malik, M.: Quantum speedup for aero science and engineering. AIAA J. **58**(8), 3715–3727 (2020). https://doi.org/10.2514/1.J059183

12. Gottschalk, F., van der Aalst, W.M.P., Jansen-Vullers, M.H., la Rosa, M.: Configurable workflow models. Int. J. Cooper. Inf. Syst. **17**(02), 177–221 (2008). https://doi.org/10.1142/S0218843008001798

13. Kumara, I., et al.: The do's and don'ts of infrastructure code: a systematic gray literature review. Inf. Softw. Technol. **137**, 106593 (2021). https://doi.org/10.1016/j.infsof.2021.106593, https://www.sciencedirect.com/science/article/pii/S0950584921000720

14. Kumara, I., Han, J., Colman, A., Nguyen, T., Kapuruge, M.: Sharing with a difference: Realizing service-based SAAS applications with runtime sharing and variation in dynamic software product lines. In: 2013 IEEE International Conference on Services Computing, pp. 567–574 (2013)

15. Kumara, I., et al.: Sodalite@rt: orchestrating applications on cloud-edge infrastructures. J. Grid Comput. **19**(3), 29 (2021)

16. Kumara, I., et al.: Towards semantic detection of smells in cloud infrastructure code. In: Proceedings of the 10th International Conference on Web Intelligence, Mining and Semantics (WIMS 2020), Association for Computing Machinery, New York (2020). https://doi.org/10.1145/3405962.3405979

17. Leymann, F., Barzen, J., Falkenthal, M., Vietz, D., Weder, B., Wild, K.: Quantum in the cloud: application potentials and research opportunities. In: Proceedings of the 10th International Conference on Cloud Computing and Services Science - Volume 1 (CLOSER), pp. 9–24. INSTICC, SciTePress (2020)

18. Liu, Y., Arunachalam, S., Temme, K.: A rigorous and robust quantum speed-up in supervised machine learning. Nat. Phys. (2021). https://doi.org/10.1038/s41567-021-01287-z

19. McIlraith, S.A., Son, T.C., Zeng, H.: Semantic web services. IEEE Intell. Syst. **16**(2), 46–53 (2001)

20. Mintz, T.M., McCaskey, A.J., Dumitrescu, E.F., Moore, S.V., Powers, S., Lougovski, P.: Qcor: a language extension specification for the heterogeneous quantum-classical model of computation. J. Emerg. Technol. Comput. Syst. **16**(2). (2020). https://doi.org/10.1145/3380964

21. Papazoglou, M.P., Heuvel, W.: Blueprinting the cloud. IEEE Internet Comput. **15**(06), 74–79 (2011)

22. Papazoglou, M.: Web Services: Principles and Technology. Pearson Education, Harlow(2008)

23. Papazoglou, M.P., Van Den Heuvel, W.J.: Service-oriented design and development methodology. Int. J. Web Eng. Technol. **2**(4), 412–442 (2006)

24. Preskill, J.: Quantum computing in the NISQ era and beyond. Quantum **2**, 79 (2018)

25. Sodhi, B., Kapur, R.: Quantum computing platforms: assessing the impact on quality attributes and sdlc activities. In: 2021 IEEE 18th International Conference on Software Architecture (ICSA), pp. 80–91 (2021). https://doi.org/10.1109/ICSA51549.2021.00016
26. Staab, S., Studer, R.: Handbook on ontologies. Springer Science & Business Media (2010)
27. Weder, B., Breitenbücher, U., Leymann, F., Wild, K.: Integrating quantum computing into workflow modeling and execution. In: 2020 IEEE/ACM 13th International Conference on Utility and Cloud Computing (UCC), pp. 279–291 (2020)
28. Weder, B., Barzen, J., Leymann, F., Salm, M., Vietz, D.: The quantum software lifecycle. In: Proceedings of the 1st ACM SIGSOFT International Workshop on Architectures and Paradigms for Engineering Quantum Software (APEQS 2020), pp. 2–9. Association for Computing Machinery, New York (2020)
29. Wild, K., Breitenbücher, U., Harzenetter, L., Leymann, F., Vietz, D., Zimmermann, M.: TOSCA4QC: two modeling styles for TPSCA to automate the deployment and orchestration of quantum applications. In: 2020 IEEE 24th International Enterprise Distributed Object Computing Conference (EDOC), pp. 125–134 (2020). https://doi.org/10.1109/EDOC49727.2020.00024

Automating the Comparison of Quantum Compilers for Quantum Circuits

Marie Salm[✉][iD], Johanna Barzen[iD], Frank Leymann[iD], Benjamin Weder[iD],
and Karoline Wild[iD]

Institute of Architecture of Application Systems, University of Stuttgart,
Universitätsstraße 38, Stuttgart, Germany
{salm,barzen,leymann,weder,wild}@iaas.uni-stuttgart.de

Abstract. For very specific problems, quantum advantage has recently been demonstrated. However, current NISQ computers are error-prone and only support small numbers of qubits. This limits the executable circuit size of an implemented quantum algorithm. Due to this limitation, it is important that compiled quantum circuits for a specific quantum computer are as resource-efficient as possible. A variety of different quantum compilers exists supporting different programming languages, gate sets, and vendors of quantum computers. However, comparing the results of several quantum compilers requires (i) deep technical knowledge and (ii) large manual effort for translating a given circuit into different languages. To tackle these challenges, we present a framework to automate the translation, compilation, and comparison of a given quantum circuit with multiple quantum compilers to support the selection of the most suitable compiled quantum circuit. For demonstrating the practical feasibility of the framework, we present a prototypical implementation.

Keywords: Quantum computing · NISQ · Decision support · Compiler · NISQ analyzer

1 Introduction

Quantum computing is a highly discussed and emerging technology in research and industry [17]. Quantum advantage has already been demonstrated for specific problems [3,36]. Furthermore, a variety of quantum algorithms exists promising further beneficial breakthroughs in different areas such as computer and natural sciences [17]. Nevertheless, the *Noisy Intermediate-Scale Quantum (NISQ)* era is not yet overcome [19]. Existing gate-based quantum computers still only offer small numbers of qubits and high error rates. This strongly limits the circuit sizes of implemented quantum algorithms executable on existing quantum computers [11]: The number of required qubits, i.e. the *width*, has to be less than or equal to the number of qubits offered by the quantum computer. In addition, the number of sequential executable gates, i.e. the *depth*, can only be executed in a certain time frame, often in the range of micro seconds, otherwise too many errors would accumulate and interfere the results.

© Springer Nature Switzerland AG 2021
J. Barzen (Ed.): SummerSOC 2021, CCIS 1429, pp. 64–80, 2021.
https://doi.org/10.1007/978-3-030-87568-8_4

The width and depth of a quantum circuit is significantly influenced by (i) the qubit topology of the quantum computer, i.e. the connectivity between the qubits, (ii) the implemented gate set of the quantum computer, and (iii) the mapping and optimization algorithm of the used quantum compiler [4, 25]. The quantum compiler maps the qubits and gates of the quantum circuit to the qubits and implemented gates of the real quantum computer [13].

Today, a great variety of quantum compilers exists [14]. They all differ in their implemented mapping and optimization algorithms. Especially in the NISQ era, the selection of the most suitable, i.e., the best optimizing quantum compiler for a given quantum circuit and quantum computer is tremendously important to make optimal use of the currently limited quantum resources. However, quantum compilers are accessed via *software development kits (SDKs)* providing libraries for implementing and executing quantum circuits on quantum computers or simulators [13, 24]. These SDKs differ in their (i) supported programming languages, (ii) supported gate sets, and (iii) supported vendors of quantum computers for execution. Vendor-independent SDKs, such as pytket [30], exist facilitating the import of quantum circuits in various programming languages and a variety of gate sets with the respective hardware access. Nevertheless, several quantum compilers are accessed via vendor-specific SDKs, such as Qiskit [1] from IBM and Forest SDK [23] from Rigetti, only supporting vendor-specific languages, gate sets, and hardware access. As a result, it cannot simply be tested which compiler generates the most suitable compilation of a given quantum circuit and not every circuit can be compiled and executed on every existing quantum computer, because (i) the programming languages are not compatible and (ii) the gate sets differ between the different vendors. Thus, for comparing the results of quantum compilers deep technical knowledge about the SDKs and large manual effort for the translation of the quantum circuit into the different supported programming languages and gate sets is required. Several works, such as [15, 16, 30], already compare quantum compilers. However, they focus on presenting the overall strength of their compilation approaches with certain prepared benchmarks.

In this paper, we present a framework to compare the compilation results of different quantum compilers for a particular quantum circuit and quantum computer. Therefore, the framework enables to *(i) translate* the quantum circuit into the required programming languages of the SDKs of the given quantum compilers, *(ii) execute* the compilation with the selected compilers, and *(iii) analyze* the compilation results. Thus, the user can select the most suitable compilation. With the translation, we enable the decoupling of the SDK used for implementing a certain quantum circuit and the vendor used for execution. As basis for our framework, we analyze existing SDKs and their compilers, their supported programming languages, specification features, and quantum computers. For comparing the compiled circuits, metrics, such as width and depth, are chosen. To demonstrate the practical feasibility of the framework, a prototypical implementation is presented supporting the t|ket⟩ compiler [30], the Qiskit Transpiler [1], and the Quilc compiler [23]. The framework is plug-in based, such that the support of further metrics, programming languages, compilers, and SDKs can be added.

The remainder of the paper is structured as follows: In Sect. 2 the fundamentals and the problem statement are introduced. In Sect. 3 existing SDKs and their compilers are analyzed and compared. Furthermore, the suitability of compilations is discussed. Section 4 describes the concept of the framework. Section 5 presents the system architecture and prototype. Section 6 validates the framework with a case study. Section 7 discusses the concept of the framework. Section 8 presents related work and Sect. 9 concludes the work and gives an outlook.

2   Fundamentals and Problem Statement

In this section, we introduce the fundamentals about quantum compilation and present current challenges using quantum compilers. Finally, we present the problem statement and the research questions of this work.

2.1   Quantum Circuits and Quantum Compilers

For gate-based quantum computing, quantum circuits represent implemented quantum algorithms [18]. A quantum circuit is described by qubits and quantum gates manipulating the states of the qubits as well as the order in which the gates are performed. For the execution on a certain quantum computer, also called *quantum processing unit (QPU)*, a quantum compiler has to map the defined quantum circuit to the properties of the quantum computer [13]. In general, gate-based quantum computers differ in their implemented gate set, the number of qubits, the qubit topology, and errors that can occur during the execution of a quantum circuit [4,22,25]. In a first step, the quantum compiler replaces non-implemented gates of a defined quantum circuit by a sequence of implemented gates [11,13]. Moreover, due to the non-complete topology graph of the selected quantum computer, further gates and qubits are required for the usage of multi-qubit gates [5,33]: The state of non-directly connected qubits has to be transferred over connected qubits. During the compilation (i) the qubits limiting the maximum width and (ii) the error rates of the gates and the decoherence time of the qubits limiting the depth of a quantum circuit have to be considered [30,33]. Therefore, quantum compilers perform several optimizations, such as parallelizing gates and replacing gates with high error rates [30]. The mapping procedure is NP-complete [29]. Also, it can lead to a significant increase of the depth of a circuit challenging a successful execution on today's NISQ computers with high error rates and small qubit numbers [5,11,19].

Today, a large number of quantum compilers exist and is still growing [14]. Each compiler performs another mapping and optimization algorithm. Hence, the resulting compiled quantum circuits of a given input circuit for a certain quantum computer differ in their properties. This makes it difficult to predict which compiler suits best for a certain quantum circuit and quantum computer. However, as we are still in the NISQ era, it is important to optimize a quantum circuit by reducing its depth and width [25], to minimize the impact of increasing errors and use the quantum resources efficiently.

Besides the width and depth, further circuit properties, i.e. metrics, exist and are commonly used to compare compiled circuits describing the inner structure of a circuit, e.g., the number of two-qubit gates with their high error rates or the total number of gates [30]. Another proposed metric roughly estimates if an execution of a circuit with a certain width and depth could be successful dependent on the effective error rate of the given quantum computer [4, 11, 19, 25]. Nevertheless, for sharpening and applying this metric the effective error rate of the quantum computer has to be determined which is challenging as the exact composition of the effective error rate is not yet known [21, 25, 33]. Thus, the two metrics width and depth build a solid expandable set for describing the decisive size of a circuit enabling a concise overview to compare between multiple compilations of different quantum compilers [25, 30].

2.2   Quantum Software Development Kits

A quantum compiler is often accessed via an SDK. An SDK provides tools and libraries for developing a quantum circuit, to compile it, and, finally, execute it on a quantum computer [10]. Most of the current vendors of quantum computers, such as IBM and Rigetti, provide proprietary SDKs, e.g. Qiskit [1] and Forest SDK [23], for accessing their quantum compilers and quantum computers [24]. However, a few SDKs exist supporting several vendors, such as pytket [30] and ProjectQ [32]. Each SDK offers a different set of supported programming languages, customizable quantum computer specifications, and gate sets [34]. Thus, a circuit is not necessarily interchangeable between different SDKs. This denies the flexibility of testing several compilers and executing on a wide range of quantum computers. An overview about the features of existing SDKs and their compilers is given in Sect. 3. Thereby, many properties of the SDKs are taken into account as they determine, e.g., import and export programming languages.

2.3   Problem Statement

It is hard to estimate in advance which quantum compiler returns the most suitable compilation, in terms of smallest width and depth, for a given quantum circuit and quantum computer. However, simply testing every compiler with a certain quantum circuit and quantum computer is challenging. First, the circuit has to be written in a programming language and gate set supported by the SDK providing the specific quantum compiler, otherwise it has to be rewritten. In addition, for a compilation on the desired quantum computer, its vendor has to be supported by the SDK. Hence, the first research question (RQ) is as follows:

> **RQ 1**: *How can potentially relevant quantum compilers be identified for the compilation of a certain quantum circuit on a certain quantum computer?*

While a detailed analysis of programming languages and vendors supported by existing quantum compilers and their SDKs builds a good basis, comparing existing quantum compilers to find the most suitable compiled circuit for a specific quantum computer demands a lot of manual effort and deep technical knowledge from the user. Therefore, the second RQ is as follows:

> **RQ 2**: *How can the comparison of compiled circuits of different quantum compilers for a given quantum circuit and quantum computer be automated?*

For addressing the formulated RQs, we analyzed quantum compilers and SDKs and realized a compilation comparison framework, presented in the following.

3   Analysis of Quantum Compilers

In this section, we present an analysis of SDKs and their quantum compilers, as seen in Table 1. Furthermore, we discuss the suitability of compiled circuits.

Table 1. Compiler-specific criterion on SDKs.

	SDKs (compilers)	Import languages	Export languages	Backend vendors	Custom QPUs	Custom compilation gate set
Propr. SDKs	Cirq	OpenQASM, Cirq-JSON, Quirk-JSON	OpenQASM, Quil, Cirq-JSON	Google, AQT, Pasqal	Yes	Yes
	Forest (Quilc)	PyQuil*, Quil	Quil	Rigetti	Yes	No
	Qiskit (Transpiler)	OpenQASM, Qiskit*	OpenQASM	IBM	Yes	Yes
Independent SDKs	pytket (t|ket⟩)	OpenQASM, Qiskit*, PyZX*, PyQuil*, Cirq*, Quipper	OpenQASM, Qiskit*, PyZX*, PyQuil*, Cirq*, Qulacs*, Q#, ProjectQ*	AQT, Amazon Braket, Honeywell, Rigetti, IBM, Microsoft QDK	Yes	Yes
	staq	OpenQASM	OpenQASM, ProjectQ*, Quil, Q#, Cirq*	No	No	No
	ProjectQ	ProjectQ*	ProjectQ*	IBM, AQT, Amazon Braket, IonQ	No	Yes

3.1   Compiler-Specific Analysis of SDKs

To address **RQ 1**, different SDKs and their quantum compilers are analyzed (see Table 1). This analysis focuses on the integration and configuration properties for certain compilers. Thus, the support of different programming languages, vendors, custom quantum computers, and custom compilation gate sets is considered. Note that vendors of simulators are excluded. The selected set is only an excerpt of open-source accessible SDKs and serves for exemplary purposes showing their distinct properties. Detailed analyses of SDKs have been shown, e.g., by [7,10,34].

Most of the analyzed SDKs support the import and export of multiple programming languages. In general, the supported languages can be split in high-level programming languages, such as Python, and assembly languages, such as Quil [31] and OpenQASM [6,34]. However, most SDKs offer their own Python libraries (marked with *), such that implemented circuits are not interchangeable. Most SDKs, except Forest SDK [23] and ProjectQ [32], support Open-QASM.

From the vendor-specific SDKs, only Cirq [20] supports multiple vendors, as shown in Table 1. Pytket [30] supports a great variety of vendors. Staq [2] supports many export languages but considers only mocked quantum computers.

Many of the considered SDKs support the specification of custom quantum computers, their qubit topologies, gate sets, and error rates for experimental compilation in their proprietary format. But less quantum compilers natively support customizing the target gate set, such that the previously specified gates cannot be retrieved in the compiled quantum circuit.

Thus, for comparing the outcomes of a wide range of existing quantum compilers, the given quantum circuit has to be translated into several programming languages. In addition, tackling **RQ 1**, the SDK of a considered quantum compiler must natively support the given quantum computer for comparison. Otherwise, the SDK needs to offer the possibility to specify custom quantum computers. However, a complete specification is often associated with a lot of manual effort. The analysis is the basis of the framework introduced in the following Sect. 4.

3.2   Suitability of Compiled Quantum Circuits

After compiling a quantum circuit with a compiler, its compilation result is assumed to be *suitable* if it is successfully executable such that the correct result is clearly identifiable and not too much interfered by errors [11,25]. Therefore, the number of qubits, decoherence times, and error rates of the quantum computer determine the maximum width and depth of an executable and, thus, suitable quantum circuit. However, a general prioritization of width or depth cannot be determined. Quantum computers can have a great number of stable qubits but only support the execution of circuits with small depths, or vice versa [11]. Moreover, if, e.g., two compiled circuits are suitable, i.e. have a smaller or equal width and depth than the number of qubits and the maximum executable depth of the quantum computer, it cannot simply be determined which circuit is to be preferred. Thus, selecting the most suitable compilation depends on multidimensional aspects and, currently, cannot be solved by automation.

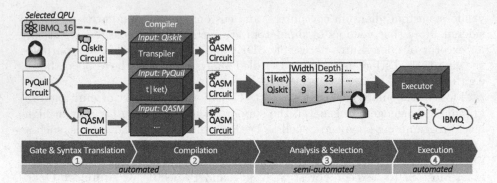

Fig. 1. Automated compilation and comparison of circuits with multiple compilers.

4   Framework for Compilation Comparison

To address **RQ 2**, we present a framework to compare the compiled circuits of different quantum compilers for a certain quantum circuit and quantum computer. The overall approach is shown in Fig. 1. The phases 1, 2, and 4 are completely automated while phase 3 is semi-automated. First, the given circuit is translated into the programming languages and gate sets supported by the SDKs of the selected compilers. The translated circuits and the information about the selected quantum computer serve as input for the compilation in the second step. After compilation, the widths and depths of the resulting circuits are analyzed and suitable results are recommended to the user. The user, then, manually selects the most suitable compilation. Finally, the selected circuit is executed. The details about each phase are provided in the following.

4.1   Gate and Syntax Translation

The basis for translation is the quantum circuit and selected quantum computer. Based on Sect. 3, the SDKs of suitable quantum compilers (i) have to support the selected quantum computer and (ii) determine the required programming languages. Thus, in the *(1) Gate and Syntax Translation* phase, the circuit for compilation, its programming language, e.g. Python for *PyQuil*, and the desired quantum computer, e.g. *IBMQ_16*, serve as input for the automated translation, compilation, and comparison, as seen in Fig. 1. For each SDK, the supported vendors are specified. Thus, based on the selected quantum computer the matching quantum compiler can be determined. Then, it is identified which languages are supported by the selected SDKs. For an SDK not supporting the language of the given circuit, the syntax of the circuit is mapped to the syntax of the supported language. For example, the circuit is mapped to the Python library Qiskit, as the SDK *Qiskit* and its Transpiler does not support PyQuil. Thereby, an intermediate format reduces the number of possible translation combinations. For the gate translation, a mapping table is defined for each language. Gates that are not supported by the SDK, e.g. hardware-specific or custom gates, are either replaced by a subroutine of supported gates or unitary matrices defining the specific gates as custom gates. A simple example is the SWAP gate, that, if not supported, can be replaced by three CNOT gates [18]. For defining a matrix, the target SDK has to support custom gates. In general, an arbitrary gate can be approximated by using a universal set of quantum gates [18].

4.2 Compilation

In the *(2) Compilation* phase, the circuit in the respective input language as well as the information about the quantum computer, i.e. its name, are taken as input for each compiler. Then, the selected quantum compilers compile in parallel. The returned compilations are in the programming language required for the later execution on the selected quantum computer, e.g. for IBM machines OpenQASM is required [6]. As SDKs and their compilers are selected dependent on their vendor support, they natively support their required languages and gates.

4.3 Analysis and Selection

In the *(3) Analysis and Selection* phase, the compiled quantum circuits are analyzed to determine their widths and depths. Therefore, the *NISQ Analyzer* is used to compare the depth of the compiled quantum circuits with the estimated maximum executable depth of the quantum computer [24]. The NISQ Analyzer is a tool that selects suitable quantum circuit implementations based on the chosen quantum algorithm and input values and determines if they are executable on available quantum computers. The maximum executable depth of a quantum computer is estimated by dividing the average decoherence time of all available qubits through the maximum gate time [26]. In general, if the width of a quantum circuit is greater than the number of qubits of the quantum computer, existing quantum compilers automatically reject the circuit. If width and depth of a compilation is less than or equal to the maximum depth and the number of qubits of the quantum computer, it is executable and recommended to the user as suitable compiled circuit. All other compilations are filtered out automatically beforehand in the analysis. If multiple compiled circuits are suitable, the user, then, can manually select the most suitable compiled quantum circuit based on their comparable widths and depths, as discussed in Sect. 3.2.

4.4 Execution

In the *(4) Execution* phase, the most suitable compilation selected by the user is executed on the quantum computer, as shown in Fig. 1. As the SDKs containing the quantum compilers also provide access to the considered quantum computer, the respective SDK is used for the automated execution. Therefore, the user does not have to manually deploy the required SDK and compiled circuit for execution. Instead, the *Executor* supports all SDKs used for compilation and automates the execution of compilations. Finally, the execution result is presented to the user.

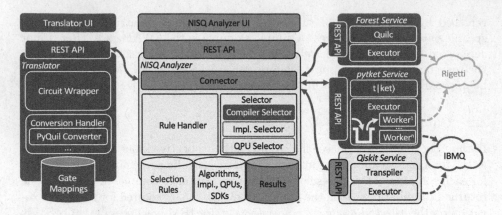

Fig. 2. Architecture for translating, compiling, and comparing quantum circuits.

5   System Architecture and Prototype

In this section, the overall system architecture is presented, as seen in Fig. 2. Furthermore, the prototypical implementation of the framework is described.

5.1   System Architecture

In Fig. 2 the overall architecture of the comparison framework is shown. It consists of an extension of the NISQ Analyzer [24] as well as new components for the translation and a set of compilation and execution services. Thereby, new components are dark, extended components are middle and already existing components are light grey. The *Translator* on the left side of Fig. 2 provides an HTTP REST API used by the *Translator User Interface (UI)* offering the modeling and translation of quantum circuits in multiple programming languages. The *Circuit Wrapper* component inside the Translator controls the import, conversion, and export of a given quantum circuit in the defined programming language. For the conversion between the import and the export languages an intermediate format is used. Therefore, the *Conversion Handler* component invokes the language-specific converter plug-in for converting from the language of the given circuit into the intermediate format and vice versa. For example, the *PyQuil Converter* supports the import and export of circuits written with PyQuil and in Quil. For converting the language and gate set supported by an SDK to the other, the defined gate mappings are stored in a repository.

For the compilation, analysis, and execution, the *NISQ Analyzer*, in the middle of Fig. 2, is extended. The HTTP REST API and the NISQ Analyzer UI are extended triggering the comparison and selection process. The new *Compiler Selector* component in the NISQ Analyzer backend identifies available SDKs and, thus, compilers supporting the vendor of the selected quantum computer and required languages. It also verifies the executability of compilations on the quantum computer. The *Connector* enables the interaction with the Translator and the *Compilation and Execution (Com&Ex) Services*. The analysis and execution results, including the transpiled circuits, are stored as provenance data in a repository enabling the learning of compilations and executions in the future [13].

On the right side of Fig. 2, three exemplary Com&Ex Services are shown. Each supported SDK is wrapped by an interface enabling the compilation and execution with the accessible quantum compiler on a supported quantum computer.

To start the compilation with available quantum compilers, the user inserts the quantum circuit using the NISQ Analyzer UI, selects its programming language and chooses the desired quantum computer. The Compiler Selector identifies the Com&Ex Services supporting the vendor of the quantum computer. Then, the Compiler Selector invokes the Connector to call the Translator if a Com&Ex Service requires another language than the circuit is written in. The circuit, information about its own language and the required language are passed to the Translator. The Circuit Wrapper invokes the Conversion Handler for the translation into the syntax and gate set of the required language and returns the resulting circuit to the NISQ Analyzer. The Compiler Selector passes the circuits to the respective Com&Ex Services for compilation. After compilation, each Com&Ex Service analyzes the width and depth of its compiled circuit and returns the information to the NISQ Analyzer [24]. Then, the Compiler Selector compares the depth of the compilations with the estimated maximum executable depth of the quantum computer proofing executability. Thereby, non-suitable circuits are filtered out and all suitable circuits, their widths and depths are returned to the user. Then, the user can select the most suitable compilation for execution. Therefore, the compiled circuit is passed to its respective Com&Ex Service, where it is sent to the cloud service of the vendor. Finally, the execution result is shown. The NISQ Analyzer can be extended by plug-ins to support further metrics besides comparing width and depth. The Connector can be extended to support further Com&Ex Services implementing the defined interfaces. Additional languages can be supported by implementing respective converters.

5.2   Prototype

The Translator UI and the NISQ Analyzer UI are implemented in TypeScript. The Translator and the Com&Ex Services are written in Python with the framework Flask. The NISQ Analyzer is written in Java with the framework Spring Boot. A detailed discussion of the implementation of the NISQ Analyzer and the Com&Ex Services can be found in [24]. The entire prototype is available open-source[1,2,3].

The intermediate format of the Translator is based on *QuantumCircuit*[4] from Qiskit. As shown in Sect. 3, Qiskit enables defining custom gates. It also supports a great set of standard gates natively. Thus, the import and export of

---

[1] https://github.com/UST-QuAntiL.

[2] https://github.com/UST-QuAntiL/nisq-analyzer-content.

[3] https://youtu.be/I5l8vaA-zO8.

[4] https://qiskit.org/documentation/stubs/qiskit.circuit.QuantumCircuit.html.

OpenQASM and the import of Python for Qiskit is natively supported, as the SDK Qiskit provides respective functions. Exporting a circuit to Python for Qiskit requires additional functions for extracting the *QuantumCircuit* instructions into the required Python-based syntax. Additionally, as proof-of-concept, Quil and Python for PyQuil are supported by the Translator. For example, when importing a circuit written with PyQuil to *QuantumCircuit*, first, the implemented PyQuil Converter uses the Forest SDK returning a PyQuil-specific *Program*[5]. Then, the PyQuil Converter iterates over the *Program* constructing an equivalent *QuantumCircuit*. Exporting from a circuit defined as *Quantum-Circuit* to a circuit written with PyQuil works vice versa. By iterating over the instructions, defined qubit registers and classical bits of a circuit are transferred. For transferring a gate, possible gate parameters and the qubits on which the gate is applied are extracted. The gate mapping itself is stored in a dictionary. Thereby, (i) an equivalent gate, (ii) a subroutine of gates, or (iii) a matrix is defined supported by the target language.

For proof-of-concept, currently three SDKs and their quantum compilers are supported for compilation and execution: Forest SDK with its Quilc compiler [23], pytket with its t|ket⟩ compiler [30], and Qiskit with its Transpiler [1].

6   Case Study

In this section, the prototype of the framework from Sect. 5 is validated. Thus, two use cases are presented. In the first use case, a Quil circuit implementing the Shor algorithm [27] is used for the compilation on the *ibmq_16_melbourne* [9] offering 15 qubits and an estimated maximum gate depth of 32 levels. In the second use case, a Qiskit circuit implementing the Grover algorithm [8] is compiled on a mocked Rigetti quantum computer supporting a fully connected 9-qubit-topology with a maximum depth of 120 levels. Since we cannot access real quantum computers of Rigetti, the usage of the Quilc compiler is shown with a mocked Rigetti quantum computer. Each circuit is provided in our GitHub repository (see Footnote 2).

6.1   Compilation on IBM Hardware

The Shor algorithm factorizes an odd integer and computes its prime factors exponentially faster than a classical counterpart [27]. The considered circuit *shor-15-quil* in Quil factorizes 15. As *ibmq_16_melbourne* is the target, the Qiskit Service and the pytket Service are automatically selected for compilation, as Forest SDK [23] does not support IBM. Both Com&Ex Services do not natively support Quil. Thus, for the pytket Service, the Quil circuit is translated into PyQuil which is one of the supported languages of pytket presented in Sect. 3. For the Qiskit Service, it is translated into Python for Qiskit. Then, the quantum computer and the translated circuits are passed to the respective Com&Ex

---

[5] https://pyquil-docs.rigetti.com/en/latest/apidocs/program.html.

Services. The resulting depth and width of the compilations can be seen in Table 2. Both are executable on the *ibmq_16_melbourne* according to the NISQ Analyzer and are recommended to the user. Based on the widths and depths of the compilations, the user can select which should be executed.

Table 2. Compilation results for *shor-15-quil*.

Compiler	Width	Depth	Backend	Executable
Qiskit Transpiler	4	10	ibmq_16_melbourne	Yes
t|ket⟩	5	8	ibmq_16_melbourne	Yes

6.2   Compilation on Rigetti Hardware

The Grover algorithm, in general, searches items in unsorted lists and has a quadratic speed up compared to a classical algorithm [8]. The algorithm is also applied to more specific problems, such as the *Boolean satisfiability problem (SAT)*. The implemented circuit *grover-SAT-qiskit* in Qiskit solves the SAT problem $(A \lor B) \land (A \lor \neg B) \land (\neg A \lor B)$. The target is a mocked Rigetti quantum computer. Thus, the Forest Service and the pytket Service are automatically selected. The quantum computer and the circuit are directly passed to the pytket Service. For the Forest Service, the circuit is translated into Quil. The mocked Rigetti and the translated circuit are, then, passed to the Forest Service. As we set the maximum depth of the mocked Rigetti to 120, the compilation of the Quilc compiler is not executable according to the NISQ Analyzer, see Table 3. Thus, only the compilation of the t\|ket⟩ compiler is recommended to the user. Finally, the user can trigger the automated execution of the recommended compilation.

Table 3. Compilation results for *grover-SAT-qiskit*.

Compiler	Width	Depth	Backend	Executable
Quilc	8	164	mocked Rigetti	No
t|ket⟩	8	117	mocked Rigetti	Yes

7   Discussion and Limitations

The presented framework enables the decoupling of quantum circuits and their SDKs and the comparison of compilation results of quantum compilers for arbitrary circuits. Thereby, the automated (i) translation, (ii) compilation, and (iii) analysis of a given quantum circuit and quantum computer is provided to support the selection of the most suitable compilation. As discussed in Sect. 3, automatically prioritizing a compiled circuit if, e.g., one executable compilation has the smallest depth but another has the smallest width, is a multidimensional challenge and is currently not yet supported. However, all non-suitable compilation results in terms of width and depth are filtered out and, thus, only suitable compilation results are returned to the user for the final selection.

At present, we only consider quantum compilers if the selected quantum computer is natively supported. However, as shown in Sect. 3, some quantum compilers support the specification of custom quantum computers. The framework could be further extended to retrieve quantum computer specifications from a certain vendor and to translate them into the format to custom define this quantum computer for the compiler. By iterating over the individual instructions for translating a defined circuit into another programming language, non-optimal replacements can occur which can also affect the resource efficiency of the compiled circuit. Furthermore, no automated equivalence verification of translated circuits is currently supported. Nevertheless, the translated circuits presented in Sect. 6 were verified by comparing their execution results with those of the initial quantum circuits. Currently, only the programming languages OpenQASM and Quil and the Python libraries Qiskit and PyQuil are supported. However, as our framework bases on a plug-in based system, additional plug-ins can be implemented supporting further languages, SDKs, metrics, and compilers.

We currently use Com&Ex Services to support all SDKs and their compilers utilized for the compilation of quantum circuits and the automated execution of their compilations. For the automated deployment and execution also existing deployment automation technologies can be used [35].

8   Related Work

Comparing quantum compilers is covered in several works. Sivarajah et al. [30] present their software development platform to access the quantum compiler t|ket⟩ supporting multiple programming languages and vendors, as shown in Sect. 3. They compare their compiler with the Quilc compiler and the Qiskit Transpiler. Therefore, several test circuits are used as benchmarks and executions on quantum computers were performed. Also, in the work of [2, 15, 16] the performance of the presented compilation and optimization algorithms were compared with the Qiskit Transpiler and the Quilc compiler, by several test circuits and certain quantum algorithm implementations. Thus, their focus is on showing the overall performance of their compilers using defined benchmarks. The focus of our framework is on supporting the selection of the most suitable compilation situation-based for an arbitrary quantum circuit on a certain quantum computer.

In the work of Mills et al. [14] the t|ket⟩ compiler and the Qiskit Transpiler are compared. Thereby, they are investigating their different compilation and optimization algorithms in consideration of the physical properties of implemented qubits on quantum computers. Nevertheless, their focus is on aspects considered during the compilation process on quantum computers. Thus, they do not support the generic approach of comparing and selecting compilations of quantum compilers for arbitrary quantum circuits.

Arline[6] introduces a framework for the automated benchmarking of quantum compilers[7]. For the implementation of quantum circuits, the framework offers its own programming language but also supports the import and export of Open-QASM circuits. Thereby, gate sets from quantum computers of IBM, Rigetti, and Google are supported. Currently, compilers of Qiskit and Cirq are considered and can be combined for compiling quantum circuits. The benchmarking analysis of the quantum compilers and its compilations bases on metrics, e.g. the depth of the compiled circuit, the gate count, and the compiler runtime. However, analyzing the executability on a certain quantum computer afterward is not considered. Instead of accessing real quantum computers, properties are hard-coded. Thus, no execution is supported. Furthermore, no support of several programming languages and its translations is given.

9 Conclusion and Future Work

In this paper, we presented a framework to compare the compilations of different quantum compilers for a certain quantum circuit and quantum computer. Answering **RQ 2**, the framework automatically (i) translates the quantum circuit into the programming languages required by the SDKs of the available compilers, (ii) compiles with selected quantum compilers, and (iii) analyzes the compilations. Thereby, the dependency between quantum circuits and their SDKs are solved, such that the execution on an arbitrary quantum computer is enabled. For the comparison of the compilations, the widths and depths of the resulting circuits are determined and their executability on the chosen quantum computer is examined. The most suitable quantum circuit can, then, directly be executed on the respective quantum computer. As basis of our framework, several SDKs and their compilers are analyzed towards compilation answering **RQ 1**.

The framework extends the NISQ Analyzer [24] which is part of the platform PlanQK[8] focusing on sharing and executing quantum software [12,13]. In the future, we plan to implement further Com&Ex Services wrapping additional SDKs to increase the variety of available quantum compilers. Additionally, we plan to support an automated equivalence verification framework to verify the Translator component systematically and ensure the equivalence of its translations [28]. Furthermore, we plan to investigate in an intermediate format to support the specification of arbitrary quantum computers for SDKs supporting custom quantum computers. We also plan to offer further metrics, e.g. the count of multi-qubit gates and the estimation of a successful executability [25], to improve the comparison of compiled quantum circuits.

Acknowledgements. We would like to thank Thomas Wangler for the implementation of the Translator.

This work was partially funded by the BMWi project *PlanQK* (01MK20005N) and the DFG's Excellence Initiative project *SimTech* (EXC 2075 - 390740016).

---

[6] https://www.arline.io.

[7] https://github.com/ArlineQ.

[8] https://planqk.de/en/.

References

1. Aleksandrowicz, G., Alexander, T., Barkoutsos, P., Bello, L., Ben-Haim, Y., et al.: Qiskit: an open-source framework for quantum computing (2019). https://doi.org/10.5281/zenodo.2562111

2. Amy, M., Gheorghiu, V.: staq–a full-stack quantum processing toolkit. Quantum Sci. Technol. **5**(3), 034016 (2020). https://doi.org/10.1088/2058-9565/ab9359

3. Arute, F., Arya, K., Babbush, R., Bacon, D., Bardin, J.C., et al.: Quantum supremacy using a programmable superconducting processor. Nature **574**(7779), 505–510 (2019). https://doi.org/10.1038/s41586-019-1666-5

4. Bishop, L., Bravyi, S., Cross, A., Gambetta, J., Smolin, J.: Quantum volume, March 2017

5. Cowtan, A., Dilkes, S., Duncan, R., Krajenbrink, A., Simmons, W., et al.: On the qubit routing problem. In: 14th Conference on the Theory of Quantum Computation, Communication and Cryptography (TQC 2019). Leibniz International Proceedings in Informatics (LIPIcs), vol. 135, pp. 5:1–5:32. Schloss Dagstuhl-Leibniz-Zentrum fuer Informatik (2019). https://doi.org/10.4230/LIPIcs.TQC.2019.5

6. Cross, A.W., Bishop, L.S., Smolin, J.A., Gambetta, J.M.: Open quantum assembly language (2017)

7. Fingerhuth, M., Babej, T., Wittek, P.: Open source software in quantum computing. PLOS ONE **13**(12), 1–28 (2018). https://doi.org/10.1371/journal.pone.0208561

8. Grover, L.K.: A fast quantum mechanical algorithm for database search. In: Proceedings of the Twenty-Eighth Annual ACM Symposium on Theory of Computing, pp. 212–219 (1996)

9. IBMQ Team: 15-qubit backend: IBM Q 16 Melbourne backend specification V2.3.6 (2021). https://quantum-computing.ibm.com

10. LaRose, R.: Overview and comparison of gate level quantum software platforms. Quantum **3**, 130 (2019). https://doi.org/10.22331/q-2019-03-25-130

11. Leymann, F., Barzen, J.: The bitter truth about gate-based quantum algorithms in the NISQ era. Quantum Sci. Technol. **5**(4), 1–28 (2020). https://doi.org/10.1088/2058-9565/abae7d

12. Leymann, F., Barzen, J., Falkenthal, M.: Towards a platform for sharing quantum software. In: Proceedings of the 13th Advanced Summer School on Service Oriented Computing, pp. 70–74 (2019). IBM technical report (RC25685), IBM Research Division (2019)

13. Leymann, F., Barzen, J., Falkenthal, M., Vietz, D., Weder, B., et al.: Quantum in the cloud: application potentials and research opportunities. In: Proceedings of the 10th International Conference on Cloud Computing and Services Science (CLOSER 2020), pp. 9–24. SciTePress (2020)

14. Mills, D., Sivarajah, S., Scholten, T.L., Duncan, R.: Application-motivated, holistic benchmarking of a full quantum computing stack (2021). https://doi.org/10.22331/q-2021-03-22-415

15. Murali, P., Baker, J.M., Javadi-Abhari, A., Chong, F.T., Martonosi, M.: Noise-adaptive compiler mappings for noisy intermediate-scale quantum computers. In: Proceedings of the Twenty-Fourth International Conference on Architectural Support for Programming Languages and Operating Systems, ASPLOS 2019, pp. 1015–1029. ACM (2019). https://doi.org/10.1145/3297858.3304075

16. Murali, P., Linke, N.M., Martonosi, M., Abhari, A.J., Nguyen, N.H., et al.: Full-stack, real-system quantum computer studies: architectural comparisons and design insights. In: Proceedings of the 46th International Symposium on Computer Architecture, ISCA 2019, pp. 527–540. ACM (2019). https://doi.org/10.1145/3307650.3322273

17. National Academies of Sciences, Engineering, and Medicine: Quantum Computing: Progress and Prospects. The National Academies Press (2019)

18. Nielsen, M.A., Chuang, I.L.: Quantum Computation and Quantum Information, 10th edn. Cambridge University Press, Cambridge (2011)

19. Preskill, J.: Quantum computing in the NISQ era and beyond. Quantum **2**, 79 (2018). https://doi.org/10.22331/q-2018-08-06-79

20. Quantum AI team and collaborators. Cirq (2020)

21. Resch, S., Karpuzcu, U.R.: Benchmarking quantum computers and the impact of quantum noise (2019)

22. Rieffel, E., Polak, W.: Quantum Computing: A Gentle Introduction, 1st edn. The MIT Press, Cambridge (2011)

23. Rigetti: Docs for the Forest SDK (2021). https://pyquil-docs.rigetti.com/

24. Salm, M., Barzen, J., Breitenbücher, U., Leymann, F., Weder, B., Wild, K.: The NISQ analyzer: automating the selection of quantum computers for quantum algorithms. In: Dustdar, S. (ed.) SummerSOC 2020. CCIS, vol. 1310, pp. 66–85. Springer, Cham (2020). https://doi.org/10.1007/978-3-030-64846-6_5

25. Salm, M., Barzen, J., Leymann, F., Weder, B.: About a criterion of successfully executing a circuit in the NISQ era: what $wd \ll 1/\epsilon_{eff}$ really means. In: Proceedings of the 1st ACM SIGSOFT International Workshop on Architectures and Paradigms for Engineering Quantum Software (APEQS 2020), pp. 10–13. ACM (2020). https://doi.org/10.1145/3412451.3428498

26. Sete, E.A., Zeng, W.J., Rigetti, C.T.: A functional architecture for scalable quantum computing. In: 2016 IEEE International Conference on Rebooting Computing (ICRC), pp. 1–6 (2016). https://doi.org/10.1109/ICRC.2016.7738703

27. Shor, P.W.: Polynomial-time algorithms for prime factorization and discrete logarithms on a quantum computer. SIAM J. Comput. **26**(5), 1484–1509 (1997). https://doi.org/10.1137/S0036144598347011

28. Singhal, K., Rand, R., Hicks, M.: Verified translation between low-level quantum languages. In: The First International Workshop on Programming Languages for Quantum Computing (2020)

29. Siraichi, M.Y., dos Santos, V.F., Collange, S., Quintão Pereira, F.M.: Qubit allocation. In: CGO 2018 - International Symposium on Code Generation and Optimization, pp. 1–12 (2018). https://doi.org/10.1145/3168822

30. Sivarajah, S., Dilkes, S., Cowtan, A., Simmons, W., Edgington, A., et al.: t|ket⟩: a retargetable compiler for NISQ devices. Quantum Sci. Technol. **6** (2020). https://doi.org/10.1088/2058-9565/ab8e92

31. Smith, R.S., Curtis, M.J., Zeng, W.J.: A practical quantum instruction set architecture (2017)

32. Steiger, D.S., Häner, T., Troyer, M.: ProjectQ: an open source software framework for quantum computing. Quantum **2**, 49 (2018). https://doi.org/10.22331/q-2018-01-31-49

33. Tannu, S.S., Qureshi, M.K.: Not all qubits are created equal: a case for variability-aware policies for NISQ-era quantum computers. In: Proceedings of the Twenty-Fourth International Conference on Architectural Support for Programming Languages and Operating Systems, ASPLOS 2019, pp. 987–999. ACM (2019). https://doi.org/10.1145/3297858.3304007

34. Vietz, D., Barzen, J., Leymann, F., Wild, K.: On decision support for quantum application developers: categorization, comparison, and analysis of existing technologies. In: Paszynski, M., Kranzlmüller, D., Krzhizhanovskaya, V.V., Dongarra, J.J., Sloot, P.M.A. (eds.) ICCS 2021. LNCS, vol. 12747, pp. 127–141. Springer, Cham (2021). https://doi.org/10.1007/978-3-030-77980-1_10

35. Wild, K., Breitenbücher, U., Harzenetter, L., Leymann, F., Vietz, D., Zimmermann, M.: TOSCA4QC: two modeling styles for TOSCA to automate the deployment and orchestration of quantum applications. In: 2020 IEEE 24th International Enterprise Distributed Object Computing Conference (EDOC). IEEE Computer Society (2020). https://doi.org/10.1109/EDOC49727.2020.00024

36. Zhong, H.S., Wang, H., Deng, Y.H., Chen, M.C., Peng, L.C., et al.: Quantum computational advantage using photons. Science **370**(6523), 1460–1463 (2020)

Advanced Application Architecture

Towards Taming the Adaptivity Problem
Formalizing Poly-/MultiStore Topology Descriptions

Daniel Glake[ID], Felix Kiehn[✉][ID], Mareike Schmidt[ID], and Norbert Ritter

Working Group DBIS, Department of Informatics, Universität Hamburg,
Vogt-Kölln-Str. 30, 22846 Hamburg, Germany
{dbis-research.inf,felix.kiehn}@uni-hamburg.de
https://vsis-www.informatik.uni-hamburg.de/dbis/

Abstract. Systems following the Polyglot Persistence paradigm are on the rise and with them come new problems and challenges. A major challenge is the ability to automatically self-adapt to changing requirements and workloads. The most difficult and as yet rarely discussed form of adaptivity relates to cahanges to the underlying data composition and topology. The search for a topology suited best for a given set of requirements can be modelled as a complex optimization problem.

This paper proposes and formalizes *Blueprints*, which we define as graphs representing functional units composed of (heterogeneous) data stores. Blueprints can be used as manageable, predefined building blocks to form the highly complex system topologies Poly- and MultiStores use internally. Subsequently, the optimization search space can be limited to a set of Blueprints, which can be matched against the Poly-/MultiStores' requirements. Furthermore, we discuss System requirements and their impact on adaptivity decisions and identify future research directions building upon our Blueprint concept.

Keywords: Polyglot persistence · Multi-/Polystore · Adaptivity · Data migration · System topology · Cloud data management

1 Introduction and Motivation

In a sense, the last decade was a gold rush for the database community. The ever-growing amount of data made it necessary to reevaluate best practices and proven solutions at the time and triggered a shift within big tech companies towards fundamentally different data models and cheaper general-purpose hardware. This gave rise to a variety of new database systems that did not follow the previous dominant relational paradigm and, amongst others, paved the way for the NoSQL movement we see since 2009. Today, these NoSQL systems are ubiquitous and enrich the database landscape with various data storage and management solutions, each with its particular advantages and disadvantages. Consequently, the formerly postulated *one size fits all* mind set is no longer valid [23,24] and developers see themselves confronted with a hard decision: Which

© Springer Nature Switzerland AG 2021
J. Barzen (Ed.): SummerSOC 2021, CCIS 1429, pp. 83–99, 2021.
https://doi.org/10.1007/978-3-030-87568-8_5

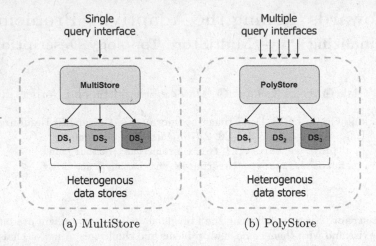

Fig. 1. System Types (Based on: Tan et al. [25])

system fits my use case best and am I experienced enough to get the best out of this system? While the first problem can be solved more efficiently by providing guidelines and decision aids [10], the second problem is more complex, especially if a developer needs to use multiple different systems at once. Polyglot persistence tries to prove a solution to this problem [19].

Systems following the idea of polyglot persistence incorporate multiple data storage solutions to combine their strength and balance out their weaknesses. These systems handle the coordination of the underlying (heterogeneous) database systems themselves. Based on the number of query interfaces these systems provide, one can distinguish between two distinct variants: A MultiStore (Fig. 1a) has one single query interface, whereas PolyStores (Fig. 1b) offer multiple query interfaces at once.

But of course, polyglot persistence comes with its own share of problems and challenges. One of these is how Poly- and Multistores manage their underlying systems and provide forms of self-adaptivity, e.g. to react to changes in workloads or data requirements.

In this paper, we want to address what self-adaptivity means w.r.t. to polyglot persistence and how it could be achieved. Since self-adaptivity is complicated to achieve, we want to break the problem down into smaller, better solvable pieces and provide ideas towards self-adaptivity in Poly- and MultiStore systems. Thus, we introduce the concept of *Blueprints*, which are designed to model and formalize the underlying structure of database systems, auxiliary systems and storage nodes within a Poly-/MultiStore, and we discuss how Blueprints can be used as a stepping stone towards self-adaptivity.

The remainder of this paper is structured as follows: In Sect. 2, we motivate the need for self-adaptivity in Poly-/MultiStores and identify different basic kinds of self-adaptivity. Based on this categorization, we explore and discuss approaches for topology changes in Sect. 3. After that, we discuss how Poly- and MultiStores can leverage System Requirements for Adaptivity in Sect. 4. In Sect. 5, we describe our contribution towards self-adaptivity in the Form of *Blueprints*, which will be discussed further in Sect. 6. After that, we give an overview of topics for future work in Sect. 7. Section 8 concludes the paper.

2   Forms of Adaptivity

A major selling point of Multi- and PolyStores is their ability to continuously provide a system to users capable of adapting itself to needs to be postulated by predefined requirements or demands derived from a potentially ever-changing query workload. Different methods can be used to modify a system to meet these demands and requirements to face these challenges. In different current systems, we see many approaches that involve adaptivity for various reasons and design goals. For example, the general-purpose cross-platform data processing system RHEEM [1] allows for temporary or permanent data migration to find efficient query plans over multiple databases. Other approaches like the online partitioning software Clay [21] aim at re-partition data based on incoming queries to identify semantically connected data to co-locate them together to speed up future operations. Based on both existing adaptivity approaches and our own ideas, we divide the different forms of self-adaptation that such a system can provide into the following four levels:

- **Level 1:** performing automatic temporary data migrations to execute domain-specific operations or to *split* workload across the data stores to run operations concurrently,
- **Level 2:** permanently migrating data between systems to rearrange the distribution of data and locating it on stores better suited for its usage,
- **Level 3:** changing store-parameters and hardware configuration of a given data store (e.g., in-/decrease resource-limits or quorum-configs) to achieve a higher read- or write-throughput,
- **Level 4:** and, ultimately, changing the Poly-/MultiStore composition of underlying data stores (changing the store's topology),e.g. starting and interconnecting new DB instances or by replacing databases.

Even if these problems are not as trivial as they look at first glance, some of the current Poly- and MultiStore systems already incorporate (partial) solutions for the first three levels. Table 1 gives an overview of these systems and their ability to provide the presented levels of self-adaptivity.

While level 1 (temporary data migration) is widely considered in current systems, level 2 is rarely implemented (exceptions are MuSQLE and RHEEM), and level 3 is not addressed in the literature. Further, to the best of our knowledge, there is currently no system that supports level 4. To some extend, Polypheny-DB is an exception. However, this information is primarily based on a vision paper, making it difficult to evaluate the current state of implementation and property set. Because permanent data migration is a whole other topic already covered by a considerable amount of research, we focus on the levels 3–4.

Table 1. Self-Adapting capabilities of existing Poly-/MultiStores

System	Level 1	Level 2	Level 3	Level 4
BigDAWG [7,8]	✓	✗	⑦	✗
Polybase [6]	✓	✓	✓	✗
BigIntegrator [29]	✗	✗	⑦	✗
CloudMdsQL [14]	✓	✗	⑦	✗
Myria [28]	✓	✗	⑦	✗
ESTOCADA [2]	✓	✗	⑦	✗
FORWARD [17]	✗	✗	⑦	✗
MuSQLE [11]	✓	✓	⑦	✗
RHEEM [1]	✓	✓	⑦	✗
Polypheny-DB[a] [26]	✓	✓	✓	✓

[a]The information about Polypheny-DB is based on a vision paper

Especially level 4 is a consequential direction for Poly- and MultiStore systems, given their proposed ability to handle changing requirements and workload challenges. A given setup of datastores can only be optimized by data migration or replication to a certain degree and changes the underlying data store structure inevitably w.r.t. to performance or functionality optimizations.

Addressing this problem outlined by adaptivity level 4, the following questions need to be answered: (I) When must a system adapt and trigger adaption actions? (II) How does a system perform an adaption, especially on the system's topology? (III) How does a system measure the success of an adaption and prevent alternating between similar good system compositions?

A system adaption can be triggered by a wide variety of possible causes and related events. In contrast to manually triggering changes (*offline*), systems can react proactively (*online*) by comparing the system state divergence of the current workload against specified constraints (SLAs) [19] or by using a prediction model [26]. Based on the heterogeneous nature of polyglot data stores, the adaption needs to be able to support different migration strategies across the underlying store models: (i) Depending on the data or the processing context, only a subset of the data objects must be moved. (ii) The migration can perform *lazy* or *eager* to a set of queries. Furthermore, data can be migrated online or offline as well as during a more inactive system state. (iii) The migration strategy should consider the direction within *homogeneous store subsets* and *schema versions* or between *heterogeneous stores*.

To determine how a system should adapt, a classic optimization problem needs to be solved: How can the operational costs be minimized while still satisfying the requirements imposed on the system in an optimal way? In case of of the levels 1–2, this mainly focuses on migrating and partition data accordingly to increase the overall system performance (cf. [21]). Regarding level 3 and 4, the optimization task becomes significantly more difficult because of the sheer amount of parameters and compositions of databases, additional (auxiliary) systems and their configuration (both software and hardware configuration). Thus, to satisfy (non-)functional requirements users may impose upon a Poly-/MultiStore, one is confronted with a vast search space to find optimal/satisfying solutions.

In order to do this, the system has to select the datastore solutions and their configurations suited best for its optimization factors. To reduce the search space for this optimization problem, we propose the concept of *Blueprints*, graphs representing (heterogeneous) database system configurations of arbitrary complexity tailored for specific use cases or requirements (e.g. read scalability or spatio-temporal capabilities). These graphs can be used as building blocks to craft complex Poly-/MultiStore topologies and, therefore, reduce the optimization search space to a more manageable set of predefined Blueprints (see Fig. 2).

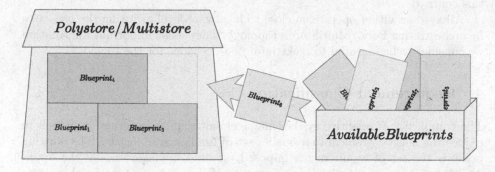

Fig. 2. Blueprints as building blocks towards a larger Poly- or MultiStore system

Additionally, we explore how system and performance requirements can be addressed during solving the mentioned optimization problem and how they can be incorporated into our Blueprint approach.

3 Related Work

As they will be defined in Sect. 4.3, Blueprints fall into the category of meta-models. Few systems/models can be found in the literature, focusing on the same niche as our graph model. One of these is TOSCA[1], a standard for meta-modelling cloud services and topologies [22] and part of the standardization efforts of OASIS[2]. TOSCA focuses on describing service structures on a very high level and a very abstract view of how systems handle requirements in service level agreements. Despite the fact that the meta-model of TOSCA serves

---

[1] https://docs.oasis-open.org/tosca/TOSCA/v2.0/TOSCA-v2.0.html.
[2] https://www.oasis-open.org/.

to describe services with their agreements and restrictions the user can expect, it does not imply any kind of optimization. Assumptions around non-functional requirements are plainly described with a specified threshold, and no background is provided to observe and compare these states. However, the meta-model has extensively been used in practice, serving a description model with the relevant requirements, even if the domain is limited to data management. Practical aspects are considered as well (e.g., security consequences). In addition, TOSCA descriptions are specified in machine-readable formats (XML, YAML).

On a more hardware and deployment focused abstraction level, deployment plans are used heavily in the industry. Orchestration systems such as Kubernetes[3] use deployment plans written in data-serialization languages YAML or JSON to describe and deploy containerized services with its virtual network. Similarly, infrastructure-as-code (short: IAC) systems use description languages to orchestrate the hardware node and virtual machines. Solutions like Chef[4], Ansible[5], Puppet[6], Terraform[7] or Saltstack are a few examples to be named in this context.

All systems either operate on close to hardware-level or fitting the use-cases by orchestrating Poly-/MultiStore's topology. They mask important information we consider to be essential to make informed decisions for the topology.

4   Requirement Classification

The complexity of adaptive system management requires a formal approach to reduce the holistic problem to a smaller set of fundamental factors. The starting point is the set of requirements imposed on data management by the application and given as functional requirements (FRs) and non-functional requirements (NFRs). There is a broad consensus regarding the definition of functional requirements (FRs) [27]. FRs express what a product must do, can do, or does in the face of a given software specification. Other views refine this description to include resulting and desired behaviours for FRs in the form of fulfilled use cases [12]. When defining non-functional requirements (NFRs), this consensus does not exist [5,12,15]. Different domains consider NFRs as quality features [13], goals [18], and constraints [5,12]. Linguistic approaches [16] provided a different view, stating that non-functional requirements are defined with predicates such as "must" and "at least", e.g. *the system must allow filtering by username* or *the username's length must be at least ten characters*.

In contrast, non-functional requirements have different definitions and have only gained importance since the early 2000s due to their relevance to closer system development [3]. Work in the area represents the consensus that NFRs, unlike FRs, describe how the system achieves its goals and purposes, not how

---

[3] https://kubernetes.io/.
[4] https://www.chef.io/.
[5] https://www.ansible.com/.
[6] https://puppet.com/.
[7] https://www.terraform.io/.

it functions explicitly. Common examples of requirements classified as NFRs include abstract demand for reliability, performance, safety, accuracy and maintainability, as well as other descriptors that do not necessarily describe actions to be performed by the system [4]. Thus, there is no consensus on the definition of NFRs.

Based on these different perspectives, it becomes clear that the distinction between FRs and NFRs with the various subcategories of the latter is a fuzzy classification concept. Upon closer examination concerning data management systems, it becomes evident that this fuzziness mixes three different concepts: first classification by type (e.g., whether a requirement is a function, a performance requirement, a constraint), second by soft or hard fulfilment, and third by representation (e.g., whether a requirement is represented operationally, quantitatively, or qualitatively). For this reason of fuzziness and the fact that the model is used as a structured basis for a concrete system, we propose a more structure-oriented classification of requirements that overcomes traditional fuzziness and separates them by their aspects type, satisfiability, and representation.

4.1 Type

Requirements can be binary, discrete-valid or, continuous-valid. Binary conditions comprise whether a property (e.g., a function or an operator's existence) is fulfilled. Discrete-valid requirements depend on a use case that specifies constraints on its quality (read and write speed of data objects of a specific type, maximum latency for a request to a sensor data system for a current value). Continuous requirements describe constraints on the system that must be valid across multiple use cases. With this point of view, requests are linked to a requirement and a state that the data management system tries to fulfil.

4.2 Satisfiability

Verification of requirements has to determine whether or not the actual system state satisfy the requirements. Therefore, we distinguish two cases, meeting their satisfaction type with *hard* and *soft* requirements (FRs are usually *hard* requirements; NFRs usually soft target measures) and by the current workload's applicability. *Hard* requirements are represented as *step-functions*, with values either 0 or 1. Soft requirements specify the value more flexibly via a discontinuous, for example, a *sigmoid* or *trapezoidal* function with *ordinal* scaled value range in [0, 1] range. The more quality is required, the more it costs. However, it often does not increase linearly.

4.3 Representation

When checking the satisfiability, we need to represent them for data-management under their fulfilment. *Operational* requirements induce behaviour that the system is supposed to provide. These can be formed abstractly over the specification and examination of the input and desired output state, e.g. a database-specific function (spatial-join). However, such state descriptions also include *declarative* representations with logical conditions. This logic refers to existence checks of an, e.g., database operator or the topology's current structure. Regarding the satisfiability, requirement's costs are mapped to an ordinal-scaled value range, implying a *quantitative* description. Quantitative descriptions have to be checked via measurements, whereas the final form concerning qualitative requirements with generally valid data-management objectives. These requirements cannot be verified directly but are subjective assessments such as the usability of the available language (e.g., SQL interface) (Table 2).

Table 2. Different types of system requirements based on [20] extended by the proposed classification.

Requirement	Type	Representation
Availability	Continuous	Quantitative
Latency	Continuous	Quantitative
Throughput	Continuous	Quantitative
Scalability	Discrete	Quantitative
Consistency	Discrete	Operational
ACID transactions	Functional	Operational
Joins	Functional	Operational
Stream processing	Functional	Operational
Spatio-temporal queries	Functional	Declarative
Range query	Functional	Declarative
Analytics integrations	Functional	Declarative, Qualitative

5   Blueprint Description

In this section, we want to introduce a theoretical concept called *Blueprint*. Each of these Blueprints represents a set of systems combined to provide a set of functionalities and fulfil a set of non-functional requirements for a specific use case (e.g. a caching system or a system providing access to Spatio-temporal data). A basic example of a Blueprint can be found in Fig. 3. The overall topology of a Poly-/MultiStore consists of these block-like Blueprints, able to be added, removed or replaced as required. Using these building blocks will reduce the search space of optimizing the topology of a Poly-/MultiStore to the set of available Blueprints.

When talking about the topology of a Poly-/MultiStore, we distinguish between three different classes of systems within one Blueprint:

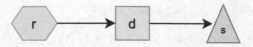

Fig. 3. Basic illustration of a Blueprint containing a dedicated root (r/⬡), a database management system (d/▪) and a storage system (s/△).

Database Management Systems provide data models, certain functionalities and persist incoming data. Representatives of this class are among others PostgreSQL, MongoDB, Neo4j and Redis but also systems such as Apache Spark, Hadoop or Kafka.

Auxiliary Systems provide additional functionalities but do not persist incoming data. Furthermore, this class contains systems that are necessary for the operation of some Database Mangemant Systems. Additional functionalities, amongst others, can be Caching (ORESTES[9], Hazelcast[8]), Load Balancing (Porter[9], Ingress[10]), Monitoring (Prometheus[11], Jaeger[12]), Coordination and Consensus (Zookeeper[13]) as well as failure recovery (Istio[14], Linkerd[15]).

Storage Systems define the type of Storage used by the Database Management Systems or the Auxiliary Systems. Possible storage systems might be HDD and SSD-disk storage, Block-Storage, Network- and Cluster-File Systems.

It should be noted that some systems such as Redis can be assigned to the first and to the second class depending on the specific usage. However, the same instance can never belong to both types at the same time. Redis, for example, is part of the Database Management Systems when used as a datastore and part of the Auxiliary Systems when used for caching.

To simplify the adaptivity problem, Blueprints can be used to construct a topology. Blueprints are defined as follows:

Definition 1 (Blueprint). *Let D, A and S be disjoint sets of databases, auxiliary systems and storage systems, respectively.*

A Blueprint B is a graph tuple B = <V, E> where:

– *V is the set of components (nodes):*

$$V = D \cup A \cup S \cup \{r\}$$

with r representing the coordinator (root node)

---

[8] https://hazelcast.com/.
[9] https://github.com/kubesphere/porterlb.
[10] https://kubernetes.io/docs/concepts/services-networking/ingress.
[11] https://prometheus.io/.
[12] https://www.jaegertracing.io/.
[13] https://zookeeper.apache.org/.
[14] https://istio.io/.
[15] https://linkerd.io/.

– E is the set of directed dependencies (edges):

$$E \subseteq (\{r\} \times (D \cup A)) \cup (D \times (V \setminus \{r\})) \cup (A \times (V \setminus \{r\}))$$

Furthermore, a Blueprint satisfies the following conditions:

1. The Graph consists of at least one database node: $|D| \geq 1$
2. The Graph consists of at least one storage node: $|S| \geq 1$
3. Every node can be reached from the root node:

$$\forall v \in V \setminus \{r\} : \exists n \in \mathbb{N} : \exists p = (v_0, ..., v_n) :$$
$$(v_0 = r \text{ and } v_n = v \text{ and } (\forall i \in \{0, ..., n-1\} : v_i \in V \text{ and } (v_i, v_{i+1}) \in E))$$

4. Databases depend on exactly one Storage System:

$$\forall d \in D : \exists! s \in S : (d, s) \in E$$

According to this definition, a Blueprint consists of database management systems, auxiliary systems, storage systems and a control node (root). The database management systems provide a set of available data models and functional and non-functional requirements that can be fulfilled. Auxiliary systems provide additional functionalities or may be needed for the operation of some database management systems. The Blueprint illustrates dependencies using directed edges between database management systems and auxiliary systems. Furthermore, the Blueprint contains information about the storage structures employed by database management and auxiliary systems.

Apart from this basic graph structure, we defined several criteria that a Blueprint has to fulfil. First, storage systems do not have outgoing edges as they do not depend on other systems. Second, any Blueprint has to possess at least one database management system and one storage system. Otherwise, functionalities could not be granted. Auxiliary systems are optional. Third, there always has to be a path from the destined root to any other node (independent of its kind) in the graph so that the complete graph is connected. Last but not least, every database management system is related to precisely one storage system to be able to persist data.

To provide information about the Blueprint's functional and non-functional capabilities, we first define a set of requirements as follows:

Definition 2 (Requirements). Let R be a set of requirements. $R_f \subseteq R$ and $R_n \subseteq R$ define sets of functional and non-functional requirements respectively. R_f and R_n are disjoint.

The set of requirements is provided by the Poly-/MultiStore. In addition, the scoring is defined as:

Definition 3 (Blueprint scoring). Let f_{Bscore_f} and f_{Bscore_n} two static scoring function mapping each tuple $(b, r) \in (B \times R)$ to a score $s \in S \subseteq \mathbb{R}_0^+ \cup \{\bot\}$ with $\bot$ denoting "unknown".

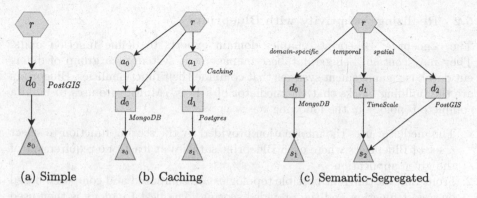

(a) Simple   (b) Caching   (c) Semantic-Segregated

Fig. 4. Exemplary blueprints for different application-cases. The root nodes are represented by green hexagons (⬡), database management systems by blue squares (◼), auxiliary systems by yellow circles (●) and storage systems by red triangles (▲)

$$f_{Bscore_f} : (B \times R_f) \to \{0, 1, \bot\} \tag{1}$$

$$f_{Bscore_n} : \begin{cases} (B \times R_n) \to [0, 1] \cup \{\bot\}, & \textit{if requirement is normalizable} \\ (B \times R_n) \to \mathbb{R}_0^+ \cup \{\bot\}, & \textit{else} \end{cases} \tag{2}$$

The function assigns a given Blueprint and a given requirement a static quality value independent of the current workload. Functional requirements are mapped to 0 (not supported) or 1 (supported). Non-functional requirements are mapped to an arbitrary positive value or, if possible, to a value between 0 and 1. If there is no information available on whether or not a requirement is supported, it will be mapped to $\bot$. Hence, each Blueprint forms a scoring vector where each element is related to one requirement.

5.1 Examples

To illustrate the Blueprint description, we have defined three real-world examples in Fig. 4. Each Blueprint represents a different distribution approach used to satisfy a subset of requirements. Blueprint 4a describes the simplest possible structure with a sample PostGIS database d_0 and associated storage s_0 that ensures the persistence of application data. The root node r delegates queries in this topology state only to Postgres. Blueprint 4b extends the topology by an aggregate-driven *denormalized* property in the form of a MongoDB node. Highly normalized data sets with higher data consistency requirements are still stored in the relational database, whose intermediate caching layer a_1 has been specified for certain partial queries to increase the throughput (e.g., divergent join operations). An extra monitor auxiliary system a_0 observes the system state. Blueprint 4c specifies an exemplary topology in which data is decomposed against spatio-temporal properties to execute spatial, temporal or domain-related partial queries in the respective databases and integrate its results in the mediation system r.

5.2   Realizing Adaptivity with Blueprints

The concept of Blueprints enables domain experts to define function units. They may contain a single database management system or a group of different database management systems that combine their functionalities. Blueprints are the building blocks that the mediator of a Poly-/MultiStore uses to build a complete topology in the following way:

1. The mediator uses the information provided by the scoring function to select a set of Blueprints where each Blueprint satisfies at least one requirement of the given application.
2. From this set, different possible topologies are computed and compared based on a cost function and the provided scoring. The best topology is then used for the system.

When a new adaption process is triggered by the user or by the monitoring system, the mediator can easily change the existing topology by adding and removing one or more Blueprints or replacing a current set of Blueprints with a better suitable one. Furthermore, domain experts may extend the global set of available Blueprints if they encounter new requirements.

Apart from the role of an abstract building block for computing topologies, Blueprints can also be transferred into concrete deployment plans. Based on these plans, it is possible to start-up, shut down and (re-)configure existing systems and services. When exchanging one Blueprint with another, a Poly-/MultiStore could, for instance, first re-configure all systems that are part of both Blueprints. Then it could start all systems and services that are missing in the current deployment. The Blueprints systems are now running in parallel, and data is migrated online from its original datastores to its new destinations. As soon as the migration process is finished, all systems that are not part of the new Blueprint are shut down, and adaptation from one topology to another is successful.

The Kubernetes (K8) metamodel is one solution, providing relevant elements to specify topologies from the Blueprint as set goals. The K8 controller attempts to fully achieve this specification by observing and comparing deployed landscapes, retrying to applied start, stop or reschedule systems satisfying deployment conditions (e.g., required CPU cores). The goals are given externally and can be retrieved from interactions with *cyclically* active *monitoring* of incoming traffic and deriving requirements from formulated database queries. Such database queries offer the functional requirement context, concerning referenced *sources* and applied *operations* and are delimited by given non-functional requirements.

6   Discussion

Blueprints focusing on data management systems are used to achieve FRs and NFRs. We have tried to reduce the complexity with a structured description to a suitable framework for adaptivity measures according to expectations.

We have proposed a classification for system requirements tailored to our polyglot persistence use case, removing the uncertainty and preparing automatic processing requirements. We proposed a form of representation for each variant (automatic and manual). Compared to service level agreements (SLA) used in cloud computing, the focus is solely on data management. While SLAs strictly define conditions for validity period and expectable conditions, including mutually exclusive NFRs. For example, there are no SLAs with 100% availability, consistency and fail-safe services. The Blueprint requirements focus only on data management and are less strict since NFRs are defined as target parameters without warranties for the application.

Adaptive Changes can be differentiated into multiple levels (see Sect. 2). Triggering an adaptive action depends on to which extent a Blueprint is acceptable for the required FRs and NFRs in the current situation. However, the essential factor is the validity of the change to prevent expensive changes for a one-time use case - or outliers in runtime behaviour. Triggers should therefore only be activated/considered if the currently relevant requirements result in a longer-term improvement. It follows that FRs and NFRs need to be determined first, e.g. FRs from the operators used in the request.

An evaluation of the Blueprint results in reducing the search space of our optimization problem by first considering operational and declarative characteristics. Afterwards, the optimum for the fulfilment of soft quantitative requirements are determined. This, however, requires data collected from the current Blueprint or concluded from its transfer to another. For example, knowledge about the data volume is an indicator for utilizing a distributed No-SQL backend, but what is the corresponding threshold? Manually defined experimental values or costs of Blueprint scenarios determined from the previous runtime may help to answer this question.

We must discuss different trade-offs between the simplification performed by the Blueprint concept on the one side and a wide range of functionalities on the other side to find the appropriate balance in setting up a new Blueprint with database and auxiliary systems. For instance, if Blueprints consist of precisely one database, the resulting deployment plan is simple, but the complete set of functionalities is limited only to this system. Unfortunately, such simple Blueprints do not reduce the search space, making it inevitable to use more complex Blueprint structures. However, if a few (very) complex Blueprints are used, the resulting deployment plans may be complex. Furthermore, some functional capabilities of the included database systems may cancel each other out.

The optimum lies in between these two extremes and depends currently on the knowledge of domain experts. Appropriate and informed sizing of Blueprints will result in full functional capabilities, a proper deployment plan and a reasonable effort to construct the best possible topology.

7   Blueprints, Blueprints, Whatcha Gonna Do, Whatcha Gonna Do When They Come for You?

Based on the foundational role we envisioned for our Blueprint approach, it paves the way for many possible ways to work on next. In this Section, we want to elaborate on a few of these future directions further.

Currently, our approach does not directly consider where data is located and how it is distributed. However, data migration, especially the permanent one, and the management of data locality mappings is crucial due to its importance for Poly-/MultiStore performance, as we already discussed in Sect. 2. Aspects of data locality need to be included in a more sophisticated Blueprint scoring. Furthermore, it needs to be discussed how the scoring of a Blueprint can be enriched and enhanced in general. One possibility is the evaluation of each Blueprint by a domain expert. A more refined approach may exploit monitoring and benchmarking processes to measure a Blueprint's (non-)functional capabilities. A machine learning approach could also be feasible for this topic and should be investigated in the future. Regardless of the scoring source, it is indispensable to find a way to merge the capabilities of each of the Blueprint's embedded systems into one single scoring for the Blueprint itself.

Additionally, we have to decide when and how to adapt to the impact of migration of data objects and their mapping to the database systems in one Blueprint. These decisions need to be extended to determine which FRs are required and the degree to which NFRs can be targeted for current and future runtime behaviour.

The scoring function does not mean an end in itself but must be used in some clever way. This is the moment when the orchestration of Poly- and MultiStore systems come into play. Thus, it has to be examined how Blueprint scorings can be adopted in these systems, how they can be compared and how they can benefit adaption efforts in the larger picture.

Last but not least, it has to be determined - not only for the scoring but in general - how all this groundwork can be incorporated into Poly-/MultiStore systems themselves, which in itself is a whole new amount of exciting research adventures ahead.

8   Conclusion

This paper postulated the demand for self-adaptivity in Poly- and MultiStore systems and pointed out the lack of permanent data migration/reorganization and adaptivity in the systems' topologies. We discussed the role of system requirements on a polyglot persistence system and how it may trigger its self-adaptivity. We are convinced that adaptivity is the crucial feature to guarantee future-proof, long-term usability of polyglot data stores in a world of ever-changing applications and data requirements.

We introduced Blueprints, a graph structure for representing a reduced system composition to tackle this complex problem. Blueprints can be used as building blocks in a highly complex Poly-/MultiStore topology. Thus, Blueprints help to solve the topology optimization problem. To illustrate the advantages of our approach, we demonstrated how Blueprints can be used to build concrete examples for specific purposes and functionalities and discussed ways to measure them against system requirements using scoring functions.

We think that Blueprints are a well-suited stepping stone towards taming the beast that is self-adaptivity in Poly- and MultiStores systems. The Blueprint approach narrows down complexity. By utilizing a set of (predefined) Blueprints, the adaptivity problem becomes less convoluted and opens the research on smaller parts and segments in the field.

References

1. Agrawal, D., et al.: Rheem: enabling multi-platform task execution. In: Proceedings of the 2016 International Conference on Management of Data, SIGMOD 2016, pp. 2069–2072. Association for Computing Machinery, New York (2016). https://doi.org/10.1145/2882903.2899414
2. Alotaibi, R., Bursztyn, D., Deutsch, A., Manolescu, I., Zampetakis, S.: Towards scalable hybrid stores: constraint-based rewriting to the rescue. In: Proceedings of the 2019 International Conference on Management of Data, SIGMOD 2019, pp. 1660–1677. Association for Computing Machinery, New York (2019). https://doi.org/10.1145/3299869.3319895
3. Borg, A., Yong, A., Carlshamre, P., Sandahl, K.: The bad conscience of requirements engineering: an investigation in real-world treatment of non-functional requirements. In: Third Conference on Software Engineering Research and Practice in Sweden, pp. 1–8 (2003)
4. Broy, M.: Rethinking nonfunctional software requirements. IEEE Ann. Hist. Comput. **48**(05), 96–99 (2015). https://doi.org/10.1109/MC.2015.139
5. Chung, L., do Prado Leite, J.C.S.: On non-functional requirements in software engineering. In: Borgida, A.T., Chaudhri, V.K., Giorgini, P., Yu, E.S. (eds.) Conceptual Modeling: Foundations and Applications. LNCS, vol. 5600, pp. 363–379. Springer, Heidelberg (2009). https://doi.org/10.1007/978-3-642-02463-4_19
6. DeWitt, D.J., et al.: Split query processing in polybase. In: Proceedings of the 2013 ACM SIGMOD International Conference on Management of Data, SIGMOD 2013, pp. 1255–1266. Association for Computing Machinery, New York (2013). https://doi.org/10.1145/2463676.2463709
7. Duggan, J., et al.: The BigDAWG polystore system. ACM SIGMOD Rec. **44**(2), 11–16 (2015)
8. Gadepally, V., et al.: The BigDAWG polystore system and architecture. In: 2016 IEEE High Performance Extreme Computing Conference (HPEC), New York, USA, pp. 1–6. IEEE (2016). https://doi.org/10.1109/CSC.2011.6138543
9. Gessert, F., Friedrich, S., Wingerath, W., Schaarschmidt, M., Ritter, N.: Towards a scalable and unified rest API for cloud data stores. In: 44. Jahrestagung der Gesellschaft für Informatik, Informatik 2014, Big Data - Komplexität meistern, 22.-26. September 2014 in Stuttgart, Deutschland, vol. 232, pp. 723–734. GI Bonn (2014). https://dl.gi.de/20.500.12116/2975
10. Gessert, F., Wingerath, W., Friedrich, S., Ritter, N.: NoSQL database systems: a survey and decision guidance. CSRD **32**(3), 353–365 (2017)
11. Giannakouris, V., Papailiou, N., Tsoumakos, D., Koziris, N.: Musqle: Distributed SQL query execution over multiple engine environments. In: 2016 IEEE International Conference on Big Data (Big Data), New York, USA, pp. 452–461. IEEE (2016). https://doi.org/10.1109/BigData.2016.7840636
12. Glinz, M.: On non-functional requirements. In: 15th IEEE International Requirements Engineering Conference (RE 2007), pp. 21–26. IEEE (2007). https://doi.org/10.1109/RE.2007.45

13. Gross, D., Yu, E.: From non-functional requirements to design through patterns. Requirements Eng. **6**(1), 18–36 (2001). https://doi.org/10.1007/s007660170013
14. Kolev, B., Bondiombouy, C., Valduriez, P., Jimenez-Peris, R., Pau, R., Pereira, J.: The CloudMdsQL multistore system. In: Proceedings of the 2016 International Conference on Management of Data, SIGMOD 2016, pp. 2113–2116. Association for Computing Machinery, New York (2016). https://doi.org/10.1145/2882903. 2899400
15. Kotonya, G., Sommerville, I.: Requirements Engineering: Processes and Techniques. Wiley, Hoboken (1998)
16. Lash, A., Murray, K., Mocko, G.: Natural language processing applications in requirements engineering. In: International Design Engineering Technical Conferences and Computers and Information in Engineering Conference, vol. 45011, pp. 541–549. American Society of Mechanical Engineers (2012). https://doi.org/10. 1115/DETC2012-71084
17. Ong, K.W., Papakonstantinou, Y., Vernoux, R.: The SQL++ semi-structured data model and query language: a capabilities survey of SQL-on-Hadoop, NoSQL and NewSQL databases. CoRR abs/1405.3631 (2014). https://arxiv.org/abs/1405.3631
18. Roman, G.C.: A taxonomy of current issues in requirements engineering. IEEE Ann. Hist. Comput. **18**(04), 14–23 (1985). https://doi.org/10.1109/MC.1985. 1662861
19. Sadalage, P.J., Fowler, M.: NoSQL Distilled: A Brief Guide to the Emerging World of Polyglot Persistence. Pearson Education, Boston (2012). https://books.google. com/books?id=AyY1a6-k3PIC
20. Schaarschmidt, M., Gessert, F., Ritter, N.: Towards automated polyglot persistence. In: Seidl, T., Ritter, N., Schöning, H., Sattler, K., Härder, T., Friedrich, S., Wingerath, W. (eds.) Proceedings of the 2015 German National Database Conference (BTW 2015). LNI, Bonn, Germany, vol. P-241, pp. 73–82. GI (2015). https:// subs.emis.de/LNI/Proceedings/Proceedings241/article46.html
21. Serafini, M., Taft, R., Elmore, A.J., Pavlo, A., Aboulnaga, A., Stonebraker, M.: Clay: fine-grained adaptive partitioning for general database schemas. Proc. VLDB Endow. **10**(4), 445–456 (2016). https://doi.org/10.14778/3025111.3025125
22. Standard, O.: Topology and orchestration specification for cloud applications version 1.0 (2013)
23. Stonebraker, M., et al.: One size fits all? part 2: benchmarking studies. In: Third Biennial Conference on Innovative Data Systems Research (CIDR 2007), CIDR Conference, Asilomar, California, USA, pp. 173–184 (2007). http://cidrdb.org/ cidr2007/papers/cidr07p20.pdf
24. Stonebraker, M., Çetintemel, U.: "one size fits all": an idea whose time has come and gone (abstract). In: Aberer, K., Franklin, M.J., Nishio, S. (eds.) Proceedings of the 21st International Conference on Data Engineering, ICDE 2005, Washington, DC, USA, pp. 2–11. IEEE (2005). https://doi.org/10.1109/ICDE.2005.1
25. Tan, R., Chirkova, R., Gadepally, V., Mattson, T.G.: Enabling query processing across heterogeneous data models: a survey. In: 2017 IEEE International Conference on Big Data (Big Data), New York, USA, pp. 3211–3220. IEEE (2017). https://doi.org/10.1109/BigData.2017.8258302
26. Vogt, M., Stiemer, A., Schuldt, H.: Polypheny-DB: towards a distributed and self-adaptive polystore. In: 2018 IEEE International Conference on Big Data (Big Data), New York, USA, pp. 3364–3373. IEEE (2018). https://doi.org/10.1109/ BigData.2018.8622353

27. Walden, D.D., Roedler, G.J., Forsberg, K.: INCOSE systems engineering handbook version 4: updating the reference for practitioners. In: INCOSE International
Symposium, vol. 25, pp. 678–686. Wiley Online Library (2015). https://doi.org/
10.1002/j.2334-5837.2015.00089.x

28. Wang, J., et al.: The Myria big data management and analytics system and cloud
services. In: 8th Biennial Conference on Innovative Data Systems Research (CIDR
2017). CIDR Conference, Asilomar, California, USA (2017). http://cidrdb.org/
cidr2017/papers/p37-wang-cidr17.pdf

29. Zhu, M., Risch, T.: Querying combined cloud-based and relational databases. In:
2011 International Conference on Cloud and Service Computing, New York, USA,
pp. 330–335. IEEE (2011). https://doi.org/10.1109/CSC.2011.6138543

Towards Feedback Loops in Model-Driven IoT Applications

Daniel Del Gaudio$^{(\boxtimes)}$ and Pascal Hirmer

University of Stuttgart, Universitätsstraße 38, 70569 Stuttgart, Germany
{daniel.del-gaudio,pascal.hirmer}@ipvs.uni-stuttgart.de,
https://www.ipvs.uni-stuttgart.de

Abstract. The Internet of Things is a thriving paradigm that makes people's lives easier. In the IoT, devices equipped with sensors and actuators communicate through standardized Internet protocols to reach common goals. In Smart Homes, for example, monitoring the current state of an environment, such as the room temperature, could lead to an automated triggering of actions, such as activating the heating system. Small IoT applications, e.g., in Smart Homes, are usually more easy to manage since they do not include a large amount of devices. However, in larger and more complex IoT environments, e.g., Smart Cities and Smart Factories, management and control become a tedious task, especially since IoT devices do not offer the robustness of traditional computer systems. In case of device failures, IoT applications could become unstable or even fail completely. To make matters even worse, faulty sensor measurements could lead to an undesired behavior of IoT applications, even though there are no obvious errors that are detectable by monitoring systems. Therefore, in this paper, we introduce a first approach that aims at improving IoT applications' fault tolerance throughout their whole lifecycle by introducing feedback loops ranging from application modeling, to deployment and operation, until their retirement.

Keywords: IoT · Robustness · Failure tolerance · Model-driven

1 Introduction

The *Internet of Things* (IoT) is an evolving paradigm in which heterogeneous devices attached with sensors and actuators communicate via standardized internet protocols to reach common goals [18]. Famous applications of the IoT include Smart Homes, Smart Cities, and Smart Factories. In the IoT, data is typically gathered from sensors, is filtered and processed, and then interpreted, e.g., to control actuators [16] or to display the data in dashboards. IoT applications can be developed in a model-driven way using tools for application modeling, deployment and configuration [9,10] and can then be executed in IoT environments in a distributed manner [5,14].

Using this model based approach, IoT applications can be set up with low-effort in contrast to a traditional software development approach. However, when

© Springer Nature Switzerland AG 2021
J. Barzen (Ed.): SummerSOC 2021, CCIS 1429, pp. 100–108, 2021.
https://doi.org/10.1007/978-3-030-87568-8_6

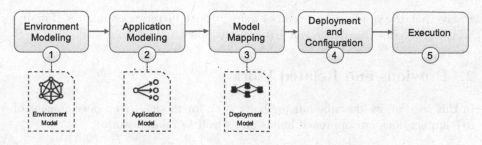

Fig. 1. Model-driven IoT application development method.

IoT environments become bigger and more complex, e.g., in Smart Cities or Smart Factories, new challenges arise, especially ensuring robustness of the modeled applications. IoT devices and applications tend to be very unstable since they are usually cheap and cannot provide the robustness of traditional computer systems. Hence, IoT applications need to consider this and react on device failures, data loss, or connectivity issues. To make matters even worse, wrong sensor measurements due to faulty sensors are nearly impossible to detect by monitoring systems and can lead to an undesired application behavior.

In this paper, our focus lies on increasing failure tolerance of model-driven IoT applications, especially when processing data in IoT environments, by introducing feedback loops to our model-driven IoT application development process. These feedback loops are depicted on top of the model-driven development method in Fig. 1. As depicted, during each step of an application's lifecycle, a robustness validation is conducted that can lead to valuable insights to improve the application's models. For example, data validation techniques can be applied to check whether processed sensor data could be faulty, leading to the suggestion to replace the sensor and adjust the environment model accordingly. Furthermore, introducing redundant sensors could be suggested in the application modeling step to prevent the danger of faulty sensor measurements by considering more than one measurements.

Our contributions of this paper include: (i) a categorization of common failures in the lifecycle of IoT applications based on intensive literature research and practical experience as well as approaches how to cope with a selection of these failures, and (ii) a first approach that introduces feedback loops in our approach for model-based IoT application development to detect and avoid costly failures during the applications' lifecycle. The feedback loops should enrich the model-driven development process to create more robust applications.

The remainder of this paper is structured as follows: Sect. 2 describes our previous work in the area of model-driven IoT application development and further related work. In Sect. 3, categories of failures in IoT environments are introduced. It furthermore gives an overview of methods how these types of failures can be detected to be coped with. In Sect. 4, we introduce feedback loops to the model-driven IoT application development process. Our aim is to use feedback from the execution of the application to improve the models in such a way that the application becomes more robust in terms of failures. Finally, Sect. 5 concludes this paper and gives an outlook on our future work.

2   Previous and Related Work

In this section, we describe our previous work for model-driven development of IoT applications our approach builds on as well as related work.

2.1   Previous Work: Model-Driven Development of IoT Applications

Figure 1 shows five steps, which we introduced in previous work [5–7], to enable model-driven development of IoT applications. In step 1 *Environment Modeling*, the so-called *Environment Model* is created that contains all devices, offering a set of capabilities (computing resources, network bandwidth, etc.), and the (network) connections between these devices. This information can be used in the next step *Application Modeling*, in which the business logic of the IoT application is modeled based on the IoT environment. The result of this step is the *Application Model*, which is based on the pipes-and-filters pattern, connecting abstract data processing operations with each other to form a direct graph from the sources (the sensors) to the sinks (e.g., actuators). These operations allow processing of IoT data (e.g., to filter or transform) and are attached with a set of requirements. In step 3 *Model Mapping*, every operation in the application model is mapped to a device in the environment model. Therefore, an operation can be mapped to a device, and, thus, will be executed by it, if the device has a matching capability for each requirement of the operation. In step 4 *Deployment and Configuration*, software for each operation is deployed on the chosen device and is configured accordingly. In step 5, the modeled application can be executed on the devices. We use a *Messaging Engine* [5] for device-to-device communication according to the models. Thus, we are able to keep control of the execution despite of the distribution, and, we can obtain information and metrics about the execution from each device, e.g., the current workload. This paper builds on the model-based approach for IoT application development and operation.

2.2   Related Work

Seeger et al. [14] propose an approach to process data in IoT environments in a decentralized way by adapting the concept of choreographies to the IoT. Their work also includes distributed monitoring techniques to detect failing IoT devices. However, there focus does not lie on robustness in general. They provide one technique to detect the failure of devices. In this paper, we aim at increasing the scope by also considering other kinds of failures, including also network or even software failures.

Chakraborty et al. [3] propose a method to detect failing sensors by measuring the sensors voltage response while the sensor' is turned off. In our paper, we do not focus explicitly on sensors in particular but also consider failure of IoT devices or network issues.

Su et al. [17] propose mechanism for fault tolerance in the IoT by utilizing the heartbeat protocol and duplicated services. Similar to other related work, we consider a wider range of failures to increase the scope of our approach.

Kodeswaran et al. [11] present a method to increase robustness especially in Smart Homes by using a centralized system that provides means to monitor sensor failures and a planning component for maintenance. In contrast, in our paper, our goal is omitting a centralized system to decrease network overhead and increase response times, i.e., our approach is tailored to decentralized systems.

Another approach to detect sensor failures is proposed by Sharma et al. [15]. They apply rule-based methods, estimation methods, time-series-analysis-based methods and learning-based methods to real-world sensor datasets to identify sensor faults. Nonetheless, they do not consider IoT environments as a whole but only sensors.

These related works propose methods and approaches to detect specific types of failures in IoT environments. Opposed to this, we regard failure tolerance not only during the execution of the application, but during the whole model-driven IoT application development process, by introducing feedback loops. We also aim to create a foundation for further research in the area of developing failure-tolerant IoT applications with the model-driven approach. Some of the related work can be integrated in our approach.

3   Overview of IoT Failures

To support future research and consolidate our concept of feedback loops, we created a categorization of IoT failures that is described in this section. Based on intensive literature research and our own experience in IoT related research projects, we elaborated several categories of IoT failure scenarios. In the following, we define a *failure* as an *"unintended deviation of intended behavior of a system or parts of it"*. Furthermore, we define *IoT failures* as *"failures that occur in IoT environments, involving utilization of one or more IoT devices"*. Note that we do not regard failures that occur in non-IoT systems, e.g., in cloud-based virtual machines. We divided failure scenarios into hardware, software and network failures. The categories are further divided and described in the following.

Note that failures do often not occur isolated but usually in combination or as the result of another failure. Hence, finding the root cause of failures can become very complex, especially when many failures occur at the same time. Especially in security critical applications, finding errors in a timely manner is essential to keep the downtime of the IoT application as low as possible.

3.1   Hardware Failures

We identified three types of hardware failures that could occur: *device failures*, *sensor failures* and *actuator failures*. A device failure is a failure of a device's hardware, not including attached or connected sensors or actuators. This failure occurs, e.g., when a device is involuntarily detached from its energy source or is damaged by physical impact. In most cases, it is not possible to recover from such failures remotely. We distinguish device failures from the sensor failures, since a sensor failure can still be detected by evaluating the sensor values, since the device itself is still working. However, in some cases, validating solely the sensor values is not sufficient, for example, a zero output of a light sensor could mean that the sensor is broken or that it is working correctly and is just covered. In this case, it is necessary check the hardware manually, e.g., by measuring the sensor's voltage output.

A hardware failure may lead to non-responding or, in case of mobile devices, even to lost devices. Failures, that do not lead to a non-responding device can be detected by additional sensors and monitoring to a certain degree. A consequence of a device failure can be loss of locally stored data. A sensor failure may lead to false sensor values or no sensor values at all. Thus, a sensor failure can be the origin of a data failure (cf. Sect. 3.2). Actuator failures comprise every misbehavior in terms of actuators, which can include broken or blocked actuators, e.g., an obstructed robot arm. Since such actuator failures can be detected by applying corresponding sensors, we do not further regard actuator failures.

Conventional methods to detect failures in IoT environments utilize a central controller to monitor the reachability of devices periodically [4], e.g., using *heartbeats*. Yet, the approach is not scalable in respect to an increasing number of devices. Seeger et al. [14] propose a distributed solution to failure detection in IoT environments based on work of Défago et al. [8]. Using the same principle based on device's sensor values instead of a heartbeat, can also lead to detection of possible sensor or data failures. Chakraborty et al. [3] describe another approach that can be used to specifically detect sensor failures, without the need for investigating the data the sensor produces. In their approach, they measure the voltage output of a sensor when it is powered off. The resulting *fall-curve* is characteristic for each sensor and a deviation implies a failure of the sensor.

3.2   Software Failures

Concerning software failures, in the scope of this paper, we only regard software that is running on the IoT devices. Software that runs on a device to collect, filter, and pass sensor data can fail like every other software. Such failures can be recognized when faulty or no more data from the device is received, however, the device could still be responding. Nevertheless, this can have the same symptoms as a sensor failure [13], which might make it harder to detect. Since many IoT devices run standard operating systems that are usually Linux based (e.g., Ubuntu IoT, Raspian), they can also fail on the operating system level. *Data Failures* can be the result of application failures, sensor failures, or errors during data transmission. Some data failures can be easily detected when the data is obviously corrupted or values are out of bound. Other data failures are harder to detect, when a value is within an expected range although is not correct [13]. Furthermore, Sharma et al. [15] categorize data faults, i.e. data failures, in short, noise, and constant faults. We also categorize a loss of data as a data failure. We also refer to data failures that can only be detected by regarding their semantics as *semantic failures*, e.g., a robot arm performing an unexpected action. These failures occur even if devices and their software components are running properly. Traditional monitoring systems do not recognize failures that are misbehavior in terms of the semantics of the data. The detection of semantic failures in distributed IoT environments is still a huge challenge. We see the opportunity to tackle this challenge in model-driven application development and execution since detecting or omitting semantic errors needs to be considered already in the models, i.e., the IoT applications goes into operation. Semantic failures are similar to byzantine faults, that can be detected using hypothesis testing [12].

3.3   Network Failures

Network failures typically occur when wireless connections, such as WiFi, Bluetooth, or LORA are utilized, which is usually necessary due to requirements of most IoT scenarios demanding high flexibility regarding location of IoT devices (e.g., in Smart Cities). We divide network failures into *lossy* and *lost connections*.

When the delay between a device and another device is untypically high, the network connection between them might be lossy. This might occur when a mobile device is at the "corner" of its wireless connection range, e.g., when using WiFi. Packages get lost during transmission and transfer of data takes a considerably higher amount of time. Depending on the applications requirements, this may be highly critical, e.g., in security related, real-time applications.

When a device does not respond anymore, it could be a hardware failure or the network connection could be lost completely. We distinct between a lossy connection and a lost connection since a lost connection usually cannot be easily distinguished from a device failure that led to a non-responding device.

To detect network failures, traditional network monitoring techniques and QoS measures (e.g., acknowledgments for guaranteed delivery) can be applied to the IoT [1]. Also, measuring heartbeats pursuant to Seeger et al. [14] can be used to determine variations in networking. Brattstrom and Morreale [2] compare agentless network monitoring to agent-based network monitoring. Despite that they prefer the agentless solution, since it needs less configuration overhead, they admit that the agent-based approach is superior in terms of scalability.

4   Feedback Loops for Model-Driven IoT Application Development

We introduce the concept of feedback loops for model-driven development of IoT applications which uses runtime information of the application in order to make IoT applications more robust in terms of the failures introduced in Sect. 3. We connect the execution of distributed IoT applications with the application development process by generating *feedback* during the execution and return it to the earlier steps of our method. The top of Fig. 1 shows the four feedback loops that are explained in the latter. To enable such feedback from the execution phase, we must be able to control and monitor the execution on the device level and change the models accordingly. The principle of the feedback loops is to (i) detect a failure, (ii) choose a mechanism to cope with the failures, (iii) automatically cope with the failure or propose a solution to a human to prevent the failure in the future. We define the following four feedback loops:

Feedback Loop 1 (FL1). FL1 concerns failures that can be handled in the deployment and configuration step. This includes application failures and maybe OS failures. These kinds of failures can be coped with by re-deploying, re-starting, or re-configuration of software. This feedback loop can be triggered by a monitoring agent on the device or by the messaging engine on another device that tries to communicate with it. FL1 does not change the models but rather re-runs particular steps of the deployment or configuration of specific software components.

Feedback Loop 2 (FL2). FL2 can be applied to improve the deployment model, i.e., the mapping of the application model and the environment model. For example, when a device is working to capacity, other devices could give feedback about bottlenecks, so that operations running on the device can be deployed on other devices additionally. This way, software failures due to misplacement of software can be prevented.

Feedback Loop 3 (FL3). FL3 concerns failures that result from decisions during the application modeling. For example, when a device is working to capacity because of an operation, FL3 can trigger creating and using another instance of the operation for load balancing, or include a filtering operation prior to the overwhelmed operation, to reduce the amount of data that has to be processed. Mostly, this can be done automatically, in case of critical failures, human interaction might be necessary. Furthermore, handling semantic failures can be suggested in FL3. The application developer can be encouraged to include a data validation step into the application model.

Feedback Loop 4 (FL4). FL4 conducts information about devices that have been added to the environment, or suggestions to add a device with specific capabilities to the environment, i.e., changes in the environment model. Furthermore, when a new device enters the environment, it can trigger FL4 to include it into the environment model and, thus, into the running application by repeating the Steps 3 and 4 of the development method. Hence, FL4 does not only react on failures but also aims at improving the whole system by adding newly appearing devices.

Depending on the mechanism to cope with the failure, human interaction might be required. For example, when a device failure is recognized and the device must be exchanged, a user can be alerted to perform this task. Then, the environment model can be changed, which we regard as part of FL4 itself, triggered by the new device [7]. Another example of a human interaction is when an optimization in the application model is suggested via FL3. Since it might change the behavior of the application, a confirmation by the user is mandatory.

Feedback loops can be triggered directly from devices, e.g., by monitoring agents as utilized by Seeger et al. [14], or by model-driven execution systems like the messaging engine described in our previous work [5]. It can also be triggered by central monitoring components that implement concepts to detect hardware, software or network failures.

Detected software failures can be used to create feedback FL1 or FL2 to re-deploy the software or to choose another device to deploy the software.

Semantic failures as described in Sect. 3.2 are hard to detect, but suspicious behavior as, e.g., sensor values that are constantly out of range and, thus, lead to that a succeeding operation is never performed, can create feedback on FL2 to suggest additional validation operations to the application model.

Detected network failures can be used to suggest to include a device to bridge the gap, or to suggest verification operations into the application model.

5   Conclusion and Future Work

In this paper, we introduced the following contributions: (i) a categorization of common failures in the lifecycle of IoT applications as well as approaches how to cope with a selection of these failures, and (ii) a first approach that introduces feedback loops in our approach for model-based IoT application development to detect and avoid costly failures during the applications' lifecycle.

We categorized potential failures in IoT environments and summarized different already existing solutions to detect failures of each category. Yet we do not offer solutions to cope with all these failures, we propose an approach to increase tolerance to such failures constantly during the execution of the application by iteratively improving the models with feedback loops. Therefore, we proposed to insert feedback loops to the model-driven development method for IoT applications to use feedback from the execution step to iterate specific steps of the method and use the feedback to improve the models. Therefore, we defined four feedback loops, one from the execution step to each previous step of the method.

In the future, we aim to refine each feedback loop with specific mechanisms, building on our previous work in [5–7] and integrate selected approaches we introduces in Sect. 3. Especially regarding FL3, the state-of-the-art lacks of concepts to improve an application model based on information from the execution. Nonetheless, this information could help application developers to improve their applications in terms of failure tolerance. We furthermore intend to evaluate our approach in a real-world scenario.

References

1. Aceto, G., Botta, A., De Donato, W., Pescapè, A.: Cloud monitoring: a survey. Comput. Netw. **57**(9), 2093–2115 (2013)
2. Brattstrom, M., Morreale, P.: Scalable agentless cloud network monitoring. In: Proceedings - 4th IEEE International Conference on Cyber Security and Cloud Computing, CSCloud 2017 and 3rd IEEE International Conference of Scalable and Smart Cloud, SSC 2017, pp. 171–176 (2017)

3. Chakraborty, T., et al.: Fall-curve: a novel primitive for IoT Fault detection and isolation. In: SenSys 2018 - Proceedings of the 16th Conference on Embedded Networked Sensor Systems, pp. 95–107 (2018)
4. Chetan, S., Ranganathan, A., Campbell, R.: Towards fault tolerance pervasive computing. IEEE Technol. Soc. Mag. **24**(1), 38–44 (2005)
5. Del Gaudio, D., Hirmer, P.: A lightweight messaging engine for decentralized data processing in the Internet of Things. SICS Softw.-Intens. Cyber-Phys. Syst. **35**(i) (2019)
6. Del Gaudio, D., Hirmer, P.: Seamless integration of devices in industry 4.0 environments. Internet Things **12**, 100321 (2020)
7. Del Gaudio, D., Reichel, M., Hirmer, P.: A life cycle method for device management in dynamic IoT environments. In: Proceedings of the 5th International Conference on Internet of Things, Big Data and Security (2020)
8. Défago, X., et al.: The phi accrual failure detector. In: RR IS-RR-2004-010, Japan Advanced Institute of Science and Technology, pp. 66–78 (2004)
9. Hirmer, P., Behringer, M.: FlexMash 2.0 – flexible modeling and execution of data mashups. In: Daniel, F., Gaedke, M. (eds.) RMC 2016. CCIS, vol. 696, pp. 10–29. Springer, Cham (2017). https://doi.org/10.1007/978-3-319-53174-8_2
10. Hirmer, P., Breitenbücher, U., da Silva, A.C.F., Képes, K., Mitschang, B., Wieland, M.: Automating the provisioning and configuration of devices in the internet of things. Complex Syst. Informatics Model. Q. **9**, 28–43 (2016)
11. Kodeswaran, P., Kokku, R., Sen, S., Srivatsa, M.: Idea: a system for efficient failure management in smart IoT environments. In: MobiSys 2016 - Proceedings of the 14th Annual International Conference on Mobile Systems, Applications, and Services, pp. 43–56 (2016)
12. Panda, M., Khilar, P.: Distributed byzantine fault detection technique in wireless sensor networks based on hypothesis testing. Comput. Electr. Eng. **48**, 270–285 (2015)
13. Ranjan, R., et al.: The next grand challenges: integrating the internet of things and data science. IEEE Cloud Comput. **5**(3), 12–26 (2018)
14. Seeger, J., Deshmukh, R.A., Sarafov, V., Broring, A.: Dynamic IoT choreographies. IEEE Pervasive Comput. **18**(1), 19–27 (2019)
15. Sharma, A.B., Golubchik, L., Govindan, R.: Sensor faults: detection methods and prevalence in real-world datasets. ACM Trans. Sensor Netw. **6**(3), 1–39 (2010)
16. Franco da Silva, A.C., Hirmer, P., Wieland, M., Mitschang, B.: SitRS XT-towards near real time situation recognition. J. Inf. Data Manage. **7**(1), 4 (2016)
17. Su, P.H., Shih, C.S., Hsu, J.Y.J., Lin, K.J., Wang, Y.C.: Decentralized fault tolerance mechanism for intelligent IoT/M2M middleware. In: 2014 IEEE World Forum on Internet of Things, WF-IoT 2014, pp. 45–50 (2014)
18. Vermesan, O., Friess, P.: Internet of Things: Converging Technologies for Smart Environments and Integrated Ecosystems. River Publishers, Aalborg (2013)

Investigating the Use of Machine Learning Techniques in a Random Physical System

George T. Stamatiou[1] and Kostas Magoutis[2,3]

[1] University of Ioannina, 45110 Ioannina, Greece
gstam@cc.uoi.gr
[2] Department of Computer Science, University of Crete, 70013 Heraklion, Greece
[3] Institute of Computer Science, FORTH, 70013 Heraklion, Greece
magoutis@ics.forth.gr

Abstract. Machine learning (ML) techniques have seen increasing use in recent years in complementing traditional HPC solutions to physical systems problems. While the scientific community has been rapidly adopting such techniques, it is still unclear how different ML techniques compare in terms of accuracy. In this paper we address this question by designing and training a neural network and comparing its performance to traditional classification models using as a case study a non-interacting quantum system on a graph structure. We build a classifier with the ability to distinguish extended from localized quantum states based on their different structure and compare it with other commonly used ML classifiers. Our results show high accuracy for certain ML models in most cases, whereas others are less effective.

Keywords: Machine learning · High performance computing · Quantum Physics · Random systems

1 Introduction

During the last few years a significant amount of research has been conducted on the field of machine learning (ML), a subfield of artificial intelligence (AI) based on the premise that computers can learn patterns in datasets gathered from various fields of human activity. The data analysis process helps the systems to perform well in specific tasks without being explicitly programmed and leads to improvement in their decision-making process, which can minimize or even remove the human factor in certain aspects. The application of ML algorithms covers a range of topics such as computer vision, speech and audio recognition, search-engine recommendations, medical technology, social networks and even

Supported by the Greek Research Technology Development and Innovation Action "RESEARCH - CREATE - INNOVATE", Operational Programme on Competitiveness, Entrepreneurship and Innovation 2014–2020, Grant T1EΔK-04819.

© Springer Nature Switzerland AG 2021
J. Barzen (Ed.): SummerSOC 2021, CCIS 1429, pp. 109–118, 2021.
https://doi.org/10.1007/978-3-030-87568-8_7

quantum computing just to name few [1,2]. From the physics perspective, data processing tasks may include classification between different phases of matter, random systems, neural network representation of quantum many-body states, quantum information, topological states in exotic materials and more [3–8]. This paper aims to demonstrate the benefits of a new generation of tools for computational scientists in studying physical systems. High-performance computing (HPC) has evolved significantly in terms of computation power in recent years. The convergence of new technologies such as ML and cloud computing with HPC led to the creation of frameworks such as Google Colaboratory[1], a hosted notebook service, which enables the integration of various research methodologies in a unified manner. In this work we demonstrate the value of such a framework in facilitating research combining ML with traditional HPC computations.

In this work our case study is the phenomenon of Anderson localization in a non-interacting quantum system, which constrains a single-particle wavefunction to a finite region of space due to disorder [10]. The Anderson model describes a single electron which is hopping in a disordered lattice and feels a random potential of strength W on each lattice site. In three dimensions a metal-insulator transition occurs at a critical disorder value $W_c \sim 16.5$ and separates the extended states from the localized ones. In the presence of interactions and disorder in isolated systems the phenomenon of many-body localization [11] cause the many-body states to be confined in a finite region of the exponentially large many-body Hilbert space. The many-body localized quantum states seem to play a key role in quantum computing research as they could be robust to decoherence. The Anderson transition occurs also on the Bethe lattice, an infinite hierarchical lattice where each site is connected to Z nearest-neighbors [12]. In this exploratory study we construct the triangular Husimi Cactus (Fig. 1 Left), a generalization of the Bethe lattice where the number of sites grows exponentially with distance in analogy to the dimension of the many-body Hilbert space.

During the last decade the ML methods have increasingly become useful in industrial applications and have shown an interesting potential in fundamental physics research. In reference [15] the authors apply the Support Vector Machines (SVM) in order to predict the whole phase diagram for studying the transition between extended and many-body localized phases in a many-body problem related to the current work. Another example for the prediction of different phases comes from the field of image recognition where use of the so called Convolutional Neural Networks (CNN) show interesting results on image classification tasks [7,8]. In this work, we follow a simpler approach which focuses on the two limiting cases only (extended and localized states) and an investigation of several methods is made. This procedure can also be generalized to other random systems in which a transition from extended to localized behavior can be shown. Recent related works have proposed quantum algorithms to simulate disordered systems using quantum computers [16] and also the exploration of Quantum Machine Learning methods using digital humanities data [17].

---

[1] https://colab.research.google.com/.

The paper is organized as follows: In Sect. 2 we describe the graph and the Hamiltonian for our numerical approach. Moreover, we introduce the quantities which are going to be studied and a step-by-step description of the classification algorithm. In Sect. 3 we present our analysis and results and conclude in Sect. 4.

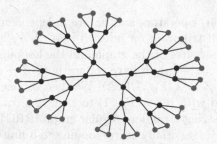 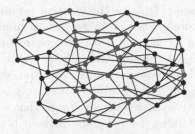

Fig. 1. (Left) Triangular Husimi Cactus with $N = 61$. (Right) Random Regular Graph with $N = 61$. The boundary sites are colored with red. (Color figure online)

2   Methodology

We first describe our NN-based implementation of a simple binary classification algorithm. The code is written in a Jupyter notebook and can be executed in the Google Colab environment. The main steps are:

1. Import Packages. We use the software library *Tensorflow*[2], the NN library *Keras*[3], *numpy*, *pandas* for data processing, and *matplotlib* for plotting.

2. Load the Dataset. The dimension of our dataset is 2900×1024. The rows correspond to different wavefunctions and the columns correspond to each one of the N sites of the graph. The last 3 columns contain the corresponding IPR values, the max amplitude and the Class variable (0: extended, 1: localized).

3. Construct the NN Model. We choose the rectified linear unit (ReLU) as the activation function for the sequential layers and the sigmoid function for the output layer. The architecture of the designed NN is 1021-5-2-1.

4. Configure the Model. We use *binary crossentropy* as the loss and the Adam algorithm as the optimizer.

5. Fit the Model. The process of training the NN, to identify the relationship between the wavefunction amplitudes per graph site and their class (0 or 1).

6. Plot the Loss and Accuracy in order to check the performance of the model on the training and test-validation data.

We next present our use case and how we create our dataset. We begin by considering the Anderson tight-binding model of a particle hopping on a

---

[2] https://www.tensorflow.org/.
[3] https://keras.io/.

triangular Husimi Cactus graph of N sites in a potential disorder described by the Hamiltonian

$$H = \sum_{n=1}^{N} V_n c_n^\dagger c_n + t \sum_{\langle n,m \rangle} (c_n^\dagger c_m + c_m^\dagger c_n), \tag{1}$$

where $c_n^\dagger (c_n)$ are the creation (annihilation) operators and V_n are independent random variables taken from a uniform distribution on interval $[-W/2, W/2]$. The second sum is over the nearest-neighbor sites of the graph and the hopping is $t = 1$ constant. Initially, the bulk sites of the graph have connectivity $Z = 4$ and the boundary sites have connectivity $Z = 2$ (Fig. 1 Left). We then connect randomly the boundary sites only (colored with red in Fig. 1) to achieve a connectivity $Z = 4$ for all sites so that we construct a random regular graph (RRG), an almost treelike graph without boundary, essentially corresponding to a finite portion of a Husimi cactus wrapped into itself (Fig. 1 Right). The triangular Husimi cactus is constructed as follows. The number of sites in the l-th layer of the graph is

$$N_l = 2^{l+1}, \quad l = 1, 2, ..., b \tag{2}$$

where b denotes the boundary layer. Therefore the total number of sites is

$$N = 1 + \sum_{l=1}^{b} N_l = 2^{b+2} - 3. \tag{3}$$

For the first 10 layers, the sizes are $N = 5, 13, 29, 61, 125, 253, 509, 1021, 2045$ and 4093. The graphs have been generated using the networkx[4] Python module.

For example, the Hamiltonian of Eq. 1 for the triangular Husimi graph of size $N = 5$ can be written in matrix form as

$$H = \begin{pmatrix} V_1 & 1 & 1 & 1 & 1 \\ 1 & V_2 & 1 & 0 & 0 \\ 1 & 1 & V_3 & 0 & 0 \\ 1 & 0 & 0 & V_4 & 1 \\ 1 & 0 & 0 & 1 & V_5 \end{pmatrix}. \tag{4}$$

The exact diagonalization of real symmetric random matrices for different sizes N is performed using the dsyevx LAPACK routine[5]. The procedure of diagonalization of large matrices and their scaling with size N is typically achieved with HPC systems and for this work the ARIS infrastructure is used[6]. First, we study the correlations between the eigenvalues E_n with methods from random matrix theory. A concise statistical measure which highlights the degree of level correlation is the ensemble-averaged ratio of consecutive level spacings $\langle r_n \rangle = \frac{min(S_n, S_{n+1})}{max(S_n, S_{n+1})}$ where $S_n = E_{n+1} - E_n$ are the spacings of consecutive

---

[4] https://networkx.github.io/documentation/stable/tutorial.html.
[5] http://www.netlib.org/lapack/lapack-3.1.1/html/dsyevx.f.html.
[6] https://hpc.grnet.gr/en/.

energy levels. In the case of a chaotic system the energy levels follow the Wigner statistics whereas instead a localized system is characterized by Poisson level statistics. The ensemble-averaged ratio takes values between $\langle r_n \rangle_P = 0.386$ and $\langle r_n \rangle_W = 0.53$ for the Poisson and Wigner limits respectively [13]. Second, the analysis of the fluctuations in the corresponding wavefunctions is done using the inverse participation ratio (IPR), $IPR = \sum_{n=1}^{N} |\psi_n|^4$. This measure characterizes the localization properties of a wavefunction. A perfectly extended (delocalized) wavefunction has probability amplitudes $\psi_n = 1/\sqrt{N}$ over all graph sites N, has $IPR = N^{-1}$, whereas a perfectly localized wavefunction on just one graph site has $IPR = 1$.

3 Analysis and Results

We first present the analysis for the statistics of energy levels and the wavefunctions and show how the two different phases emerge by varying the disorder strength W. Second, we evaluate the NN classification algorithm and finally the performance of the NN is compared with other ML classification algorithms.

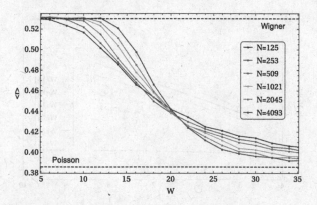

Fig. 2. Ensemble-averaged ratio of consecutive level spacings $\langle r_n \rangle$. The crossover point is estimated near the disorder value $W \sim 21$ for the sizes considered.

3.1 Energy Level and Eigenfunction Statistics

In Fig. 2 we present our numerical result for the energy level statistics parameter $\langle r \rangle$ as a function of disorder strength W for different sizes $N = 125$ to $N = 4093$. We study the middle of the spectrum keeping $1/10$ of the eigenstates around $E = 0$ with disorder realizations about 10^5. Our simulations show a distinction between two qualitatively different statistics. For small values of W the statistics is close to the Wigner limit $\langle r_n \rangle_W = 0.53$ whereas for larger values of W the statistics is closer to the Poisson limit $\langle r_n \rangle_P = 0.386$ showing delocalization and localization, respectively. The crossover point is estimated near $W_c \sim 21$ for the sizes considered. Figure 3 depicts the numerical result for the eigenfunction statistics. For the delocalized phase ($W < W_c = 21$) the quantity $N\langle IPR \rangle$ is expected to show saturation to a point which will be larger for larger W and N whereas for the localized phase ($W > W_c = 21$) a linear behavior is expected [14]. For the sizes considered here, the trend towards saturation is apparent up to $W = 18$, in accordance with the estimated crossover point $W_c \sim 21$. The behavior can be further clarified by considering larger N. We observe the linear increase with size further away from W_c ($W = 24, 36$).

Now that we have estimated the crossover point at $W \sim 21$, we select two values for the disorder in order to acquire our wavefunction dataset that is going to be passed as input in the neural network and the other classification algorithms. For the delocalized case ($W < W_c = 21$) we choose $W = 6$ and for the localized case ($W > W_c = 21$) we choose $W = 36$. In Fig. 4 we show two wavefunctions (extended, localized) for the graph structure of system size $N = 125$. This size is chosen for visualization purposes. In the localized state (right) the amplitude $|\psi|^2$ is almost one and concentrates at the only site colored red.

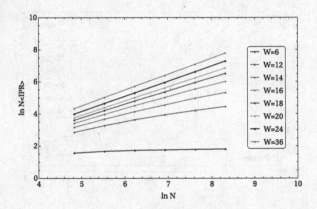

Fig. 3. $\ln N\langle IPR \rangle$ vs. $\ln N$ for different values of disorder strength W.

3.2   Evaluation of Neural Network Classification

We now examine if the neural network is able to distinguish between the two types of states based only on their structure. Following the steps for the algorithm discussed previously, we choose the intermediate system size $N = 1021$ so that the proposed NN takes 1021 variables per wavefunction as input which correspond to the absolute squares of the amplitudes $|\psi_n|^2$ per graph site n. The total number of examples is 2900 (1450 for each one of the 2 classes). The first hidden layer has 5 nodes, the second hidden layer has 2 nodes and the output

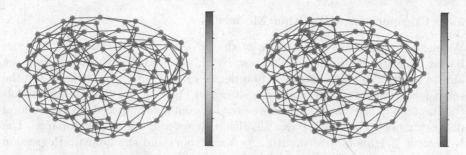

Fig. 4. (Left) $|\psi|^2$ of an *extended* quantum state with $IPR = 0.03$ and $W = 6$. (Right) $|\psi|^2$ of a *localized* quantum state with $IPR = 0.9$ and $W = 36$. The color bar takes values between 0 (dark blue) and 1 (dark red). System size $N = 125$. (Color figure online)

layer has 1 node. The hidden layers use ReLU as the activation function and the output layer uses the sigmoid activation function. The initial dataset is separated into the training and the test/validation sets with a ratio of 90% and 10%, respectively. The learning rate is set to 0.01, the batch size is 1450 and the training data are shuffled before each epoch. In Fig. 5 (Left) we observe how the loss the decreasing and at epoch = 100 the train loss is 0.0689 and the test loss is 0.1481. Both these values approach 0 which is our aim during the learning process. The Fig. 5 (Right) shows the accuracy of the model for both training and test-validation data. More specifically, at epoch = 100 the train accuracy is 1.0 and the test accuracy is 0.9517. As a consequence, the classifier works well with both the training and the validation/test sets and is also able to generalize to unknown cases. We expect these values to vary slightly with a larger/smaller dataset or when reconfiguring the model.

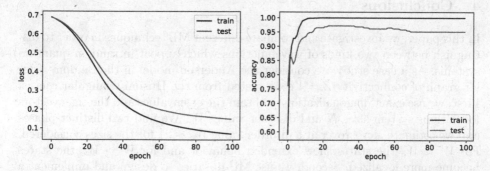

Fig. 5. NN model loss (Left) and accuracy (Right) for the training (black) and test/validation (red) sets as a function of the epochs. (Color figure online)

3.3   Comparison with Other Models

We next compare the performance of the NN to other ML models (Random Forest, Logistic Regression, K-Nearest Neighbors and Naive Bayes) with the aim to identify the best classifier. In order to implement the models we use the scikit-learn tool[7] and the results are shown in Fig. 6. From the studied models the Random Forest shows an improvement in accuracy compared with the neural network model. The Naive Bayes algorithm shows also a high performance. The K-Nearest Neighbors, tested with k = 3 neighbors and the Logistic Regression performs almost equally low, mislabeling a significant percentage of cases.

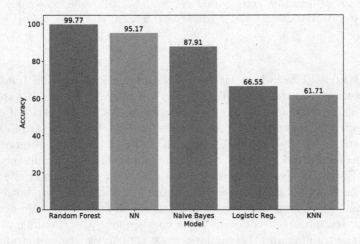

Fig. 6. Accuracy of wavefunction classification for several ML algorithms.

4   Conclusions

In this paper, we investigate and compare different ML techniques in order to distinguish between two kinds of wavefunctions which appear in random quantum systems. As a case study, we consider the Anderson model in the random regular graph of connectivity $Z = 4$ constructed from the Husimi triangular cactus. First, we use exact diagonalization to obtain the eigenvalues and the eigenvectors for various system sizes N and disorder values W. We find two distinct phases and we estimate a crossover at a disorder value $W_c \sim 21$ for the sizes considered. For $W < W_c$ the states show extended behavior and for $W > W_c$ the states become more localized. Second, we use ML libraries to design and implement a NN binary classifier for the two kinds of states. After the learning process the model is shown to have a quite good overall performance with high accuracy and decreasing loss. Third, we explore other ML models and their comparison

---

[7] https://scikit-learn.org/stable/.

reveals almost equally high accuracies for Random Forest as in the NN case. The Naive Bayes performs quite well whereas the Logistic Regression and KNN are significantly less accurate. We thus conclude that the choice of learning algorithm does matter in the use-case we studied. As a future perspective it would be interesting to expand the classification algorithm in order to include other kind of quantum states such as the critical states and check how the model will perform in that case. Moreover, it will be interesting to investigate the case of an unlabeled wavefunction dataset in the context of unsupervised learning. We hope that our results can be useful for the exploration of disordered materials in general [6,7] and for studying similar problems exhibiting phase changes.

References

1. LeCun, Y., Bengio, Y., Hinton, G.: Deep learning. Nature **521**, 436–444 (2015). https://doi.org/10.1038/nature14539
2. Biamonte, J., Wittek, P., Pancotti, N. et al.: Quantum machine learning. Nature **549**, 195–202 (2017). https://doi.org/10.1038/nature23474
3. Carrasquilla, J., Melko, R. G.: Machine learning phases of matter. Nat. Phys. **13**, 431–434 (2017). https://doi.org/10.1038/nphys4035
4. Carrasquilla, J.: Machine Learning for Quantum Matter. arXiv:2003.11040 (2020) https://arxiv.org/abs/2003.11040
5. Carleo, G., et al.: Machine learning and the physical sciences. Rev. Mod. Phys. **91**, 045002 (2019). https://doi.org/10.1103/RevModPhys.91.045002
6. Schmidt, J., Marques, M.R.G., Botti, S. et al.: Recent advances and applications of machine learning in solid-state materials science. NNI Comput Mater **5**, 83 (2019). https://doi.org/10.1038/s41524-019-0221-0
7. Yu, S., Piao, X., Park, N.: Machine learning identifies scale-free properties in disordered materials. Nat. Commun. **11**, 4842 (2020). https://doi.org/10.1038/s41467-020-18653-9
8. Ohtsuki T., Mano T.: Drawing of phase diagrams random quantum systems by deep learning the wave functions. J. Phys. Soc. Jpn. **89**, 022001 (2020). https://doi.org/10.7566/JPSJ.89.022001
9. Preskill, J.: Quantum Computing in the NISQ era and beyond. Quantum **2**, 79 (2018). https://doi.org/10.22331/q-2018-08-06-79
10. Anderson, P.W.: Absence of diffusion in certain random lattices. Phys. Rev. **109**, 1492 (1958). https://doi.org/10.1103/PhysRev.109.1492
11. Altman, E.: Many-body localization and quantum thermalization. Nat. Phys. **14**, 979–983 (2018). https://doi.org/10.1038/s41567-018-0305-7
12. Altshuler, B. L., Cuevas, L., Ioffe, L. B., Kravtsov, V. E.: Nonergodic phases in strongly disordered random regular graphs. Phys. Rev. Lett. **117**, 156601 (2016). https://doi.org/10.1103/PhysRevLett.117.156601
13. Atas, Y.Y., Bogomolny, E., Giraud, O., Roux, G.: Distribution of the ratio of consecutive level spacings in random matrix ensembles. Phys. Rev. Lett. **110** 084101 (2013). https://doi.org/10.1103/PhysRevLett.110.084101
14. Tikhonov, K.S., Mirlin, A.D., Skvortsov, M.A.: Anderson localization and ergodicity on random regular graphs. Phys. Rev. B **94**, 220203(R) (2016). https://doi.org/10.1103/PhysRevB.94.220203

15. Zhang, W., Wang, L., Wang, Z.: Interpretable machine learning study of the many-body localization transition in disordered quantum using spin chains. Phys. Rev. **B** 99, 054208 (2019). https://doi.org/10.1103/PhysRevB.99.054208
16. Alexandru, A., Bedaque, B. F., Lawrence, S.: Quantum algorithms for disordered physics. Phys. Rev. A **101**, 032325 (2020). https://doi.org/10.1103/PhysRevA.101.032325
17. Barzen, J., Leymann, F.: Quantum humanities: a vision for quantum computing in digital humanities. SICS Softw.-Inten. Cyber-Phys. Syst. **153**–158 (2019). https://doi.org/10.1007/s00450-019-00419-4

Validated Data Quality Assessment with "Skin in the Game": A Smart Contract Approach

Stefan W. Driessen[1]([✉])[ID], Geert Monsieur[1][ID], Willem-Jan van den Heuvel[1][ID], and Damian A. Tamburri[2][ID]

[1] Jheronimus Academy of Data Science - Tilburg University, Sint Janssingel 92, 5211 's-Hertogenbosch, DA, The Netherlands
s.w.driessen@jads.nl

[2] Jheronimus Academy of Data Science - Eindhoven University of Technology, Sint Janssingel 92, 5211 's-Hertogenbosch, DA, The Netherlands

Abstract. Data Markets are becoming increasingly popular but are very challenging to deploy and maintain successfully. We discuss some of the challenges related to the success of data markets, focusing particularly on the diverse challenge of assessing data quality. We introduce a novel, holistic approach whereby a blockchain-based smart contract called a *Quality Assessment contract* allows an actor called the *quality assessor* to assess the quality of a data asset, provide immutable proof of their efforts on the blockchain, and get rewarded for their efforts proportionally to the value of their quality assessment efforts. We discuss how such an approach could be used in practice to assess the quality of different data assets and discuss some architectural considerations for using a quality assessment contract.

Keywords: Data markets · Quality assessment · Blockchain · Smart contracts

1 Introduction

There has been an explosive rise in the availability of data [12,24,32], an accompanying increase in analytical tools [27,29] and, above all, the growing interest in data as a tradeable, valuable good which can be leveraged to improve or enable business processes [3,38]. Consequently, data markets have become both heavily investigated by the academic community as well as industry [30]. The potential value of leveraging big data has been estimated to grow from $138.9 billion in 2020 to $229.4 billion by 2025 [13]. Anticipating this, initiatives have been put forward to build the infrastructure necessary for complex data markets [6,19,21].

It seems, however, that data markets are very challenging to deploy and operate successfully, as demonstrated by the large number of data markets that have come and gone in the last decade alone [28,31,33]. Existing literature has

© Springer Nature Switzerland AG 2021
J. Barzen (Ed.): SummerSOC 2021, CCIS 1429, pp. 119–130, 2021.
https://doi.org/10.1007/978-3-030-87568-8_8

identified a multitude of challenges for data markets: On the one hand there are economic and societal challenges, such as a lack of willingness amongst customers to pay for data [10, 22, 33] and the inability of legal codes and law enforcement to cover the intellectual rights or address privacy concerns [11, 20]. On the flip side there are challenges that concern the design and mechanisms of data markets, which are of a more technical nature. Based on our understanding of existing literature in data markets, these challenges come in four general categories:

1. Maintaining *data sovereignty*: Data is, by its very nature, easy to duplicate and manipulate. This makes it hard to verify how, where and by whom the data, once it has left the data seller's control, will be used. A lack of data sovereignty can mean violation of privacy or legal requirements, unauthorised reselling of a data product or unintended use of the data [7, 20]. This challenge is also tied to data security, as the more data is shared, the more vulnerable it becomes to being stolen.
2. *Data quality* assessment: Data is an *experience good*, meaning that its value is highly dependent on the user, the application and their context [11]. Because of this, we view data quality in this context as more than simply a measure of how complete, feature-rich or frequently updated a data asset is. Instead we informally define data quality as a measure for how well-suited the data is for its intended purpose. This definition is in line with previous work that has noted that *"Data characteristics have no judgemental value. Without considering them in a specific context ..., they are neither good nor bad and describe only characteristic properties."* [25]. Taking this approach to data quality allows us to consider different aspects of data quality appropriately such as: on the one hand, a real-time streaming data asset for financial trading applications, which prioritises speedy access over completeness and, on the other hand, a large, feature-rich data set on household income in a nation used for finding economic trends, which might be only updated once every year.
3. *Product recommendation and querying*: As in any (digital) market, potential data buyers need a means to browse and select from amongst all possibilities those data assets that best suit their needs. Because of their prevalence outside the scope of data and data markets, recommender systems are perhaps the best understood, and certainly the most researched of all challenges, see e.g. [26].
4. *Price determination algorithms*: The challenge of accurately assessing data quality, as well as a lack of precedent on pricing comparable products make it hard to set a price for data assets [11].

In this paper we aim to address the challenge of data quality assessment, which we deem to be crucial for both price determination and developing an optimal querying mechanism. After all, in an ideal scenario the price of a data asset is highly dependent on its quality and any recommender system should prefer high-quality data assets over lower quality data assets. We find current literature on quality assessment for data markets to be lacking. With this paper, we hope to take a careful first step towards changing that.

We introduce a novel, holistic, approach, whereby a blockchain-based smart contract, called a *Quality Assessment (QA) contract*, allows an actor called the *quality assessor* to assess the quality of a data asset, provide immutable proof of their efforts on the blockchain and get rewarded for their efforts proportionally to the value of their quality assessment efforts. We believe that the QA contract should be easy to incorporate in any data market platform which leverages blockchain and smart contract technology as part of its design.

One of the major strengths of our approach is that the contract poses few restraints on quality assessment methods: We believe there does not exist a single data quality assessment approach that works well for all types of data. Instead we allocate the task of quality assessment to the quality assessor, who can prepare a variety of test plans. This makes our approach capable of addressing the many facets of data quality, doing so in a transparent, cheap-to-implement manner.

We explain our approach further in the next sections of this paper: in particular, Sect. 2.1 discusses the background behind blockchain technology in data market design, focusing on the motivations behind their use, as well as discussing the most relevant state-of-the-art work. Section 2.2 introduces the idea of staking, which we use to ensure that the quality assessor puts real effort into providing valuable insights on the data quality. In Sect. 3 we illustrate the types of quality assurance tests that our proposal enables. Next, in Sect. 4 we propose the a smart contract, called the *curation contract*, that logs the quality assessment efforts and rewards quality assessors proportionally to the value they add to the data market ecosystem. In Sect. 5 we draw a conclusion and sketch a short road-map for further research.

2 Background

In this section we explain key concepts of blockchain that are relevant for data markets as well as the concept of staking, both of which play an important role in our proposal. Smart contracts allow stakers to prove quality assessment efforts and facilitate rewarding good quality assessment, whereas staking demonstrates that the quality assessor is convinced of the quality of the data asset they have assessed.

2.1 Blockchain Technology and Data Markets

Blockchain technology has become popular in recent years as researchers and practitioners alike are starting to discover scenarios in which it makes sense to leverage its qualities (and when its downsides outweigh the pros). In essence, a blockchain is a ledger which stores information in transactions, which are added in batches called *blocks*. The key principle of blockchains is that they are maintained and manipulated in a *distributed* and *decentralised* manner. Distributed in this context means that the information in the blockchain is stored in multiple physical locations and decentralised means that no single party is in charge of the ledger, which instead is governed by a *consensus protocol*, which all participants adhere to [2]. Most public blockchains also have a *cryptocurrency* associated with them (e.g., Bitcoin [14]) which is a digital token that represents real-world value and whose ownership is tracked on the blockchain. Some blockchains, most prominently Ethereum [37], allow developers to store and manipulate pieces of code called *smart contracts*. Smart contracts are particularly interesting because the distributed and decentralised nature of the blockchain allow them to be both completely transparent and autonomous in their execution.

It can be no surprise that blockchain technology and smart contracts are actively being investigated in the context of data markets, see e.g. [1,9,12,23, 34,35]. As motivated by these researchers, blockchain- and smart contract technology bring several advantages to motivate their use for data markets. We discuss some of these advantages below:

1. The transactional nature of blockchains is well suited for implementing payments and provides an immutable record of all transactions for verification.
2. The transparency of blockchain technology adds to the transactional nature by allowing for verification of both the behaviour of buyers and sellers, as well as the inner workings and logic of those aspects of the data market that are coded in smart contracts on the blockchain.
3. Because smart contracts execute autonomously and their logic is fully transparent, they can take on the role of a trusted third party in exchange, where participants might not be inclined to trust each other.
4. Blockchain infrastructure operates similarly to cloud infrastructure and this makes it easy to deploy new smart contracts or disable old smart contracts on the fly. Automation, combined with convenient deployment can also lead to a reduction of the costs associated with operating a data market platform.

2.2   Staking on Blockchains

Staking is an activity, whereby an owner or *staker* of some cryptocurrency communicates to the blockchain network that they are locking their cryptocurrency tokens, effectively making it impossible for them to spend those tokens. Staking is usually tied to some process on the blockchain and is done to signal that the staker is committed to a positive outcome of the process, either because they will lose something if the outcome is bad, or because they stand to gain something if the outcome is good. The most prevalent example of staking is the Proof-of-Stake (PoS) consensus protocol [36] but other endeavours have been proposed to leverage staking for quality assessment, such as token-curated registries [8] (TCRs). TCRs are lists, which are curated by members (stakers) who have all staked some tokens. Members can vote on which items should be on the list, and their vote is proportional to the amount of tokens they've staked. In order to become a member, an applicant has to both buy tokens and be voted in by existing members. TCRs have been proposed to curate lists of data sources [23]; if a curated list is held in high regard, owners of data assets will want to put it on the list, in order to propose their asset they will want to become members, which means buying tokens. Thus, if the quality assessment efforts are valuable, demand for the tokens will increase leading to an increase in the value of the staked tokens.

Another example may be drawn'from the Ocean Protocol [15], which is a data market protocol with a blockchain back-end for registering, browsing and purchasing data assets. Ocean users can stake tokens on specific data assets, signalling that they believe that it is of high quality and likely to be purchased[1]. Every time a data asset is purchased, the purchaser pays a small fee which is divided amongst the stakers proportionally.

Based on these examples, we have obtained some initial evidence that the staking holds the promise to add significant value to a data market by demonstrating "investedness" in the value of quality assessment efforts, i.e., stakers who provide useful quality assessment will stand to gain from this whereas stakers who do not provide useful quality assessment might lose money. Our proposal expands upon this idea, because it enables quality assessors to not only signal investedness, but also prove that the staking is tied to some real quality assessment efforts.

3 Quality Assessment Tests

As mentioned above, one of the most important features of our suggested approach is the notion that different data assets require different types of quality assessment. Before discussing the QA contract, we illustrate some types of quality assessment methods we envision that are supported by our approach.

We believe quality assessment is best achieved when tests, captured in a set of instructions, are run against a data asset and record a result that demonstrates the quality of that data asset. We call these tests *Quality assessment (QA) tests*. When deciding on appropriate QA tests, the quality assessor considers tests that are, on the one hand, *appropriate* to demonstrate the value of the data asset and, on the other hand, *respect data sovereignty* as explained in Sect. 1.

In line with our view of quality assessment, deciding which QA tests are appropriate depends on the envisioned use of the data asset. For example, if a data asset is promoted for training machine learning algorithms, it makes sense to test one or more common algorithms on the data set and record both which algorithms were tested, as well as their resulting performance (e.g., accuracy, recall, etc.). On the other hand if a data asset provides pay-per-query real-time global weather information, a good test could simply be to request information on several different locations, compare the results to other available sources, and log the places queried, as well as the comparison on the blockchain.

Respecting data sovereignty means that not only the test results but also the tests themselves can be safely shared with potential buyers without infringing on the rights of data providers. This can be a major limitation whenever a QA test requires additional data sources: either the additional data itself should be

---

[1] In reality, staking in the Ocean data marketplace serves an additional purpose: price determination through the use of automated market makers. A full discussion of price determination is beyond the scope of this paper.

shareable (e.g., because it is in the public domain), or the data market should be able to combine multiple data assets. We illustrate this by giving some examples.

Purchasing an Entire Data Set
A very straightforward example would be a data set which, after purchase, can be downloaded as a whole and can be used, but not shared, by the data buyer. Examples of such a data set would be mailing lists (e.g., the ones offered on Data and Sons [17]). In this case, the best test would be for a quality assessor to buy the data set and manually check whether it is complete and if the metadata describing the data asset is accurate. In this case the "result" of the test would be a confirmation of the purchase, which *can* be logged on the blockchain. In this scenario the act of staking is an important signal of the quality of the data: despite the fact that the test result seemingly does not convey much information about the data asset, the quality assessor, who has demonstrably purchased the data, indicates that they believe the data set to be likely to be purchased.

Pay-Per-Query
Some data assets, such as the public data sets offered through Google BigQuery [18], can be accessed through a "pay-per-query" payment model. For such a data set, tests can be designed to assess the metadata of the data asset through aggregate results, such as number of rows, dimension of the data or the number of missing values. Additionally, if the marketplace supports it, queries can attempt to join different data assets and record the success or failure of the join operator. The test results can then validate and extend the metadata already available on the marketplace, as well as demonstrate the integrability of the offered data assets.

Real-Time-Data
We, once again, consider the example from the introduction of a real-time streaming data asset for financial applications, such as the Binance API for cryptocurrency trading [16]. In this case, test cases might be designed to assess the timeliness of the response and the test results could be timestamps, indicating the time between receiving the request and the response. Since the data quickly loses its value after publication, the data provider might not even mind if some actual query responses are shown on the blockchain which would demonstrate that the data asset works as intended.

Machine Learning with Compute-to-Data
Some data markets (e.g., [12,15,21]) aim to deliver a secure computation environment so that data never has to leave the control of the data provider. Instead the algorithmic computation is brought to the data and only aggregated results are returned to the data buyer. In this scenario our approach would be especially easy to implement, as the aggregate results can generally be considered to be the property of the data quality assessor who can share them as they please. An example for such a scenario would be to train some well-known algorithms on a data product (e.g., K-nearest neighbours, support-vector machines or random

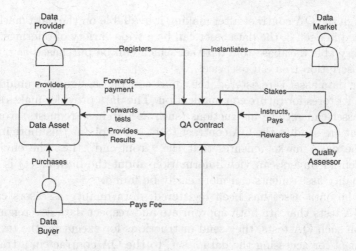

Fig. 1. The relation between the different actors, the data asset and the QA contract in the data market ecosystem

forests in the case of classification) and have test results consisting of performance metrics such as accuracy, recall, etc. The data product could even be enriched with public data sets which can be safely recorded as part of the tests.

4   The Quality Assessment Contract

In this section we introduce the QA contract, which is the key element that enables validated QA testing. Our approach has been designed to leverage the blockchain advantages mentioned in Sect. 2.1: the transactional nature facilitates, in principle, easy payment to quality assessors and makes it relatively simple to find and identify the quality assessment efforts. The transparency and trust allow us to demonstrate that quality assessment was actually conducted, and the easy deployment allows data sellers to easily leverage our solution.

We start out Sect. 4.1 by describing the relevant interactions that the different actors (e.g. data provider, data buyer, etc.) and artefacts (i.e. the data asset and QA contract) have with each other in the process of using the QA contract. The actors, artefacts and interactions are shown in Fig. 1. After outlining the interactions, we discuss some architectural considerations in Sect. 4.2, specifically we explain which parts occur on the blockchain and how these interact with the off-chain parts.

4.1   Functionality of the QA Contract

The QA contract is a smart contract which is deployed by the data market for the benefit of data providers, data quality assessors and data buyers. The choice of whether to use a QA contract lies with the data provider, who has to register their asset in the QA contract after making it available on the data marketplace. As discussed in Sect. 3, the data asset can be a wide variety of offerings, ranging from a query-able database to a data set which can be purchased as a whole or even a subscription to a data service.

When a data asset is registered, the smart contract assigns it a unique identifier, which it stores for future communication. The data provider makes sure that the data asset can receive instructions (such as purchase requests) from transactions that are send to the QA contract (Sect. 4.2 explains this more in-depth). Finally, the data market ensures that the "front-end" (i.e., the environment where potential buyers can view information about the data asset) is updated so data quality assessments can more easily be found.

After the data asset has been registered, data quality assessors can come up with QA tests that are both appropriate and respect data sovereignty. After deciding on such QA tests, they send instructions for executing the tests, along with payment for accessing the data asset, to the QA contract in a transaction on the blockchain. As discussed in Sect. 3, how these QA tests are executed and what the test results look like are highly dependent both on the type of data asset, as well as the data market, but we can assume that some appropriate result, is returned which can be logged on the blockchain.

The QA contract then forwards the payment to the data provider and the instructions for the tests to the data asset. After the tests are completed, the results are sent, in a transaction, to the QA contract[2]. Since the purchase, the test instructions and the test results are all communicated through the blockchain, they are logged in transactions to- and the smart contract which are transparent and constitute immutable proof of the purchase, the test and the test results.

After seeing the results of their tests, the staker decides whether they believe the data asset has a high quality. If they do believe the data asset has a high quality, they can decide to stake some cryptocurrency on it, through the QA contract. The QA contract verifies that the staker indeed performed some tests before accepting the stake and keeps track of which quality assessor has staked how much on each data asset.

Data buyers who are interested in the data asset can view the QA tests that have been applied, as well as the corresponding results. Since these are logged in blockchain transactions, the data buyer will know that the tests actually occurred. The QA tests can assist the data buyer in their decision on whether or not to buy the data asset. If they do decide to purchase the data asset, a small fee is charged, which is distributed amongst all quality assessors who have run tests and have staked on the data asset. The exact distribution key is an interesting problem in-and-of-itself. This will, most likely, depend partially on the size of the stake of the quality assessor.

---

[2] Of course, sending this transaction costs cryptocurrency, we presume that the quality assessor compensates the data asset for this transaction, but different implementations are also possible depending on the data market design.

4.2   Architectural Considerations

When implementing the QA contract it is important to consider which elements are on- and which are off the blockchain. The positive qualities we introduced in Sect. 2.1 come at the cost of increased cost of operation [2] and increased cost for debugging and maintenance [4]. We therefore end our discussion of the QA contract by discussing some of the architectural considerations of implementing the QA contract in a data market environment. Note, that we believe that any good data market should also offer a front-end (e.g., by using a website), which can be used to interact with the blockchain-based elements that act as a back-end. In order to further illustrate the QA contract, we provide a mock-up implementation in Solidity in our online appendix[3].

In order for the QA contract to properly function, it is important that the *payment* and the *communication* of the *QA tests* and *results* are done through the blockchain. Because of this, *at the very least*, the data asset and the quality assessor need cryptocurrency wallets on the blockchain. The quality assessor needs to be able to provably pay for the data asset and receive rewards whenever a fee is paid by a future data buyer and the data asset needs to provably receive payment and return transactions with the test results. Ideally, the data buyer would have a cryptocurrency wallet as well, so they can purchase the data asset through the blockchain, but the data market platform might offer the option to pay in fiat currency and take care of the curation fee "behind the scenes".

It was already alluded to in Sect. 4.1 that the data asset has to be able to receive instructions from the QA contract. The easiest way to achieve this, would be to have the QA contract forward a transaction to the wallet associated with the data asset each time it receives test instructions from the quality assessor. The data asset can then (automatically) search for the blockchain for the most recent transactions to the QA contract that mention its unique identifier and extract the instructions from there, for example in Ethereum, the quality assessor could include the instructions in the "data" field of its transaction to the QA contract [5].

Finally, it is important to note the data buyer can access the QA tests and results directly from the blockchain without needing their own account. Since it is not desirable potential data buyers scrape the blockchain for relevant transactions, the data market should provide links (and possibly recaps) of the relevant transactions in the overview of the data asset on the front-end of the market.

5   Conclusion

In this paper we discussed the problem of data quality assessment, taking particular notice of the multi-faceted nature of data quality. We suggested some simple quality assessment tests and showed how such tests, in combination with our QA contract have the potential to add real value to a data market ecosystem by providing provable insights into the quality of data assets.

---

[3] https://github.com/Pindapinda/QA-Contract.

In future work, we intend to evaluate the concept of a QA contract in a real-world setting by seeking out industrial partnerships. We envision that the development of appropriate and data sovereignty respecting QA tests will be particularly relevant for future data market-related research.

References

1. Bajoudah, S., Dong, C., Missier, P.: Toward a decentralized, trust-less marketplace for brokered IoT data trading using blockchain. In: Proceedings - 2019 2nd IEEE International Conference on Blockchain, Blockchain 2019, pp. 339–346 (2019). https://doi.org/10.1109/Blockchain.2019.00053
2. Butijn, B.J., Tamburri, D.A., Heuvel, W.J.V.D.: Blockchains: a Systematic Multivocal Literature Review (2019). http://arxiv.org/abs/1911.11770
3. Demchenko, Y., Cushing, R., Los, W., Grosso, P., De Laat, C., Gommans, L.: Open data market architecture and functional components. In: 2019 International Conference on High Performance Computing and Simulation. HPCS 2019, pp. 1017–1021 (2019). https://doi.org/10.1109/HPCS48598.2019.9188195
4. Driessen, S., Nucci, D.D., Monsieur, G., Tamburri, D.A., Heuvel, W.J.V.D.: AGSolT : a Tool for Automated Test-Case Generation for Solidity Smart Contracts, pp. 1–15 (2021). https://arxiv.org/abs/2102.08864
5. Eiki   (2019).   https://medium.com/@eiki1212/ethereum-transaction-structure-explained-aa5a94182ad6
6. Exner, J.P.: The ESPRESSO - Project - A European approach for Smart City Standards (2011)
7. Filippi, P.D., Mccarthy, S.: Cloud computing?: centralization and data sovereignty. Eur. J. Law Technol. **3**(2), 1–18 (2012)
8. Goldin, M.: Token-Curated Registries 1.0 (2021). https://docs.google.com/document/d/1BWWC_-Kmso9b7yCI_R7ysoGFIT9D_sfjH3axQsmB6E/edit
9. Gupta, P., Kanhere, S.S., Jurdak, R.: A decentralized IoT data marketplace (2019)
10. Hayashi, T., Ohsawa, Y.: Preliminary case study on value determination of datasets and cross-disciplinary data collaboration using data jackets. Procedia Comput. Sci. **112**, 2175–2184 (2017)
11. Koutroumpis, P., Leiponen, A., Thomas, L.D.W.: Markets for data. Ind. Corporate Change **29**(3), 645–660 (2020). https://doi.org/10.1093/icc/dtaa002
12. Koutsos, V., Papadopoulos, D., Chatzopoulos, D., Tarkoma, S., Hui, P.: Agora: a privacy-aware data marketplace. In: Proceedings - International Conference on Distributed Computing Systems 2020-Novem, pp. 1211–1212 (2020). https://doi.org/10.1109/ICDCS47774.2020.00156
13. Market Reports World: Big Data Market by Component, Deployment Mode, Organization Size, Business Function (Operations, Finance, and Marketing and Sales), Industry Vertical (BFSI, Manufacturing, and Healthcare and Life Sciences), and Region - Global Forecast to 2025. Technical Report (2020). https://www.marketsandmarkets.com/Market-Reports/big-data-market-1068.html
14. Nakamoto, S.: Bitcoin: a peer-to-peer electronic cash system (2009)
15. Ocean Protocol Foundation: The Ocean Protocol (2019). https://oceanprotocol.com/tech-whitepaper.pdf#h.uvec5xf3qzn1
16. Online: Binance   API.   https://binance-docs.github.io/apidocs/spot/en/#introduction
17. Online: Data and Sons. https://www.dataandsons.com/

18. Online: Google BigQuery Public Data Sets. https://cloud.google.com/bigquery/public-data/
19. Online: GAIA-X   (2021).   https://www.data-infrastructure.eu/GAIAX/Navigation/EN/Home/home.html
20. van Ooijen, I., Vrabec, H.U.: Does the GDPR enhance consumers' control over personal data? An analysis from a behavioural perspective. J. Consum. Policy **42**(1), 91–107 (2019). https://doi.org/10.1007/s10603-018-9399-7
21. Otto, B., et al.: Industrial Data Space - digitale Souveränität über Daten. Whitepaper (2016). https://www.fraunhofer.de/de/forschung/fraunhofer-initiativen/international-data-spaces.html
22. Potoglou, D., Patil, S., Palacios, J.F., Feijóo, C., Gijón, C.: The value of personal information online: results from three stated preference discrete choice experiments in the UK. In: ECIS 2013 - Proceedings of the 21st European Conference on Information Systems, pp. 1–12 (2013)
23. Ramachandran, G.S., Radhakrishnan, R., Krishnamachari, B.: Towards a decentralized data marketplace for smart cities. In: 2018 IEEE International Smart Cities Conference. ISC2 2018, pp. 1–8 (2019). https://doi.org/10.1109/ISC2.2018.8656952
24. Reinsel, D., Gantz, J., Rydning, J.: Data Age 2025: The Digitization of the World From Edge to Core. Seagate, IDC (November), vol. 28 (2018). https://www.seagate.com/files/www-content/our-story/trends/files/idc-seagate-dataage-whitepaper.pdf
25. Reiter, M., Breitenbucher, U., Dustdar, S., Karastoyanova, D., Leymann, F., Truong, H.L.: A novel framework for monitoring and analyzing quality of data in simulation workflows. In: 2011 IEEE Seventh International Conference on eScience, pp. 105–112. IEEE (2011)
26. Ricci, F., Rokach, L., Shapira, B.: Recommender Systems Handbook, 2 edn. Springer, Boston (2015). https://doi.org/10.1007/978-1-4899-7637-6, https://link.springer.com/book/10.1007%2F978-1-4899-7637-6#about
27. Rodríguez-Mazahua, L., Rodríguez-Enríquez, C.A., Sánchez-Cervantes, J.L., Cervantes, J., García-Alcaraz, J.L., Alor-Hernández, G.: A general perspective of big data: applications, tools, challenges and trends. J. Supercomputing **72**(8), 3073–3113 (2016). https://doi.org/10.1007/s11227-015-1501-1
28. Schomm, F., Stahl, F., Vossen, G.: Marketplaces for data: an initial survey. SIGMOD Rec. **42**(1), 15–26 (2013). https://doi.org/10.1145/2481528.2481532
29. Sharma, S.: Rise of big data and related issues. In: 12th IEEE International Conference Electronics, Energy, Environment, Communication, Computer, Control: (E3–C3). INDICON 2015, pp. 1–6 (2016). https://doi.org/10.1109/INDICON.2015.7443346
30. Spiekermann, M.: Data marketplaces: trends and monetisation of data goods. Intereconomics **54**(4), 208–216 (2019). https://doi.org/10.1007/s10272-019-0826-z
31. Stahl, F., Schomm, F., Vossen, G.: Data marketplaces: an emerging species. Front. Artif. Intell. Appl. Databases **2013**, 145–158 (2014). https://doi.org/10.3233/978-1-61499-458-9-145
32. Stahl, F., Schomm, F., Vossen, G., Vomfell, L.: A classification framework for data marketplaces. Vietnam J. Comput. Sci. **3**(3), 137–143 (2016). https://doi.org/10.1007/s40595-016-0064-2
33. Stahl, F., Schomm, F., Vossen, G., Vomfell, L.: A classification framework for data marketplaces. Vietnam J. Comput. Sci. **3**(3), 137–143 (2016). https://doi.org/10.1007/s40595-016-0064-2

34. Travizano, M., Ajzenman, G., Sarraute, C., Minnoni, M.: Wibson: A Decentralized Data Marketplace, pp. 1–6 (2018)
35. Uriarte, R.B., De Nicola, R.: Blockchain-based decentralised cloud/fog solutions?: challenges, opportunities and standards. IEEE Commun. Standards Mag. (September) (2018). https://doi.org/10.1109/MCOMSTD.2018.1800020
36. Li, W., Andreina, S., Bohli, J.-M., Karame, G.: Securing proof-of-stake blockchain protocols. In: Garcia-Alfaro, J., Navarro-Arribas, G., Hartenstein, H., Herrera-Joancomartí, J. (eds.) ESORICS/DPM/CBT-2017. LNCS, vol. 10436, pp. 297–315. Springer, Cham (2017). https://doi.org/10.1007/978-3-319-67816-0_17
37. Wood, G.: Ethereum: a secure decentralised generalised transaction ledger. Ethereum Project Yellow Paper, pp. 1–32 (2014)
38. Zech, H.: Data as a tradeable commodity-implications for contract law. In: Proceedings of the 18th EIPIN Congress: The New Data Economy between Data Ownership, Privacy and Safeguarding Competition (2017)

Service-Based Applications

What Went Wrong? Explaining Cascading Failures in Microservice-Based Applications

Jacopo Soldani$^{(\boxtimes)}$, Giuseppe Montesano, and Antonio Brogi

Department of Computer Science, University of Pisa, Pisa, Italy
`jacopo.soldani@unipi.it`

Abstract. Cascading failures can severely affect the correct functioning of large enterprise applications consisting of hundreds of interacting microservices. As a consequence, the ability to effectively analyse the causes of occurred cascading failures is crucial for managing complex applications. In this paper, we present a model-based methodology to automate the analysis of application logs in order to identify the possible failures that occurred and their causality relations. Our methodology employs topology graphs to represent the structure of microservice-based applications and finite state machines to model their expected replica- and failure-aware behaviour. We also present a proof-of-concept implementation of our methodology, which we exploited to assess its effectiveness with controlled experiments and monkey testing.

1 Introduction

Microservice-based applications integrate many heterogeneous services. Each service features a different functionality and it interacts with other services to deliver the overall application capabilities [25]. Due to the many interactions among the services of an application, cascading failures can happen: a service failing can cause the services interacting with it to fail as well, their failures can result in the failure of the services invoking their functionalities, and so on [22].

Cascading failures should be avoided/limited in microservice-based applications [23]. This requires to identify the causalities among the failures of the replicated instances of their services, e.g., which service replica failed first? Which service replicas caused failures of which other service replicas? Answering such questions requires to delve through the distributed application logs, starting from the service replicas whose failures were detected. Application operators can inspect the logs stored in the distributed environments (e.g., virtual machines or containers) used to run the service replicas, with the aim of identifying whether other service replicas have failed and whether each failure caused/was caused by some other failures [35]. The resulting process is however time-consuming and error-prone, hence making the understanding of failure causalities in microservice-based applications a concrete "pain" for application operators [31].

© Springer Nature Switzerland AG 2021
J. Barzen (Ed.): SummerSOC 2021, CCIS 1429, pp. 133–153, 2021.
https://doi.org/10.1007/978-3-030-87568-8_9

In this paper, we aim at proposing a methodology for automatically identifying failure causalities in microservice-based applications. Ours is not the first attempt in this direction, with existing solutions allowing to explain the *possible symptoms* of failures (e.g., performance anomalies) with correlation-based analyses or machine learning, e.g., [4,9,17–21,29], and [33]. The main novelties of our methodology are that (i) we consider the *failures explicitly logged* by the application services (rather than their possible symptoms), and (ii) we exploit the specification of an application to determine the possible causalities among the failures logged by its services

We rely on the widely-accepted idea of the application operator to declaratively specify their applications, by modelling the topology of multi-service applications by means of directed graphs [2]. The nodes in an application topology model the application services, each indicating the operations for managing the corresponding service, its requirements, and the capabilities it offers to satisfy other services' requirements. The oriented arcs model inter-service dependencies by connecting the requirement of a node to the capability of another node that is used to satisfy such requirement. We also rely on application operators to exploit management protocols [30] for declaratively and compositionally modelling the management behaviour of applications. Management protocols are finite state machines specifying the management behaviour of application services, including how they react to possible failures. The failure-aware management of a multi-service application is then derived by suitably composing the management protocols associated with its services, based on the application topology.

We exploit the above modelling to drive an automated analysis of the distributed logs of a microservice-based application to identify failure causalities. The core of our methodology consists of an algorithm (called WHY), which takes as input the specification of an application (viz., its topology and management behaviour), a failure whose causes are to be explained, and the logs stored while the application was running. WHY then analyses the application logs to identify the possible causes for such failure, e.g., whether it may be due to some bug causing an unforeseen failure of the service itself, or whether its failure may be due other services that have failed. In the latter case, the algorithm WHY iteratively looks for the possible causes for the identified failures of other services. In this way, WHY builds a "causality graph", i.e., a graph rooted in the failure to be explained, and whose paths model the possible causal relations among the failures that may have possibly caused such failure.

To illustrate the feasibility of our methodology, we present a PoC (Proof-of-Concept) implementation of WHY and we show how it can be used to identify failure causalities in microservice-based applications. More precisely, we show how to configure distributed log harvesting in a Docker-based application deployment to enable storing the distributed logs in a dedicated volume, after being processed by a Logstash instance to uniform their structure. We then show how our PoC can be used to automatically analyse such logs to build a causality graph representing the possible causes for a given failure to happen on a given service. Finally, we exploit our PoC to assess our methodology by means of controlled experiments and monkey testing. The results are promising in that they show that our methodology successfully identified the real causes for each failure considered in our controlled experiments and monkey testing.

The rest of this paper is organised as follows. Sections 2 and 3 provide a motivating scenario and the necessary background, respectively. Sections 4 and 5 illustrate our methodology for explaining failure causalities and its implementation, which is then used in the evaluation reported in Sect. 6. Finally, Sects. 7 and 8 discuss related work and draw some concluding remarks, respectively.

2 Motivating Scenario

Sock Shop (Fig. 1) is an open-source, microservice-based application simulating an e-commerce website[1]. External clients can connect to *Sock Shop* by interacting with an *Edge Router*, which balances the load among the possibly multiple replicas of the application *Frontend*. The *Frontend* displays a web-based graphical user interface for e-shopping socks, whose functionalities are realised by connecting to backend services, i.e., *Catalogue*, *Users*, *Carts*, and *Orders*. *Catalogue* manages the catalogue of available socks, which is stored in the *Catalogue DB*. Similarly, *Users*, *Carts*, and *Orders* manage the users of the application, their shopping carts, and their orders by connecting to the corresponding databases. *Orders* also enables simulating the payment and shipping of orders by interacting with the *Payment* and *Shipping* services. While *Payment* simulates the connection to a credit card service, *Shipping* places each order to be shipped in a message queue, i.e., *RabbitMQ*. The orders in the queue are then consumed by the service *Queue Master*, which simulates the actual shipping of orders.

Suppose now that we run *Sock Shop* with multiple replicated instances of its services. Suppose also that we observe, at some point, a functional failure of a replica of *Edge Router*. Why did this happen? Did *Edge Router* failed on its own? Was it instead because the replicas of *Frontend* were stopped or failed?

To answer the above questions, we can delve through the logs of *Edge Router* and of all replicas of *Frontend* that were running when the replica of *Edge Router* functionally failed. This indeed allows checking whether some replica of *Frontend* failed while *Edge Router* was relying on its capabilities. If this is the case, then we should check whether the failing replicas of *Frontend* were failing on their own, or whether this was because of some of the replicas of the services on which *Frontend* depends, i.e., *Catalogue*, *Users*, *Carts*, and *Orders*. This in turn requires to look at the logs of the failing replicas of *Frontend* together with those of the replicas of *Catalogue*, *Users*, *Carts*, and *Orders*. If other failure causalities are detected, then we should analyse the logs of the newly detected failing replicas, which may require to analyse the logs of other service replicas, and so on.

The above highlights how complex it can be to identify cascading failures by delving through the distributed logs of a microservice-based application.

---

[1] https://microservices-demo.github.io.

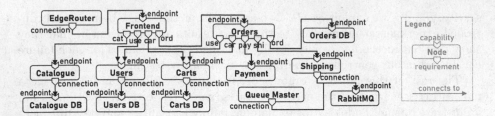

Fig. 1. The application topology of *Sock Shop*, depicted according to the TOSCA graphical notation [24]. Inter-component dependencies represented by connecting a requirement of a node to the capability of another node used to satisfy such requirement.

This holds even in a relatively simple scenario (*Sock Shop* is involving 14 services, whereas production-ready applications can involve hundreds of services), in which we did not consider the possible errors one can make while manually browsing distributed logs. For instance, we may miss some logged event, hence not detecting that a service failed and that this was causing —in cascade— the failure we wish to explain. Even worse would be the case of considering a failure as causing some other failures when this was not the case. For instance, there may be two failure cascades that happened in parallel, e.g., one starting from a replica of *Users* and the other one starting from an instance of *Payment*. By manually analysing the logs, we may wrongly consider both as possible causes for the failure of a replica of the *Edge Router*, even if only one actually caused the failures of the replicas of the *Frontend*.

To avoid those possible mistakes, as well as to intervene and limit the effects of the cascading failures that generated the failure in the replica of *Edge Router*, a representation of the failure cascades that have occurred would help. Such a representation would indeed guide us in browsing the distributed application logs. It would enable reasoning on which countermeasures to enact to avoid the elicited failure cascades to happen again. This is the purpose of our methodology, which automatically generates a causality graph modelling all cascading failures that may have possibly caused a given failure.

3   Background: Management Protocols

Multi-service applications are typically represented by indicating the states, requirements, capabilities, and management operations of the nodes composing their topology [2]. Management protocols [30] enable specifying the management behaviour of a node N (modelling an application service), by indicating (i) how each management operation of N depends on other management operations of N, (ii) how it depends on operations of the nodes that provide capabilities satisfying the requirements of N, and (iii) how N reacts when a failure occurs.

The dependencies (i) among the management operations of N are indicated by means of a transition relation τ_N. The transition relation indicates whether

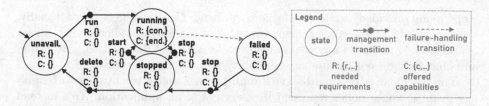

Fig. 2. Example of management protocol.

a management operation can be executed in a state of N, and which state is reached if its execution is successfully completed.

The description of (ii) whether and how the management of N depends on other nodes is instead given by associating sets of *requirements* with both states and transitions. The requirements associated with a state or transition of N must continue to be satisfied in order for N to continue residing in such state or to successfully complete executing such transition. The description of a node N is then completed by associating its states and transitions with sets of *capabilities* that indicate the capabilities that are actually provided by N (to satisfy other services' requirements) while residing in a state and while executing a transition.

Finally, (iii) a failure occurs when N is needing a requirement and the capability satisfying such requirements stops being provided by the corresponding node. To describe how N reacts to failures, a transition relation φ_N models the failure handling of N by indicating the state it reaches when a failure occurs while it is in a state or executing a transition.

Definition 1 (Management Protocols). *Let $N = \langle S_N, R_N, C_N, O_N, \mathcal{M}_N \rangle$ be a node modelling a service, with S_N, R_N, C_N, and O_N being the finite sets of states, requirements, capabilities, and management operations of N, respectively. $\mathcal{M}_N = \langle \overline{s}_N, \tau_N, \rho_N, \chi_N, \varphi_N \rangle$ is a finite state machine defining the* management *protocol of N, where*
- $\overline{s}_N \in S_N$ *is the initial state,*
- $\tau_N \subseteq S_N \times O_N \times S_N$ *models the state transition relation,*
- $\rho_N : (S_N \cup \tau_N) \to 2^{R_N}$ *indicates which requirements must hold in each state $s \in S_N$ and during each transition $\langle s, o, s' \rangle \in \tau_N$,*
- $\chi_N : (S_N \cup \tau_N) \to 2^{C_N}$ *indicates which capabilities of N are offered in each state $s \in S_N$ and during each transition $\langle s, o, s' \rangle \in \tau_N$, and*
- $\varphi_N \subseteq (S_N \cup \tau_N) \times S_N$ *models the failure handling for a node.*

Example. Figure 2 displays the management protocol of the *Catalogue* service in our motivating scenario. *Catalogue* can be in four possible states, i.e., *unavailable* (initial), *running, failed,* and *stopped*. No requirements and capabilities are associated with states *unavailable, stopped,* and *failed*, which means that *Catalogue* does not require nor provide anything in such states. The same does not hold for the *running* state, which is the only state where *Catalogue* concretely provides the *endpoint* capability, and where it assumes the *endpoint* requirement to continue to be satisfied. If *endpoint* fails (because the corresponding capability stops being provided) while *Catalogue* is *running*, *Catalogue* gets *failed*. Finally, the transitions of the management protocol of *Catalogue* indicate that all its operations do not need any requirement to be satisfied during their execution, and that they do not feature any capability while being executed.   □

The specification of a multi-service application is then given by means of topology graphs, whose nodes represent the services of an application. Arcs instead associate a node's requirements with capabilities featured by other nodes to represent the dependencies among such services, viz., they define a *binding* function associating each requirement of each node to the capability satisfying it.

Definition 2 (Application Specification). *The specification of a multi-service application is a pair $A = \langle T, \beta \rangle$, where T is a finite set of nodes modelling the application services, with each $N \in T$ such that $N = \langle S_N, R_N, C_N, O_N, \mathcal{M}_N \rangle$, and $\beta : \bigcup_{N \in T} R_N \to \bigcup_{N \in T} C_N$ is the binding function[2].*

The specification of the application in our motivating scenario is actually given by the application topology displayed in Fig. 1. In the figure, the nodes modelling the application services are depicted as boxes, associated with their requirements and capabilities. The binding function β is instead depicted by connecting the requirements of a node with the capabilities featured by other nodes. For instance, the requirements *car*, *use*, *car*, and *ord* of *Frontend* are connected to the *endpoint* capabilities of *Catalogue*, *Users*, *Carts*, and *Orders* used to satisfy them.

Application services can then be replicated into multiple replicas. All replicas of a service feature the same management behaviour, as defined by the management protocol of the node modeling such service. Different replicas of a node have different identifiers and reside in states/transitions that are possibly different from those of the other replicas of the same node.

Definition 3 (Node Replica). *Let N be a node modelling a service. A replica of N is denoted by a pair $\langle N, i \rangle$ where $i \in \mathbb{I}$ is an instance identifier[3].*

In the following, to simplify notation, we will denote a node replica $\langle N, i \rangle$ by i_N.

The states/transitions of the replicas of the nodes forming an application constitute the *global state* of the instance of a multi-service application. The management behaviour for an instance of the application specified by $A = \langle T, b \rangle$ then defines how its global state changes when nodes are horizontally scaled (viz., when replicas of a node are created or removed), when operations are executed on node replicas, and because of failure propagation and handling[4].

---

[2] To simplify notation, we assume that the names of states, requirements, capabilities, and operations of the nodes in a topology are all disjoint.

[3] $\mathbb{I}$ denotes the universe of possible instance identifiers.

[4] [30] provides further details on how management protocols enable modelling and analysing the failure- and replica-aware application management.

4   Explaining Failure Causalities

We now present the core of our methodology, viz., the algorithm WHY (Fig. 3), which enables identifying possible causalities among the failures that occurred while running a microservice-based application. The algorithm inputs an application specification A that describes an application topology and the protocols describing the management behaviour of the services forming the application. The algorithm also inputs the set L of logs stored during the run of application A. Logged events are tuples of the form $\langle i_N, t, a \rangle$ indicating that, at time t, a node replica i_N was in a state a or executed an operation a.

Definition 4 (Logged Events). *Let* $A = \langle T, \beta \rangle$ *be an application specification. A set* L *of events logged by* A *is a set of tuples of the form* $\langle i_N, t, a \rangle$ *where* i_N *is a replica of a node* $N \in T$ *(with* $N = \langle S_N, R_N, C_N, O_N, \mathcal{M}_N \rangle$*),* $t \in T$ *is a timestamp[5], and* $a \in S_N \cup O_N$*.*

Given an application specification A and a set L of logged events, the algorithm WHY identifies all the possible causes of why a node replica i_N was in a state a at time t. This is done by iteratively building a *causality graph* modelling all possible causes, taking into account also possible cascading failures. The vertices of the causality graph represent logged events as triples $\langle i_N, t, a \rangle$, where i_N is a node replica, t is a timestamp, and a denotes a state or an operation of node N, or its unexpected failure $\bot$. The (oriented) edges of the causality graph instead model causal relations between events. Namely, an edge $\langle e_1, e_2 \rangle$ indicates that event e_1 may have been caused by event e_2.

Definition 5 (Causality Graph). *Let* $A = \langle T, \beta \rangle$ *be an application specification. A causality graph* $G = (V, E)$ *for* A *is defined by a set* V *of vertices of the form* $\langle i_N, t, a \rangle$*, where* i_N *is a replica of a node* $N \in T$ *(with* $N = \langle S, R, C, O, \mathcal{M} \rangle$*),* $t \in T$ *is a timestamp, and* $a \in \bigcup_{N \in T}(S_N \cup O_N) \cup \{\bot\}$*, and by a set* $E \subseteq V \times V$ *of edges.*

The algorithm WHY (Fig. 3) inputs a logged event $\langle i_N, t, a \rangle$, where $a \in S_N$ is a state of node N, and determines all the possible causes that may have led node replica i_N to reach state a. To do so, WHY iteratively builds a (initially empty, line 1) set of *causalRelations* defining the edges of a causality graph. WHY employs two utility sets: the set of logged events still *toExplain* and the set of already *explained* logged events. These are initialised with the input event and with the empty set, respectively (lines 2–3). WHY then iteratively builds the causality graph by finding the possible explanations for all events *toExplain* (lines 4–14). Finally, it returns the (edges of the) causality graph modelling all possible causes for the node replica i_N to be in state a at time t (line 15).

  While there are events still *toExplain* (line 4), WHY picks one of such events $\langle i_N, t, a \rangle$ from the set *toExplain* (lines 5–6), and records that the corresponding state change may have been caused by an expected failure of the replica i_N itself

---

[5] $\mathbb{T}$ denotes the universe of possible timestamp identifiers.

WHY($\langle i_N, t, a \rangle, A, L$):
1   $causalRelations = \emptyset$
2   $toExplain = \{\langle i_N, t, a \rangle\}$
3   $explained = \emptyset$
4   **while** $toExplain \neq \emptyset$ **do**
5   **choose** $\langle i_N, t, a \rangle \in toExplain$
6      $toExplain = toExplain - \{\langle i_N, t, a \rangle\}$
7      $causalRelations = causalRelations \cup \{\langle\langle i_N, t, a \rangle, \langle i_N, t, \perp \rangle\rangle\}$
8   **if** $\exists \langle i_N, t_p, a_p \rangle \in L : (a_p, a) \in \varphi_N \wedge t_p < t \wedge$
                $(\forall \langle i_N, t_m, x \rangle \in L : t_m \in (t_p, t) \Rightarrow x = a)$ **then**
9   **foreach** $r \in \rho_N(a_p) - \rho_N(a)$ **do**
10   **foreach** $\langle j_M, u, b \rangle \in L : u < t \wedge \beta(r) \in C_M \wedge \beta(r) \notin \chi_M(b) \wedge$
                $(\forall \langle j_M, u_s, b_s \rangle \in L : u_s \in (u, t) \Rightarrow \beta(r) \in \chi_M(b_s))$ **do**
11              $causalRelations = causalRelations \cup \{\langle\langle i_N, t, a \rangle, \langle j_M, u, b \rangle\rangle\}$
12   **if** $(b \notin O_M \wedge \langle j_M, u, b \rangle \notin explained)$ **then**
13                 $toExplain = toExplain \cup \{\langle j_M, u, b \rangle\}$
14     $explained = explained \cup \{\langle i_N, t, a \rangle\}$
15 **return** $causalRelations$

Fig. 3. The algorithm WHY.

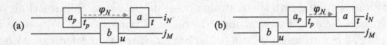

Fig. 4. Different cases considered by WHY for determining causal relations.

(line 7). Moreover, a replica i_N may have reached a state a at time t by handling a fault (with a failure-handling transition $\langle a_p, a \rangle \in \varphi_N$), which was caused by some other node replica that stopped providing some capability required by i_N to stay in a state a_p. WHY hence considers the latest time t_p before t at which i_N was (logged to be) in a state a_p different from a, if any (line 8). WHY then checks all the requirements r (line 9) of a_p that may have stopped being provided, thus leading i_N to switch from a_p to a to handle such fault. For each possibly failed requirement r, WHY checks the logs of all node replicas that could have been used to satisfy r, by determining the latest logged event $\langle j_M, u, b \rangle$ of any node replica j_M corresponding to j_M not providing the capability needed to satisfy r, if any (line 10). The event $\langle j_M, u, b \rangle$ is then added as a possible cause of $\langle i_N, t, a \rangle$ (line 11). It is also added to the set $toExplain$, if $b \notin O_M$ and if the event had not been already explained before (lines 12–13).

Note that WHY considers both cases sketched in Fig. 4, viz., the fact that the event b of node replica j_M may have occurred (a) after or (b) before event a_p of node replica i_N. This is because i_N may detect that a requirement is not satisfied only when it actually uses it, and this may occur (even much) later than the moment in which the matching capability stopped being offered by j_M.

It is finally worth observing that WHY always *terminates* since the number of possible iterations (lines 4–14) is bounded by the finite number of logged events L. WHY iterates until there are events in the set of *toExplain*, which initially contains only the input event. Each iteration always removes one event $\langle i, t, a \rangle$ from the set of *toExplain*, and it may add multiple events to the same set, each happening at a time strictly lower than t. In other words, WHY always goes back in time over logged events, hence eventually reaching the first event logged when the application was first started. This intuitively means that WHY eventually reach iterations where events under explanation have no other events happening earlier than them, hence stopping to add events to the set *toExplain*. WHY will anyhow continue removing events from the set *toExplain*, and it will terminate when no event will be in such set.

It is also worth observing that WHY relies on two main assumptions: (1) the application specification A is assumed to be correctly modelling the management behaviour of the application and (2) the set of logged events L_A is assumed to contain all state changes and all operation executions that have occurred during the run of A. We describe next how WHY can be used in practice to ensure that (1) and (2) hold (Sect. 5) and how this allows WHY finding plausible explanations for the events occurring when running an application (Sect. 6).

5 Proof-of-Concept (PoC) Implementation

To illustrate the feasibility of our methodology, we developed an open-source implementation of WHY[6]. We implemented a Java-based library that can be used to generate the causality graph modelling the possible reasons for a failure to happen in a microservice-based application. Our library relies on a standardised formatting of log events. It indeed assumes each logged event to be structured in GELF[7] (*Graylog Extended Log Format*) and to include the identifier *nodeID* of the service replica logging the event, the name *nodeName* of the corresponding service, the *timestamp* of the logged event, a *label* indicating what the logged event is about (viz., state, operation, or failure), and additional *info* on the logged event (viz., the name of a state or operation, or the causes for a failure).

Our Java-based library can be used for explaining failure causalities in microservice-based applications whose services are shipped as Docker containers (as we successfully did in our experiments—Sect. 6). This can be done by enacting the pipeline in Fig. 5. The first two steps (i.e., *Application Specification* and *Distributed Log Configuration*) are to be done only once, as the same application specification and log-enabled Docker Compose file can be reused in multiple runs of the application itself. The first two steps are to be repeated only if the application is changed, e.g., by including novel services or by changing their actual configuration or management behaviour. Instead, the steps enacting *Distributed Log Harvesting* and *Distributed Log Analysis* are to be repeated for different runs of the same application, even if this remains unchanged. Indeed, whenever

---

[6] https://github.com/di-unipi-socc/failure-causalities.
[7] https://docs.graylog.org/.

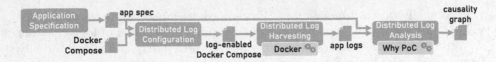

Fig. 5. A pipeline for automatically identifying failure causalities.

we are running the log-enabled Docker Compose file to deploy an application on top of Docker, the *Distributed Log Harvesting* is automatically enacted and stores the application logs. If we then wish to explain some failure that happened on an application, we can then enact the *Distributed Log Analysis* on the logs formerly stored during that particular run of the application.

Step 1: Application Specification. The first step consists of specifying the structure and management behaviour of the application to be considered. The requirements, capabilities, and management operations of the services forming the application must be elicited, and their management protocol must be specified. This obviously requires application-specific knowledge (e.g., what a service requires to run, when and how to invoke its management operations, and how it reacts to possible failures), which should typically be provided by the application developer. The various services must then be interconnected to structure the application topology, hence completing the application specification.

Step 2: Distributed Log Configuration. The *Distributed Log Configuration* essentially consists of redirecting the distributed application logs to a Logstash service storing them in an homogeneized format, based on GELF (*Graylog Extended Log Format*). This is done by including a Logstash service in the Docker Compose file specifying the application deployment, where the Docker log drivers are also configured to redirect the logs of all services to the newly included Logstash service. We chose Logstash since it natively supports transforming the heterogeneous events logged by the application services to the GELF-based format expected by our Java-based library.

The Logstash service must be configured to process the logs of service replicas and suitably label events to witness how such replicas evolved throughout their management protocol, i.e., when and which states were reached, when and which management operations were invoked, and when some failure was happening. This means that the configuration of Logstash is application-specific and driven, for each application service, by the corresponding management protocol in the application specification. A correct configuration of Logstash is indeed crucial to enable our Java-based library to effectively explain failure causalities.

As a result of this step, we obtain a log-enabled Docker Compose file, which can be reused in multiple runs of the application itself. The log-enabled Docker Compose file can indeed be reused until the application specification is to be updated, e.g., because some new service is included in the application, or since the new version of some service features a different management behaviour.

Step 3: Distributed Log Harvesting. Whenever the log-enabled Docker Compose file is run, the deployed application instance automatically enacts the distributed log harvesting. The configuration of the Docker log driver (included in the Docker Compose file during step 2) instructs the Docker runtime to automatically redirect all logs of all application services to the Logstash service. Thanks to its configuration, the Logstash service then processes logged events to marshal them to the GELF-based format expected by our Java-based library, and it stores formatted logs in a dedicated Docker volume.

The application logs can then be retrieved from the dedicated volume at any time, independendently of whether the application is undeployed or not. In the latter case, we obtain a snapshot of the logs at the time they are retrieved, as the application services continue to run and to log events.

Step 4: Distributed Log Analysis. The application logs can be processed by feeding them to a Java application exploiting our library to automatically identify the possible causes for a failure affecting the containerised instance of an application service. The Java application must first represent the application specification with an existing object model for specifying management protocols[8]. The obtained representation can then be fed to our library, together with the file with the application logs and the event to be explained. The result is a Java object modelling the causality graph, which can, e.g., be printed on the standard output to visualise all the possible causes for the event that was to be explained.

6 Experimentation

We exploited our PoC to evaluate the helpfulness of our methodology in practice. We first implemented a reference application whose services fails when subject to given events (Sect. 6.1). We then exploited our reference application to run some controlled experiments (Sect. 6.2) and monkey testing (Sect. 6.3).

The rationale for developing the reference application used in our experimentation is the following. We developed an application whose services continuously interact, and such that whenever a service stops answering to another service, the latter fails. We hence fully know how the application's service replicas behave while being operated, including when and how they can fail, as well as how failures can propagate in a running instance of the application. This provided us with a sort of "ground thruth" against which to compare the results obtained by running WHY on the application logs stored while running each controlled experiment or monkey test.

6.1 Reference Application

Our reference application is made of so-called *Pong* services, which are open source and publicly available on GitHub at https://git.io/Jtb7g. *Pong* is a containerized service offering a HTTP endpoint listening for "ping" requests, to which it answers with "pong". Each instance of *Pong* can be configured to depend on other *Pong* instances by providing it with the list of their hostnames.

---

[8] https://github.com/di-unipi-socc/management-protocols

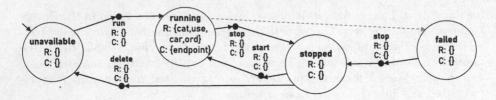

Fig. 6. Management protocol for the *Pong* service replacing *Frontend*.

Once running, the *Pong* instance will start pinging all the instances it depends on. If one of such instances stops answering, the *Pong* instance will fail and move to a state where it is no more answering with "pong" to its clients.

With such behaviour, *Pong* services can be connected to structure any possible application topology. Connecting a *Pong* service to another indeed simply requires to include the hostname of latter in the configuration of the former. To obtain a realistic application topology, we decided to interconnect 14 *Pong* services by mirroring the topology of *Sock Shop*, viz., we replaced each service in *Sock Shop* by a *Pong* service and we interconnected such services to obtain the same structure as in Fig. 1. In this way we developed *Sock Pong*, our reference application, whose deployment with Docker Compose is publicly available online at https://git.io/Jtb72. The Docker Compose file already includes a Logstash container, suitably configured to store and process the event logs as prescribed by the step 2 of the pipeline presented in Sect. 5.

We then specified *Sock Pong* by exploiting the object model for management protocols (see https://git.io/Jtb7X). We specified the topology of *Sock Pong* as in Fig. 1 and we equipped each other *Pong* service with a management protocol. We associated the *Pong* service replacing *Frontend* with the management protocol in Fig. 6. The management protocols of the other services are similar. They differ only for the requirements assumed in state *running*, where each service assumes all its requirements, which differ from service to service.

The rationale of the management protocol modelling the management behaviour of *Pong* services is the following. Coming as Docker container, a *Pong* service can be managed with the operations natively supported by Docker to *run*, *start*, *stop*, and *delete* containers. By executing the operation *run* when the service is *unavailable*, the service gets *running*. In such state, it offers its endpoint and requires all the services it depends on to be up and running, as it will send them "ping" requests. As soon as on of such services stops answering, the service gets *failed*. In addition, by executing the operation *stop* when the service is *running* or *failed*, it gets *stopped*. In the latter state, the service can get back *running* or *unavailable* by executing the operations *start* or *delete*, respectively.

6.2   Controlled Experiments

We run three controlled experiments, each enacted by deploying *Sock Pong* with Docker with one instance for each service. The three experiments represent

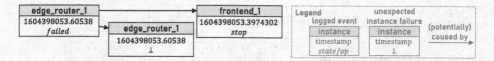

Fig. 7. Causality graph obtained by applying WHY to the logs in case 1.

different possible cases, where we exploited the stop of some service instance to inject the failure on the instances of the services depending on it, viz., (1) failure of a service instance due to stopping another service instance, (2) failure cascade resulting from the stop of a service instance, and (3) different failure cascades resulting from the stop of the instances of two different services.

The experiments were repeated various times on a Arch Linux machine (Intel i7 CPU, 16 GB of RAM). Our PoC of WHY always successfully identified the cascading failures that actually occurred. Examples of the log files generated by the different runs of each experiment are publicly available online at https://git. io/Jtb7y. They will be used hereafter as a reference to present a concrete run of each experiment.

(1) One Service Instance Failing in Cascade. We first show the case of a service instance failing due to the stop of one of the replicas of the services it depends on. We consider the case of an instance of *Edge Router* failing because of the execution of `docker stop` on the container running the instance of *Frontend* it interacts with. We show the outcomes of running WHY on the application logs obtained by executing such stop in the running instance of *Sock Pong*.

As for the reference file (`oneTwo.log`) publicly available online, the above case corresponds to running our PoC to explain why the instance of *Edge Router* got *failed* at time 1604398053.60538. The result is a JSON marshalling of the causality graph depicted in Fig. 7. The graph includes the actual cause for the failure of the instance of *Edge Router*, viz., the instance of *Frontend* was stopped at time 1604398053.3974302. The graph also includes the possibility of the instance of *Edge Router* changing its state because of an unexpected internal failure, viz., ⊥. As we already said in Sect. 4, unexpected internal errors of service replicas should never be excluded, as bugs in the code may unpredictably result in failing instances [14]. Whereas this is to be considered to explain failures, such as that leading the instance of *Edge Router* to get *failed*, the same obviously does not hold for service instances changing their state because management operations were invoked, such as the instance of *Frontend*, which changed its state because the operation *stop* was invoked.

(2) Failure Cascade after Stopping a Service Instance. The second experiment considers the case of an instance failing due to cascading failures affecting multiple services. In particular, we consider the failure of the instance of *Edge Router* after executing `docker stop` on the container running the instance of *Carts DB*. Stopping such instance indeed results in a failure of the instance of *Carts*. This in turns results in a failure of the instance of the *Frontend*, which then causes a failure in the instance of *Edge Router*. This always happens with our

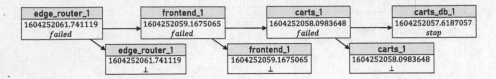

Fig. 8. Causality graph obtained by applying WHY to the logs in case 2.

implementation of *Sock Pong*, as (i) each *Pong* instance always fails when one of the instances it depends on stop answering, and since (ii) *Edge Router* invokes *Frontend*, which invokes *Carts*, which invokes *Carts DB* (Fig. 1).

In the reference application logs for this experiment (`waterfallFault.log`), we have that the instance of *Edge Router* got *failed* at time 1604252061.741119. By running the PoC of WHY to explain why this happened, we obtained the JSON marshalling of the causality graph in Fig. 8. The graph includes the expected failure cascade causing the failure on the instance *Edge Router*: it explicitly models the failure cascade starting from the *stop* on the instance of *Carts DB* and reaching the instance of *Edge Router*. It also considers the possibility for the instances of *Edge Router*, *Frontend*, and *Carts* to be affected by some unexpected internal failure.

(3) Failure Cascades after Stopping Two Service Instances. This experiment considers the case of two different services being stopped and generating two failure cascades that possibly intersect each other. In particular, we consider the case of the instance of *Edge Router* failing because of the cascading failures generated by issuing `docker stop` on the containers running the instances of two different services. We distinguished two possible cases in this experiment. We first considered the case (3.a) of stopping the instance of *Users DB* while a failure cascade due to previously stopping the instance of *Orders* was already propagating. We then considered the case (3.b) of simultaneously stopping the instances of *Users DB* and *Carts DB*, with the resulting failure cascades propagating in parallel. The rationale for 3.a and 3.b is the following: in case 3.a, we ensure that the failure cascade due to stopping the instance of *Orders* propagates earlier to the instance of *Edge Router*, hence being the only possible cause for the latter to fail. In case 3.b, the cascades due to stopping the instances of *Users DB* and *Carts DB* propagate in parallel towards the instance of *Edge Router*, hence both constituting possible causes for the failure in the instance of *Edge Router*.

As for the reference application logs in the case 3.a (`oneTwoWaterfall.log`), the event to be explained is the transition of the instance of *Edge Router* to state *failed* at time 1604400140.4041817. By running the PoC of WHY to explain why this happened, we obtained the JSON marshalling of the causality graph in Fig. 9a. The graph includes the failure cascade due to stopping the instance of *Orders* as possible cause for the failure in *Edge Router*, together with the possibility of the instances of *Edge Router* and *Frontend* to unexpectedly fail on their own. The failure cascade generated by stopping the instance of *Users DB* is instead not considered as possibly causing the failures of the instances of *Edge*

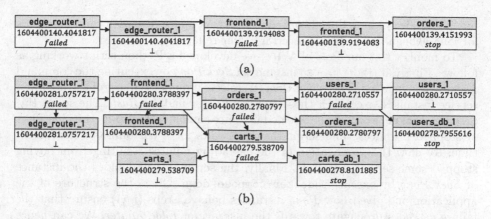

Fig. 9. Causality graph obtained by applying WHY to the logs in cases 3.a and 3.b.

Router and *Frontend*, even if the latter invokes *Users*, which in turn interacts with *Users DB* and fails when the latter is stopped. This is precisely what we expected to have, and by further inspecting the application logs we observed the reasons for this to happen: the instance of *Users* fails because of stopping the instance of *Users DB*. However, this is not causing the failure on the instance of *Frontend*, as the latter fails *before* of the failure of the instance of *Users*. WHY hence succeeded in excluding the failure of the instance of *Users* from the possible causes for the failure of the instance of *Frontend*, and subsequently for that of the instance of *Edge Router*.

For the reference logs in the case 3.b (`twoComponentWaterfall.log`), the event to be explained is the transition of the instance of *Edge Router* to state *failed* at time 1604400281.0757217. By running the PoC of WHY to explain why this happened, we obtained the JSON marshalling of the causality graph in Fig. 9b. Other than possible internal failures of service instances, the graph shows that the failure of the instance of *Edge Router* can be caused by that of the instance of *Frontend*. The latter can in turn be caused by the failures of the instances of *Users*, *Carts*, and *Orders*, with the failure of the instance *Orders* also potentially caused by those of the instances of *Users* and *Carts*. The failures of the instances of *Users* and *Carts* can instead be caused by the stopping of the instances of *Users DB* and *Carts DB*, respectively. In other words, the causality graph effectively models the two failure cascades caused by stopping the instances of *Users DB* and *Carts DB*, which we expected to propagate in parallel and to both possibly cause the failure of the instance of *Edge Router*.

6.3   Monkey Testing

To stress-test WHY, we monkey tested [1] its PoC. Monkey testing essentially consists of providing random inputs to check the behavior of applications. Depending on the context, monkey testing can be carried out in different ways, but it can always be reduced to feeding systems under test with random events for long enough to be able to ascertain their reliability.

To monkey test our PoC of WHY, we developed a Python script working as follows. Firstly, it (i) deploys an instance of *Sock Pong* by executing the command `docker-compose up`. The script then (ii) selects a random subset of the deployed service instances, except for those of *Edge Router* and *Logstash*. The script (iii) executes `docker stop` on the selected instances and it (iv) outputs the identifiers of stopped instances. The script then (v) waits for a customisable amount of time, to allow the propagation of the cascading failures resulting from having stopped some service instances. Finally, the script (vi) undeploys the instance of *Sock Pong* by executing `docker-compose down`. Given the structure of the application and given how *Pong* instances behave, steps (i–vi) ensure that the failure cascades propagate towards the instance of *Edge Router*. We can hence then run the PoC of WHY to explain the failure of the instance of *Edge Router*.

We executed the monkey testing script on a Arch Linux machine with an Intel i7 CPU and 16 GB of RAM for 30 times. We then run to the PoC of WHY to explain the failure of the instance of *Edge Router* in each of the 30 corresponding application logs. We compared the graphs generated by WHY with the ground truth given by the events logged in the 30 runs of the application. As a result, we observed that WHY was always generating a causality graph modelling the failure cascades that actually happened in each run of the application.

To ease repeating our tests/performing new ones, the Python script and the obtained application logs are publicly available at https://git.io/Jtb79.

7   Related Work

Various existing solutions tackle the rigorous engineering of failures in complex systems [6]. For instance, [26], and [34] exploit machine learning to isolate possible failures in the sources of an application. [3,16], and [28] instead enable obtaining fault-free application by iteratively refining them by identifying and handling the failures that may occur. All such solutions differ from ours as they aim at obtaining applications that "never fail", because their potential failures have already been identified and properly handled. Our methodology is instead more recovery-oriented [7]: we consider applications where services can possibly fail and we enable explaining why failures affected some services.

[12] applies adaptive interventional debugging to identify and resolve possible failures in database-backed applications. [12] shares our baseline ideas of identifying failure causalities and of explicitly modelling the possible causes for a failure to happen. At the same time, [12] differs from our methodology as it focuses only on database-backed applications, while we enable analysing microservice-based applications. Moreover, also [12] aims at obtaining applications that "never fail", while our methodology considers applications where services can possibly fail.

In the latter perspective, the solutions proposed in [10,11], and [13] are closer to ours. They all explicitly represent the failures that can possibly happen in multi-service applications. They also support the development —at design-time— of countermeasures to recover applications from failures, in the form of recovery plans to be enacted when failures are monitored at run-time. They however differ from our methodology as they focus on explicitly modelled failures, which have to be foreseen. We instead enable explaining why the services in an application failed, even if this was due to unforeseen reasons, to help operators to adopt countermeasures to limit the identified cascading failures.

Another approach worth mentioning is [8], which proposes a decentralised solution for identifying failures in component-based systems. Application components are equipped with local diagnosers, which monitor their failures and enact recovery actions. Similarly to our methodology, [8] considers possible cascading failures. Whenever a failure is diagnosed in a component, [8] interacts with the local diagnosers of the components interacting with the failed component to proactively check whether they have also failed. [8] differs from our methodology since inter-component dependencies are used to coordinate the online monitoring of failures. We instead provide an explanation the possible causes for a failure to happen, in the form of a causality graph obtained from application logs.

In this perspective, we are closer to existing approaches for determining failure root causes in microservice-based applications. For instance, [36] illustrates how to enact delta debugging on a microservice-based application to minimize the possible set of circumstances (the "deltas") that could have generated a functional failure in a service. [36] hence shares our objective of helping application operators to understand why a given service failed, but at the same time it is limited by the observability of the "deltas" in the context where the application is being run. We instead analyse the logs of the application services themselves, which are available in any context where the application can run.

[4,17,18,21,33], and [37] provide different solutions to determine the root causes of performance anomalies (which are symptoms of possible failures) in microservice-based applications, all based on the offline analysis of monitored performance metrics. [9,19,20], and [29] instead analyse monitored performance metrics while a microservice-based application is running, to detect possible performance anomalies and their root causes. Similarly to our methodology, all the above solutions can determine whether the issue affecting a service is due to the service itself or to the services it depends on. However, they all differ from our methodology since they focus on determining the root causes of the possible symptoms of failures (viz., performance anomalies) with correlation-based analysis or machine learning on monitored performance metrics. We instead consider the failures explicitly logged by the application services, and we propose a model-based methodology to determine the causalities among such failures.

In summary, to the best of our knowledge, ours is the first methodology geared towards identifying the possible reasons why functional (and possibly unforeseen) failures affected a microservice-based application. It is also the first concrete solution following the baseline ideas in [5], where we first discussed the potentials of management protocols to explain failure causalities—but without providing any concretely usable solution.

8   Conclusions

We have presented a methodology for automatically identifying failure causalities in microservice-based applications, This is done by running the algorithm WHY, for which we also provided a PoC implementation, which we used to determine the causes for failures in our controlled experiments and monkey testing.

The causality graphs obtained from WHY can be used by application operators as a sort of "map" guiding their analysis of the possibly huge amount of distributed application logs, when needing to understand why a given cascade of failures happened. Such causality graph indeed allows application operators to only focus on the logged events that could have truly been involved in a cascade of failures. For each possibly involved event, they then have to just search for the corresponding timestamp in the logs of the corresponding service instance. This is of practical value, as it enables considering only one event for each service instance that could have truly contributed to the cascading failures, rather than having to delve through the vary many events logged by possibly involved service instances before the cascading failures happened.

Continuous Integration/Continous Deployment [15] (CI/CD) could also benefit from our model-based methodology, which could be integrated with CI/CD pipelines to automatically identify the cascading failures that have generated a monitored failure in a running application. The identified cascading failures could then be limited by adopting suitable countermeasures, e.g., by including circuit breakers or bulkheads limiting failure propagation. Following CI/CD principles [15], such circuit breakers or bulkheads could then be deployed while the application continues to run. As future work, we plan to automate this by (i) integrating our methodology with CI/CD pipelines and by (ii) devising a support system exploiting the outcomes of our methodology to suggest how to refactor an application to mitigate the effects of identified cascading failures.

In this perspective, we also plan to further support application developers by extending our analysis to elicit all possible service failures in a microservice-based application and the causal relations among them. This could be done, for instance, by integrating our methodology with a technique to stress-test an application by injecting different failures on different services in different runs, and with fine-grained monitoring solutions, like those in [27] and [32], for instance. WHY could then be exploited to explain the different failures monitored in the different runs, and by then combining the obtained causality graphs in a single modelling of the possible service failures and their causalities. The obtained modelling would help in deciding whether/how to enact countermeasures mitigating the failure cascades that could possibly occur in their applications.

Finally, we plan to extend the applicability of our methodology. For instance, we shall investigate whether and how to automate the configuration of log-enabled Docker Compose files (Sect. 5). Other examples are considering replication strategies while explaining cascading failures, and enabling to apply our methodology even when some events (like state changes or operation invocations) have not been logged, when multiple services run in a same virtual environment, and when the application topology or the behavior of the application services therein dynamically change over time.

References

1. Basiri, A., et al.: Chaos engineering. IEEE Softw. **33**(3), 35–41 (2016)
2. Bergmayr, A., et al.: A systematic review of cloud modeling languages. ACM Comput. Surv. **51**(1), 1–38 (2018)
3. Betin Can, A., Bultan, T., Lindvall, M., Lux, B., Topp, S.: Eliminating synchronization faults in air traffic control software via design for verification with concurrency controllers. Autom. Softw. Eng. **14**(2), 129–178 (2007)
4. Brandón, A., Solé, M., Huélamo, A., Solans, D., Pérez, M.S., Muntés-Mulero, V.: Graph-based root cause analysis for service-oriented and microservice architectures. J. Syst. Softw. **159**, 110432 (2020)
5. Brogi, A., Soldani, J.: Identifying failure causalities in multi-component applications. In: Camara, J., Steffen, M. (eds.) SEFM 2019. LNCS, vol. 12226, pp. 226–235. Springer, Cham (2020). https://doi.org/10.1007/978-3-030-57506-9_17
6. Butler, M., Jones, C.B., Romanovsky, A., Troubitsyna, E. (eds.): Rigorous Development of Complex Fault-Tolerant Systems. LNCS, vol. 4157. Springer, Heidelberg (2006). https://doi.org/10.1007/11916246
7. Candea, G., Brown, A.B., Fox, A., Patterson, D.: Recovery-oriented computing: building multitier dependability. Computer **37**(11), 60–67 (2004)
8. Console, L., Picardi, C., Dupré, D.T.: A framework for decentralized qualitative model-based diagnosis. In: 20th International Joint Conference on Artificial Intelligence (IJCAI 2007), pp. 286–291 (2007)
9. Du, Q., Xie, T., He, Y.: Anomaly detection and diagnosis for container-based microservices with performance monitoring. In: Vaidya, J., Li, J. (eds.) ICA3PP 2018. LNCS, vol. 11337, pp. 560–572. Springer, Cham (2018). https://doi.org/10.1007/978-3-030-05063-4_42
10. Durán, F., Salaün, G.: Robust and reliable reconfiguration of cloud applications. J. Syst. Softw. **122**(C), 524–537 (2016)
11. Etchevers, X., Salaün, G., Boyer, F., Coupaye, T., De Palma, N.: Reliable self-deployment of distributed cloud applications. Softw. Pract. Experience **47**(1), 3–20 (2017)
12. Fariha, A., Nath, S., Meliou, A.: Causality-guided adaptive interventional debugging. In: 2020 ACM SIGMOD International Conference on Management of Data, pp. 431–446. ACM (2020)
13. Friedrich, G., Fugini, M.G., Mussi, E., Pernici, B., Tagni, G.: Exception handling for repair in service-based processes. IEEE Trans. Softw. Eng. **36**(2), 198–215 (2010)
14. Gray, J.: Why do computers stop and what can be done about it? TR 85.7, PN87614, Tandem Computers (1985)
15. Humble, J., Farley, D.: Continuous Delivery: Reliable Software Releases through Build, Test, and Deployment Automation. Addison-Wesley Professional, Boston (2010)
16. Johnsen, E., Owe, O., Munthe-Kaas, E., Vain, J.: Incremental fault-tolerant design in an object-oriented setting. In: 2nd Asia-Pacific Conference on Quality Software, p. 223. APAQS, IEEE Computer Society (2001)

17. Kim, M., Sumbaly, R., Shah, S.: Root cause detection in a service-oriented architecture. SIGMETRICS Perform. Eval. Rev. **41**(1), 93–104 (2013)
18. Lin, J., Chen, P., Zheng, Z.: Microscope: pinpoint performance issues with causal graphs in micro-service environments. In: Pahl, C., Vukovic, M., Yin, J., Yu, Q. (eds.) ICSOC 2018. LNCS, vol. 11236, pp. 3–20. Springer, Cham (2018). https://doi.org/10.1007/978-3-030-03596-9_1
19. Liu, P., et al.: Unsupervised detection of microservice trace anomalies through service-level deep Bayesian networks. In: 2020 IEEE 31st International Symposium on Software Reliability Engineering (ISSRE), pp. 48–58 (2020)
20. Ma, M., Lin, W., Pan, D., Wang, P.: Self-adaptive root cause diagnosis for large-scale microservice architecture. IEEE Trans. Serv. Comput. (2020, in press)
21. Meng, Y., et al.: Localizing failure root causes in a microservice through causality inference. In: 2020 IEEE/ACM International Symposium on Quality of Service (IWQoS), pp. 1–10 (2020)
22. Newman, S.: Building Microservices. O'Reilly Media Inc., Newton (2015)
23. Nygard, M.: Release It! Pragmatic Bookshelf, Design and Deploy Production-Ready Software (2007)
24. OASIS: TOSCA Simple Profile in YAML, version 1.2 (2019)
25. Pahl, C., Jamshidi, P., Zimmermann, O.: Architectural principles for cloud software. ACM Trans. Internet Technol. **18**(2), 1–23 (2018)
26. Peng, Z., Xiao, X., Hu, G., Kumar Sangaiah, A., Atiquzzaman, M., Xia, S.: ABFL: an autoencoder based practical approach for software fault localization. Inf. Sci. **510**, 108–121 (2020)
27. Phipathananunth, C., Bunyakiati, P.: Synthetic runtime monitoring of microservices software architecture. In: 2018 IEEE 42nd Annual Computer Software and Applications Conference (COMPSAC), vol. 02, pp. 448–453 (2018)
28. Qiang, W., Yan, L., Bliudze, S., Xiaoguang, M.: Automatic fault localization for BIP. In: Li, X., Liu, Z., Yi, W. (eds.) SETTA 2015. LNCS, vol. 9409, pp. 277–283. Springer, Cham (2015). https://doi.org/10.1007/978-3-319-25942-0_18
29. Samir, A., Pahl, C.: DLA: detecting and localizing anomalies in containerized microservice architectures using Markov models. In: 2019 7th International Conference on Future Internet of Things and Cloud (FiCloud), pp. 205–213 (2019)
30. Soldani, J., Cameriero, M., Brogi, A.: Modelling and analysing replica- and fault-aware management of horizontally scalable applications, Submitted for publication
31. Soldani, J., Tamburri, D.A., Van Den Heuvel, W.J.: The pains and gains of microservices: a systematic grey literature review. J. Syst. Softw. **146**, 215–232 (2018)
32. Tamburri, D.A., Miglierina, M., Nitto, E.D.: Cloud applications monitoring: an industrial study. Inf. Softw. Technol. **127**, 106376 (2020)
33. Wu, L., Tordsson, J., Elmroth, E., Kao, O.: MicroRCA: root cause localization of performance issues in microservices. In: NOMS 2020-2020 IEEE/IFIP Network Operations and Management Symposium, pp. 1–9 (2020)
34. Zakari, A., Lee, S.P.: Simultaneous isolation of software faults for effective fault localization. In: 2019 IEEE 15th Int. Colloquium on Signal Processing its Applications (CSPA), pp. 16–20 (2019)
35. Zhou, X., et al.: Fault analysis and debugging of microservice systems: Industrial survey, benchmark system, and empirical study. IEEE Trans. Softw. Eng. 1–18 (2018)

36. Zhou, X., et al.: Delta debugging microservice systems with parallel optimization. IEEE Trans. Serv. Comput. (2019, in press)
37. Zhou, X., et al.: Latent error prediction and fault localization for microservice applications by learning from system trace logs. In: 2019 27th ACM Joint Meeting on European Software Engineering Conference and Symposium on the Foundations of Software Engineering. ESEC/FSE 2019, pp. 683–694. ACM (2019)

Which RESTful API Design Rules Are Important and How Do They Improve Software Quality? A Delphi Study with Industry Experts

Sebastian Kotstein[1]([⊠])[iD] and Justus Bogner[2][iD]

[1] Herman Hollerith Zentrum, Reutlingen University, Böblingen, Germany
`sebastian.kotstein@reutlingen-university.de`
[2] Institute of Software Engineering, University of Stuttgart, Stuttgart, Germany
`justus.bogner@iste.uni-stuttgart.de`

Abstract. Several studies analyzed existing Web APIs against the constraints of REST to estimate the degree of REST compliance among state-of-the-art APIs. These studies revealed that only a small number of Web APIs are truly RESTful. Moreover, identified mismatches between theoretical REST concepts and practical implementations lead us to believe that practitioners perceive many rules and best practices aligned with these REST concepts differently in terms of their importance and impact on software quality. We therefore conducted a Delphi study in which we confronted eight Web API experts from industry with a catalog of 82 REST API design rules. For each rule, we let them rate its importance and software quality impact. As consensus, our experts rated 28 rules with high, 17 with medium, and 37 with low importance. Moreover, they perceived usability, maintainability, and compatibility as the most impacted quality attributes. The detailed analysis revealed that the experts saw rules for reaching Richardson maturity level 2 as critical, while reaching level 3 was less important. As the acquired consensus data may serve as valuable input for designing a tool-supported approach for the automatic quality evaluation of RESTful APIs, we briefly discuss requirements for such an approach and comment on the applicability of the most important rules.

Keywords: REST APIs · Design rules · Software quality · Delphi study

1 Introduction

Around 2000, Roy T. Fielding formalized the idea of "how a well-designed Web application behaves" by introducing a novel architectural style that he named "Representational State Transfer" (REST) [5]. In detail, he defined REST as a set of constraints that a Web application must fulfill to improve several quality attributes like scalability, efficiency, and reliability. The motivation for this

© Springer Nature Switzerland AG 2021
J. Barzen (Ed.): SummerSOC 2021, CCIS 1429, pp. 154–173, 2021.
https://doi.org/10.1007/978-3-030-87568-8_10

was the concern that the Web as an open platform, i.e. not being under the control of a central entity, would not scale without rules and constraints to govern interactions and information exchanges [5,13].

Although REST mainly relies on well-established Web standards like Uniform Resource Identifiers (URIs) and is aligned with the features of the Hypertext Transfer Protocol (HTTP), REST and its constraints are not an official standard [23]. Moreover, Fielding's initial formulation of REST and its constraints describe the recommended behavior of a Web application from a high-level perspective instead of providing developers with detailed instructions on how to achieve this behavior. As a consequence, REST leaves room for various interpretations [21] and different design decisions when implementing Web applications [23]. With the popularity of RESTful services in industry [1,24] and the rapid growth of publicly available Web applications and APIs over the last two decades (see e.g. the number of newly registered APIs per year at *Programmable Web*[1]), the variety of different "REST" designs were growing as well.

The popularity, diversity, and growing complexity of Web APIs make their quality evaluation and assurance very important. This is often manual work based on design rules or best practices, e.g. derived from the original REST constraints, and several works proposed guidance for developers when designing and implementing Web APIs [13,17,20]. At the same time, multiple studies analyzed the degree of REST compliance among existing real-world APIs by systematically comparing them against interface characteristics deduced from REST best practices and constraints [14,21,23]. Many of these studies concluded that only a small number of existing Web APIs is indeed *RESTful*, which means that the majority of Web APIs do not satisfy all required constraints. Nevertheless, many of the APIs classified as non REST-compliant claim to be RESTful [14], which suggests that the term "REST" may have become a synonym for every type of API that simply offers its functionality through URIs and the HTTP [21,26].

The large body of existing rules and best practices may also make it difficult for practitioners to select the most important ones. Simultaneously, the fact that only a small number of real-world APIs seems to adhere to rules and best practices for REST-compliant APIs leads us to believe that practitioners perceive many rules aligned with Fielding's REST constraints differently in terms of their importance and impact on software quality. We therefore see the need for an investigation from the perspective of industry practitioners. For that purpose, we conducted a Delphi study in which we confronted eight Web API experts from industry with a catalog of REST API design rules and asked them how they rate the importance and software quality impact of each rule. This study should answer the following research questions (RQs):

RQ1: Which design rules for RESTful APIs do practitioners perceive as important?

RQ2: How do practitioners perceive the impact of RESTful API design rules on software quality?

---

[1] https://www.programmableweb.com.

These results should provide valuable input for creating an approach for the automatic rule-based quality evaluation of real-world Web APIs. More precisely, tool support to automatically evaluate the software quality of APIs based on their conformance to important rules would assist practitioners in designing better RESTful APIs. Based on the results, we briefly discuss requirements for such an approach and comment on the applicability of the most important rules.

The remaining paper is organized as follows: as a basis for the selection of rules, we discuss the architectural style REST as well as existing literature about rules and best practices in Sect. 2. Furthermore, we present existing Web API analysis approaches, which might serve as a foundation for an automatic rule-based quality evaluation approach. Section 3 explains the details of our study design. In Sect. 4, we present the results of our study and discuss their interpretation and implications in Sect. 5. Finally, we describe threats to the validity of our study (Sect. 6) and close with a conclusion (Sect. 7).

2   Background and Related Work

In this section, we discuss the principles of the architectural style REST and the reasons why this style may lead to different interpretations and design decisions. To make a selection of rules and best practices for our study, we briefly discuss existing literature presenting rules and best practices for RESTful API design. Finally, we mention existing approaches for systematic Web API analysis that might serve as a foundation for automatic rule-based quality evaluation.

2.1   REST as an Architectural Style

In 2000, as part of his PhD dissertation [5], Fielding introduced REST as an architectural style that describes how distributed hypermedia systems like the World Wide Web (WWW) are designed and operated [26]. On the one hand, REST is a blueprint formalizing the application of existing Web techniques and standards like URIs and the HTTP [26]. On the other hand, it serves as a guideline for designing new applications such that they adopt these well-established Web concepts successfully and meet several quality attributes like scalability, efficiency, and reliability [4].

Fielding presented REST as a framework of architectural constraints that describe the proper use of these existing Web techniques and standards and, therefore, express several design decisions for building Web applications (e.g. Web APIs). In detail, he named six core constraints that a Web application must fulfill to be RESTful, namely *Client-Server, Layered System, Stateless Communication, Cache, Code-On-Demand,* and *Uniform Interface* [4]. Moreover, Fielding complemented the *Uniform Interface* by four additional constraints: *Identification of Resources, Manipulation of Resources Through Representations, Self-Descriptive Messages,* and *Hypermedia as the Engine of Application State* (HATEOAS) [4]. For detailed descriptions of these constraints, we refer to [4,6], and [13].

While some constraints like *Client-Server* and *Layered System* are automatically fulfilled because they are fundamental concepts of the WWW architecture, the concepts behind URIs and the HTTP promote other constraints like *Cache* and *Uniform Interface*, but cannot enforce their compliance [6]. In fact, a developer can ignore or misuse given mechanisms of URIs and the HTTP, which might result in a violation of these constraints. Especially in Web API design, adhering to *Uniform Interface* and its four additional constraints is crucial, since this enables developers to reuse existing client code for different APIs. Individual interface styles, however, force client-side developers to implement individual clients [14]. In our point of view, especially the *Uniform Interface* constraint and its four additional constraints leave developers too much room for different interpretations, thereby leading to various interface designs in practice.

2.2 Best Practices for REST

While Fielding's formal description of REST and its constraints mainly focus on the recommended behavior of a Web application and the naming of quality attributes that can be achieved by satisfying these constraints, several works examined the principles of REST. They translated them into rules and best practices to guide developers towards good RESTful design with instructions on how to satisfy them. The existing literature in this field includes scientific articles, e.g. by Pautasso [19], Petrillo et al. [20], and Palma et al. [16,17], as well as textbooks, e.g. by Richardson and Ruby [22], Massé [13], and Webber et al. [26]. While both [22] and [26] proposed several best practices embedded into continuous guides for designing and implementing REST APIs, Massé [13] presented a catalog of 82 rules, where each rules is described concisely and is often complemented by short examples and suggestions for its implementation. Petrillo et al. [20] compiled and presented a similar catalog, with rules inspired by the work of [13], but also incorporating rules and best practices from [22] and other sources. Unsurprisingly, most of the rules and best practices in the mentioned literature focus on *Uniform Interface* and its four additional constraints.

In addition to rules and best practices for REST API design, Leonard Richardson developed a maturity model [12] that allows one to estimate the degree of REST compliance of a Web API. More precisely, the model consists of four levels of maturity that incorporate the principles of REST:

- Web APIs complying with level 0 provide their functionality over a single endpoint (URI). Moreover, they use the HTTP solely as a transport protocol for tunneling requests through this endpoint by using HTTP POST and without leveraging any other Web mechanisms. SOAP and XML-RPC services typically rely on level 0.
- At level 1, Web APIs use the concept of resources, which means that they expose different endpoints (URIs) for different resources. However, at level 1, operations are still identified via URIs or specified in the request payload rather than using different HTTP methods for different operations.

- Web APIs at level 2 use HTTP mechanisms and semantics including different verbs for different operations as well as the interpretation of status codes. Level 2 is partially aligned with the *Uniform Interface* constraint of REST.
- Level 3 Web APIs embed hypermedia controls into responses to advertise semantic relations between resources and to guide a client through the application. This final level of the maturity model addresses the HATEOAS constraint of REST.

2.3   Studies for the Evaluation of Web APIs

Several publications analyzed the quality or conformity of existing RESTful APIs or proposed automatic approaches for their evaluation.

In [21], Renzel et al. analyzed the 20 most popular RESTful Web services listed in *ProgrammableWeb* in May 2011. For that purpose, they created a catalog of 17 metrics, which are based on the REST architecture style, relevant features of the HTTP, as well as characteristics and best practices of REST as described by [22]. This catalog contains metrics like the number of different HTTP methods used in an API or whether links are embedded into representations or not. For each of these 20 APIs, they manually read the API service description to capture the values of these metrics. The analysis revealed that nearly none of the 20 Web services were indeed RESTful (only four Web services were HATEOAS-compliant, for instance). Moreover, the study identified differences in terms of adaption and interpretation of REST principles among the analyzed Web services.

Palma et al. introduced an approach for the automatic detection of REST patterns and antipatterns called *SODA-R* [16]. They identified five patterns and eight antipatterns for REST and defined heuristics for detecting them. Palma et al. translated these heuristics into algorithms that automatically detect these (anti-)patterns on a set of APIs by invoking their interfaces. The tests against 12 real-world REST APIs revealed that developers tend to use customized headers negatively affecting the *Uniform Interface*, in particular, the *Self-Descriptive Messages* constraint. Moreover, eight out of 12 APIs did not embed hyperlinks into response payloads, thereby violating HATEOAS.

Rodríguez et al. [23] analyzed more than 78 GB of HTTP network traffic to gain insights into the use of best practices when designing Web APIs. Since the analyzed data contained any kind of Web-based traffic, they used API-specific heuristics to extract REST API related requests and responses and identified the relevant APIs based on this data. Then, they validated the extracted requests and responses against 18 heuristics, which they deduced from design principles and best practices introduced in [13,18,19]. Moreover, they mapped the heuristics to the levels of the Richardson maturity model [12] to estimate the level of compliance of the identified APIs. According to the paper, only a few APIs reached level 3 of the maturity model (embedded hyperlinks into resource representations), while the majority of APIs complied with level 2.

Petrillo et al. of [20] compiled a catalog of 73 best practices, which we already mentioned in Sect. 2.2. Based on this catalog, they manually analyzed the documentations of three cloud provider APIs and determined whether the respective cloud provider fulfilled these best practices or not. Although all three APIs fulfilled only between 56% and 66% of the best practices, Petrillo et al. assessed their maturity level as acceptable.

In [17], Palma et al. presented an approach for the detection of linguistic patterns and antipatterns addressing the URI structure of REST APIs and their compliance with best practices of REST. They tested the approach with 18 real-world APIs by invoking their endpoints and analyzing their documentations. Most of the analyzed APIs used appropriate resource names and did not use verbs within URI paths, which confirms the acceptance of this best practice. However, URI paths often did not convey hierarchical structures as it should be according to another best practice.

An extensive study for investigating the quality of real-world Web APIs and estimating the level of REST compliance was presented by Neumann et al. in [14]. The authors compared the documentations of 500 APIs claiming to be RESTful against 26 features reflecting REST principles and best practices deduced from [13,17,20,21,23] and other works. Similar like Renzel et al. [21], the authors identified a very heterogeneous adoption of REST. Especially the *Uniform Interface* constraint was barely adopted. The study came to the result that only four APIs (0.8%) fully complied with REST.

The aforementioned studies primarily focus on the analysis of Web API compliance with rules, features, and best practices aligned with the principles and constraints of REST. However, there are also two approaches by Haupt et al. [7] and Bogner et al. [2]. Rather than using best practices or rules, they analyzed Web APIs based on a set of interface characteristics and calculated metrics that provide insights about the general structure and quality of Web APIs. Both approaches run completely automatically based on machine-readable API documentation, which might be interesting for our rule-based quality evaluation approach. In detail, Haupt et al. [7] introduced a framework to provide insights about the structure of a REST API by automatically analyzing its service description. Bogner et al. [2] proposed a modular framework called *RESTful API Metric Analyzer (RAMA)* that calculates maintainability metrics from service descriptions and enables the automatic evaluation of REST APIs. Moreover, it converts the content of a service description into a canonical meta-model, which is used for the subsequent evaluation against a set of metrics.

By analyzing real-world Web APIs, the mentioned studies revealed that only a small number of Web APIs adheres to the rules and best practices of REST and, therefore, are truly RESTful. While these studies identified mismatches between theoretical concepts of REST and implementations by examining the work of developers, the reasons for these mismatches between theory and practice remain unclear. To the best of our knowledge, the opinions of developers about theoretical REST principles as well as rules and best practices for REST API design have not been investigated so far. We therefore see the need for a study from the perspective of industry practitioners: instead of analyzing their work as previous studies did, we directly want to confront them with rules and best practices for REST API design and query their perceived importance as well as the perceived impact on software quality. Furthermore, these results should enable rule-based quality evaluations of Web APIs relying not only on rules and best practices originating from theory but also incorporating opinions of practitioners to evaluate a Web API from a more practical point of view.

3   Research Design

In this section, we describe our followed methodology. We first present a general overview of our research process and then describe more design details of the most important phase, the conducted Delphi study with industry experts. For transparency and replicability, we make the most important study artifacts available online.[2]

3.1   General Process

This research took place in several distinct stages (see Fig. 1). In an initial step, we thoroughly analyzed existing rule catalogs and best practices for REST API design as well as approaches for systematic Web API analysis and related work in this area (see Sect. 2). Based on the results, we selected a comprehensive list of rules (namely the catalog from Massé [13]) and created a detailed study protocol with the necessary materials. We also recruited industry experts as participants and scheduled the study execution with them. The Delphi study took place over a period of roughly nine weeks between June and August 2020. As results, this study produced – for each rule – a consensus on its perceived importance (RQ1) as well as the quality attributes that experts perceived as positively impacted by adhering to it (RQ2). Finally, we analyzed the automation potential of this consensus data, i.e. we investigated the important rules from the perspective of using them in a tool-supported approach for the rule-based quality evaluation of RESTful APIs.

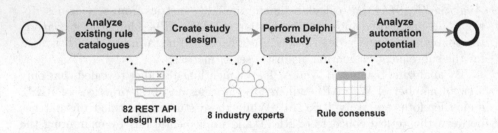

Fig. 1. Overview of the research process

---

[2] https://doi.org/10.5281/zenodo.4643906.

3.2 Delphi Study

While one-time interviews or a survey could have been used to gather relevant data for RQ1 and RQ2, we instead decided to employ the Delphi method [3], a structured communication approach originally designed as a forecasting technique by the RAND corporation in the 1950s. Within several iterations, individual expert opinions and rationales for the same set of questions are collected without experts getting in direct contact with each other, thereby avoiding issues with group dynamics. As input for the next round, participants get the anonymous results from their peers, often in aggregated form, and are encouraged to rethink their previous answers. Iterations are stopped once sufficient consensus has been reached. Dalkey and Helmer, two of the original authors, describe the advantages of this approach as follows [3]: "The method [...] appears to be more conducive to independent thought on the part of the experts and to aid them in the gradual formation of a considered opinion. Direct confrontation, on the other hand, all too often induces the hasty formulation of preconceived notions, an inclination to close one's mind to novel ideas, a tendency to defend a stand once taken, or, alternatively and sometimes alternately, a predisposition to be swayed by persuasively stated opinions of others." Delphi studies can be conducted with different objectives and several methodological variations exist. The method has been successfully used as a consensus technique in both information systems [15] and software engineering [11] research.

In our study, the objectives were to reach consensus on the importance of RESTful API design rules (RQ1) and their impact on software quality (RQ2). For each RQ, we conducted a separate Delphi process with the same experts.

Study Objects. The objects of this study were the 82 design rules for RESTful APIs compiled by Massé [13]. While several catalogs of design rules or best practices have been proposed in this area (see Sect. 2), Massé's collection comprises the vast majority of frequently mentioned rules in diverse areas. It is a comprehensive collection of industrial REST API design knowledge, which has also been cited over 440 times in scientific literature[3]. Massé organized the 82 rules nicely into five categories, namely *Interaction Design with HTTP* (29), *Identifier Design with URIs* (16), *Metadata Design* (15), *Representation Design* (13), and *Client Concerns* (9), and illustrated them with helpful examples and implementation suggestions. This pragmatic presentation makes the rules very actionable for practitioners, but also well suited for our Delphi study. Massé relied on RFC 2119[4] to incorporate a level of rule importance, in particular the three modifiers may, should, and must, optionally combined with not. For example, a rule from *Interaction Design with HTTP* prescribes that "22: POST must be used to create a new resource in a collection". Another example from *Representation Design* states that "73: A consistent form should be used to represent error responses".

---

[3] According to Google Scholar (https://scholar.google.com) in March, 2021.
[4] https://tools.ietf.org/html/rfc2119.

Study Participants. For our study participants, we set out the following requirements: (i) at least three years of experience with RESTful APIs, (ii) industry practitioners with a technical background, and (iii) from several different companies or at least divisions. This ensured that participants had sufficient practical experience and came from different backgrounds to avoid a single company-specific perspective. We used convenience sampling to recruit participants via our personal industry network and further referrals. While this may introduce some bias, it also ensured that we could rely on the participants' expertise and time commitment to the study. In the end, we were able to recruit eight participants (Table 1) with REST-related professional experience between six and 15 years (median: 11.5 years). They were from four different global IT enterprises, where they worked in seven different divisions. All participants were located in Germany.

Table 1. Delphi study participant demographics (PID: participant ID, CID: company ID, DID: company division ID)

PID	CID	Domain	# of employees	DID	REST exp. (years)
1	C1	Software & IT Services	100k–150k	D1	6
2				D2	15
3				D2	7
4				D3	13
5	C2	Software & IT Services	50k–100k	D4	6
6				D5	11
7	C3	Telecommunications	200k–250k	D6	15
8	C4	Technology & Manufact.	250k–300k	D7	12

Study Materials and Measurements. Several artifacts were used in this study. To get familiar with the rules and as a source for more details on specific rules, all participants received a digital copy of Massé's *REST API Design Rulebook*. Additionally, we extracted the rules and their description. We used this content to create Excel spreadsheets to gather participants' input. The spreadsheets also contained concrete instructions for participants and a form to gather their demographics. For RQ1, the spreadsheet contained a list of all 82 rules with a field to rate the perceived importance of each rule. Participants had to use a 3-point ordinal scale with the labels `low`, `medium`, and `high`. For RQ2, a similar spreadsheet was used, but this time with fields to associate a rule with positive impact on several different quality attributes (QAs). We used the eight top-level attributes from ISO 25010 [9], i.e. functional suitability, performance efficiency, compatibility, usability, reliability, security, maintainability, and portability. To ensure a common understanding, participants received a link to a website with descriptions about the standard[5]. For each rule, participants had to select which

---

[5] https://iso25000.com/index.php/en/iso-25000-standards/iso-25010.

QAs where positively impacted by adhering to it. The association was binary, i.e. a rule could either affect a specific QA (1) or not (0). Multi-selection was possible, i.e. a rule could affect several QAs. Both spreadsheets also contained tabs to provide the aggregated responses of the previous iteration for each rule, i.e. the number of experts who voted for the different levels of importance or the different associated QAs respectively.

Lastly, we created an analysis spreadsheet to summarize the responses and calculate *consensus* and *stability*. Since required percentage agreements of 70% and greater are common in Delphi studies [25], we defined 87.5% as consensus condition for a rule, i.e. only one of the eight experts could rate it differently than the rest. For the impact on software quality, agreement therefore meant that the exact same QAs had to be selected by seven experts. Additionally, we considered a stopping condition based on rating stability to avoid being deadlocked in iterations without significant change of votes [8]. As it is commonly used in Delphi studies, we chose Cohen's kappa coefficient (κ) to calculate the group stability between two iterations [10]. Since the ratings for rule importance were on an ordinal scale, we used a weighted kappa variant [8], i.e. the weight for changing your vote from low to high or vice versa was 2, while e.g. changing from medium to high only had a weight of 1. We used the standard variant for the impact on software quality. Landis and Koch [10] label κ-values between 0.81 and 1.00 as "almost perfect" agreement. While we did not define a strict stopping threshold and the stability has to be interpreted in conjunction with the percentage agreement, κ-values of 0.90 and greater for at least two iterations indicate that it may be advisable to stop the process.

Study Execution. Before starting the regular Delphi iterations, we scheduled personal meetings with participants to explain study procedure and provided materials. Furthermore, we addressed open questions and communicated the response timelines. We also encouraged participants to contact the study lead in case of uncertainties about the procedure or material during the iterations. After these meetings, the two consecutive Delphi processes were conducted (see Fig. 2).

The goal of the first Delphi process was to reach consensus on the perceived importance of the 82 REST API design rules (RQ1). After the first iteration, participants were in agreement about 42 of the 82 rules (51.22%). To start the second iteration, we provided them with the aggregated results from their peers, i.e. the number of times each level of importance had been chosen for a rule. Based on this feedback, participants were already able to reach full consensus on the 82 rules after two iterations, i.e. κ-based stopping was not necessary.

The goal of the second Delphi process was to reach consensus on the perceived positive rule impact on different software QAs (RQ2). To reduce the cognitive load and required effort, we only advanced the 45 rules for which the experts had rated the importance as medium or high to the final stage. Despite the substantially greater rating complexity per rule (choosing 0 or 1 for eight different QAs instead of three different importance levels), experts reached a similar

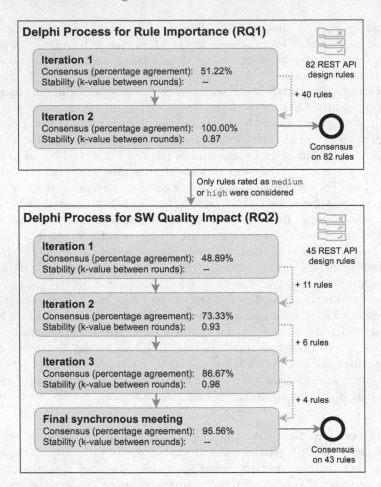

Fig. 2. Overview of the Delphi study

percentage agreement in the first iteration, with consensus on 48.89% of the rules (22 of 45). Based on the provided peer responses, consensus on an additional 11 rules could be reached in iteration #2 (73.33% agreement with a κ-value of 0.93). However, progress slowed down in the third iteration, where agreement on only six more rules could be reached (86.67% agreement, $\kappa = 0.98$). Since κ-values had been greater than 0.90 for two consecutive rounds and only six rules without consensus were left, we decided to end the iterations and instead hold a final synchronous meeting to discuss the remaining rules. While this breaks participant anonymity and might reintroduce group dynamics bias, such meetings can lead to efficient consensus finalization. They are often suggested after the third or even later iterations. All participants agreed to this virtual meeting, which took place over one hour via Microsoft Teams. During the meeting, the study lead first introduced the remaining open topics and the current state of ratings for them. Afterwards, he initiated an open discussion. As a result, consensus could be reached for four of the six rules. The two rules without consensus are "54: Caching should be encouraged" and "61: JSON should be supported for resource representation". In both cases, five experts perceived a positive impact on functional suitability, while three experts could not be convinced by this.

4 Study Results

In this section, we present the aggregated results of the conducted Delphi study, i.e. how important our eight experts judged the rules and how they perceived the rule impact on software quality.

4.1 Perceived Importance of API Design Rules (RQ1)

Of the 82 REST API design rules studied in the first Delphi process, participants rated 37 with low importance (45%), 17 with medium importance (21%), and 28 rules with high importance (34%). In other words, our experts perceived nearly half of the rules as not really important and only one third as very important. Especially rules from the smaller categories *Client Concerns* and *Metadata Design* were rated as less relevant. Most important categories were *Identifier Design with URIs* (50% of rules rated as high) and *Interaction Design with HTTP* (45% of rules rated as high), which together also make up 55% of the total rules. These findings are summarized in Table 2. Table 3 lists all rules with medium importance and Table 4 the ones with high importance.

4.2 Perceived Rule Impact on Software Quality (RQ2)

During the second Delphi process, our experts rated the impact of the 45 rules with medium or high importance on the eight software QAs of ISO 25010. As a result, 10 rules were assigned to one QA, 12 rules to two QAs, 18 rules to three QAs, and the remaining five rules to four different QAs, i.e. a bit more than half of the rules were perceived with a positive impact on three or more QAs. Most associated attributes were *usability* (35), *maintainability* (35), and *compatibility* (26). In many cases, these QAs were impacted by the same rules. Of the 35 rules linked to *usability*, 21 were also selected for *maintainability* and *compatibility*. At the same time, *functional suitability* was only perceived as impacted by seven rules. The remaining attributes were very rarely selected, with *performance efficiency* being associated with three rules, *reliability* and *portability* with one rule each, and *security* with zero rules.

Table 2. Perceived rule importance by category (RQ1), percentages represent the fractions of total rules and fractions within the category respectively

Category	Total # of rules	Importance	# of rules
Identifier design with URIs	16 (20%)	High	8 (50%)
		Medium	5 (31%)
		Low	3 (19%)
Interaction design with HTTP	29 (35%)	High	13 (45%)
		Medium	5 (17%)
		Low	11 (38%)
Representation design	13 (16%)	High	4 (31%)
		Medium	2 (15%)
		Low	7 (54%)
Metadata design	15 (18%)	High	2 (13%)
		Medium	3 (20%)
		Low	10 (67%)
Client concerns	9 (11%)	High	1 (11%)
		Medium	2 (22%)
		Low	6 (67%)

Figure 3 summarizes these findings and also includes the associated rule categories. Our experts especially perceived rules from *Interaction Design with HTTP* with a broad impact on software quality: all 18 rules from this category were associated with three or more QAs, with only five rules from other categories having a similar spread. As the second largest category, *Identifier Design with URIs* (13) was primarily associated with *maintainability* (12) and *usability* (7). Furthermore, *Representation Design* (6) spread fairly evenly among the three most impacted QAs *usability* (6), *compatibility* (5), and *maintainability* (4). Lastly, the rules from *Metadata Design* (5) were the only ones not associated with *maintainability* at all.

5 Discussion

The interpretation of the study results leads to several findings with interesting potential implications for research and practice.

Concerning the importance of rules, we identified substantial differences between Massé's provided categorization and our participants' verdict. In total, Massé classified 10 of the 82 rules with the lowest level may, 50 with should, and 22 with must. Conversely, our participants perceived 45% of proposed rules (37) to be of low importance, among them seven classified as must and 24 as should by Massé. Additionally, they only selected medium for 17 rules, but high importance for 28 rules. Among the latter, Massé classified 15 with should

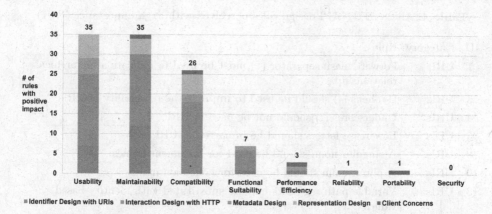

Fig. 3. Perceived rule impact on software quality (RQ2), stacked by rule category

Table 3. All 17 REST API design rules perceived with `medium` importance (RQ1)

ID	Category	Rule
2	URIs	A trailing forward slash (/) should not be included in URIs
6	URIs	File extensions should not be included in URIs
11	URIs	A plural noun should be used for store names
12	URIs	A verb or verb phrase should be used for controller names
15	URIs	The query component of a URI may be used to filter collections or stores
20	HTTP	PUT must be used to both insert and update a stored resource
26	HTTP	200 ("OK") should be used to indicate nonspecific success
31	HTTP	301 ("Moved Permanently") should be used to relocate resources
41	HTTP	406 ("Not Acceptable") must be used when the requested media type cannot be served
43	HTTP	412 ("Precondition Failed") should be used to support conditional operations
47	Meta	Content-Length should be used
51	Meta	Location must be used to specify the URI of a newly created resource
54	Meta	Caching should be encouraged
63	Repr.	XML and other formats may optionally be used for resource representation
69	Repr.	Minimize the number of advertised "entry point" API URIs
79	Client	The query component of a URI should be used to support partial response
82	Client	CORS should be supported to provide multi-origin read/write access from JavaScript

and even one with `may` ("13: Variable path segments may be substituted with identity-based values"). All in all, the verdict of our industry experts was more "extreme". Despite the intuitive expectation that such a consensus technique may lead to a more balanced compromise, participants perceived many more rules as not really important and a few more as very important in comparison

Table 4. All 28 REST API design rules perceived with **high** importance (RQ1)

ID	Category	Rule
1	URIs	Forward slash separator (/) must be used to indicate a hierarchical relationship
3	URIs	Hyphens (-) should be used to improve the readability of URIs
4	URIs	Underscores (_) should not be used in URI
5	URIs	Lowercase letters should be preferred in URI paths
9	URIs	A singular noun should be used for document names
10	URIs	A plural noun should be used for collection names
13	URIs	Variable path segments may be substituted with identity-based values
14	URIs	CRUD function names should not be used in URIs
17	HTTP	GET and POST must not be used to tunnel other request methods
18	HTTP	GET must be used to retrieve a representation of a resource
22	HTTP	POST must be used to create a new resource in a collection
23	HTTP	POST must be used to execute controllers
24	HTTP	DELETE must be used to remove a resource from its parent
27	HTTP	200 ("OK") must not be used to communicate errors in the response body
28	HTTP	201 ("Created") must be used to indicate successful resource creation
30	HTTP	204 ("No Content") should be used when the response body is intentionally empty
34	HTTP	304 ("Not Modified") should be used to preserve bandwidth
37	HTTP	401 ("Unauthorized") must be used when there is a problem with the client's credentials
38	HTTP	403 ("Forbidden") should be used to forbid access regardless of authorization state
44	HTTP	415 ("Unsupported Media Type") must be used when the media type of a request's payload cannot be processed
45	HTTP	500 ("Internal Server Error") should be used to indicate API malfunction
46	Meta	Content-Type must be used
57	Meta	Custom HTTP headers must not be used to change the behavior of HTTP methods
61	Repr.	JSON should be supported for resource representation
71	Repr.	A consistent form should be used to represent media type formats
72	Repr.	A consistent form should be used to represent media type schemas
73	Repr.	A consistent form should be used to represent error responses
74	Client	New URIs should be used to introduce new concepts

to Massé. This may suggest that practitioners prefer a small set of important rules instead of a large collection in which many rules are situational.

When analyzing rules related to the Richardson maturity model [12], participants rated the vast majority of rules necessary to reach *Level 2: HTTP Verbs* with `medium` or `high` importance. This includes the rules 17–25 about the correct usage of HTTP verbs (with the exception of `HEAD`, `OPTIONS`, and interestingly `PUT`), but also the rules 26–45 about correct status code usage. Conversely, nearly all of the rules associated with *Level 3: Hypermedia Controls* were categorized with `low` importance, including the *Representation Design* rules 65–68 and also the HATEOAS rule "70: Links should be used to advertise a resource's available actions in a state-sensitive manner". This indicates that our experts saw maturity level 2 as strongly desirable but also as sufficient, which is consistent with the results of Rodriguez et al. [23] and Neumann et al. [14]. Reaching level 3 may not be a priority for industry, even though it is one of the original RESTful constraints postulated by Fielding [5].

Concerning the rule impact on software quality, the vast majority of rules focus on usability (from an API user perspective), maintainability, or compatibility, with many rules influencing two or even all three of these QAs. Other QAs are less represented or even not at all. While it makes sense that service interface design may not be related to all QAs to the same extent, especially the absence of rules with an influence on performance efficiency and security is surprising. Intuitively, interface design should have a substantial influence on these two QAs, but the focus of Massé's rules seems to lie elsewhere. To evaluate these other QAs, different rule catalogs or approaches are therefore necessary.

Lastly, the greatest benefit should in theory be achieved by adhering to those rules that were both rated with `high` importance and associated with several QAs at once. In our sample, 17 rules with `high` importance impact at least three QAs, 13 of them from the category *Interaction Design with HTTP*, three from *Representation Design* (rules 71–73), and rule 57 from *Metadata Design*. The majority of them are again related to the correct usage of HTTP verbs and status codes, while rules 71–73 are concerned with the consistent structuring of media type formats, media type schemas, and error responses. This again highlights the fact that, in addition to consistency, our participants perceived reaching Richardson maturity level 2 as very important. These 17 rules are primary candidates for automatic evaluation approaches.

As part of our future work, we therefore plan to create tool support to evaluate Web APIs based on design rules. We start with the rules that practitioners assessed with `high` importance. This rule-based evaluation tool should assess the quality of a Web API by reporting detected rule violations and calculating individual scores for the QAs linked to these rules. Abstraction and modularity should guarantee that rules can easily be added, altered, or removed, e.g. according to new empirical data or based on company or team preferences. Reported rule violations should also be actionable for practitioners, e.g. by reporting the concrete location of findings and potential ways to address the violations. The SODA-R approach by Palma et al. [16] may serve as inspiration for our tool from both a methodological as well as a technical point of view. Similar as with SODA-R, for each rule, we will first identify REST properties and then define heuristics that indicate whether the analyzed API satisfies the respective rule. These properties can be either static and obtainable from REST API documentation (e.g. the set of URI templates indicating whether an API contains underscores (_), see rule 4) or dynamic and can be inferred from response data at runtime (e.g. a response status code). In future work, we will translate these heuristics into algorithms that automatically verify rule compliance of Web APIs. The authors of the SODA-R approach introduced heuristics for 13 REST (anti-)patterns [16] that partially overlap with some of our studied rules and, therefore, might be adaptable to our tool (e.g. heuristics for rule 26 and 46). Further heuristics applicable to the rules 4, 5, and 14 are defined by Rodríguez et al. in [23]. Moreover, in a second work by Palma et al. [17], further approaches for detecting violations of the rules 1, 4, 5, 9, 10, and 14 are presented that might be incorporated in our tool.

6   Threats to Validity

Several threats to the validity of this study have to be considered, which we discuss according to dimensions proposed by Wohlin et al. [27].

Construct validity describes the relation between the studied high-level concepts and the operationalized metrics to measure them, in other words, whether we actually measured what we wanted to measure. We studied the importance and software quality impact of design rules and measured how our Delphi participants perceived these concepts, i.e. we collected expert opinions. While experts often have solid experience-based judgment, they can also be wrong, even collectively. As long as our results are clearly treated as expert opinions, this is not an issue, especially since industry perception is important for research in this field. However, once we start to implement some of these rules, we will need more empirical data to judge their effectiveness, preferably non-opinion-based data.

Internal validity is concerned with the applied empirical rigor and potentially hidden factors that may have influenced the results. While we diligently designed our research protocol, adhered to it during the study, and relied on an established consensus technique, it is possible that confounding factors could have partially influenced the results. One such factor could be the misinterpretation of a rule or QA. To mitigate this, all participants received materials describing these concepts, and we encouraged them to ask clarifying questions. We perceive the risk of this threat as very small. A more substantial threat could be that participants knew the original rule importance level, as Massé encoded it directly into the rule text (`may`, `should`, `must`). This could have led to an anchoring effect, thereby biasing participants in their own verdict. However, as shown above, our participants were not afraid to adjust the initial importance level, leading to substantial differences between their and Massé's ratings. Since rewriting the rule texts could have introduced even greater inconsistencies, we still perceive this threat as fairly low. A last threat in this area could be the final synchronous meeting in our Delphi study. By breaking anonymity and facilitating synchronous exchange, we opened the door for potential influences related to group dynamics. Nonetheless, this was only for six of the 82 rules and only related to the QAs, not the importance. Moreover, no complete consensus was reached in this discussion, thereby reducing the probability that most participants yielded to the reputation or behavior of a few.

Lastly, *external validity* refers to the generalization potential of results, i.e. how well the results obtained in our specific setting carry over to different contexts. Only the 82 rules from Massé's catalog were considered in this study. While they provide a comprehensive collection of REST API design knowledge and substantially overlap with other catalogs, they are not the only available source and were published in 2011, i.e. roughly 10 years ago. Moreover, our software quality analysis revealed a focus on usability, maintainability, and compatibility. Rules with different focus and level of abstraction should be considered in future research. Additionally, only eight experts participated in our Delphi study. While they reached strong consensus and were from different companies and divisions, their general contexts were still fairly similar (large IT enterprises, enterprise application development, located in Germany). All in all, it is possible that experts with very different background would come to a different verdict, e.g. when considering the importance of HATEOAS-related rules.

7 Conclusion

In this paper, we presented the results of a Delphi study with the goal to analyze the perceived importance (RQ1) and positive software quality impact (RQ2) of REST API design rules from the perspective of industry practitioners. As study objects, we selected the catalog of 82 REST API design rules compiled by Massé. As participants, we recruited eight industry experts from four different IT companies with between six and 15 years of experiences with REST. As consensus results, our participants rated 37 rules with low importance (45%), 17 with medium importance (21%), and 28 rules with high importance (34%). From the 45 rules with medium or high importance, the quality attributes impacted the most were usability (35), maintainability (35), and compatibility (26). Other attributes from ISO 25010 were less impacted or not at all. Overall, the experts rated the rule importance differently than Massé, choosing the lowest level for many more rules and the highest level for a few more. They also perceived rules for reaching level 2 of the Richardson maturity model as very important, but not the ones for level 3. The acquired consensus data may serve as valuable input for designing a tool-supported approach for the automatic quality evaluation of RESTful APIs. Follow-up research should carefully analyze the automation potential of these rules, e.g. for static or dynamic analysis, as well as how to report and aggregate the findings. For finally creating such rule-based tool support, existing approaches may serve as a methodological or technical basis. To support such endeavors, we make our study artifacts available online (see Footnote 2).

Acknowledgments. We kindly thank Tobias Hallmayer for his assistance with study planning, execution, and analysis. This research was partially funded by the Ministry of Science of Baden-Württemberg, Germany, for the doctoral program *Services Computing* (https://www.services-computing.de/?lang=en).

References

1. Bogner, J., Fritzsch, J., Wagner, S., Zimmermann, A.: Microservices in industry: insights into technologies, characteristics, and software quality. In: 2019 IEEE International Conference on Software Architecture Companion (ICSA-C), Hamburg, Germany, pp. 187–195. IEEE (2019)
2. Bogner, J., Wagner, S., Zimmermann, A.: Collecting service-based maintainability metrics from RESTful API descriptions: static analysis and threshold derivation. In: Muccini, H., et al. (eds.) ECSA 2020. CCIS, vol. 1269, pp. 215–227. Springer, Cham (2020). https://doi.org/10.1007/978-3-030-59155-7_16
3. Dalkey, N., Helmer, O.: An experimental application of the DELPHI method to the use of experts. Manag. Sci. **9**(3), 458–467 (1963)
4. Fielding, R.T., Taylor, R.N.: Principled design of the modern web architecture. ACM Trans. Internet Technol. **2**(2), 115–150 (2002)
5. Fielding, R.T.: Architectural styles and the design of network-based software architectures. Ph.D. thesis, University of California, Irvine, Irvine, CA, USA (2000)
6. Haupt, F., Karastoyanova, D., Leymann, F., Schroth, B.: A model-driven approach for rest compliant services. In: Proceedings of the IEEE International Conference on Web Services (ICWS 2014), pp. 129–136. IEEE (2014)
7. Haupt, F., Leymann, F., Scherer, A., Vukojevic-Haupt, K.: A framework for the structural analysis of REST APIs. In: 2017 IEEE International Conference on Software Architecture (ICSA), Gothenburg, Sweden, pp. 55–58. IEEE (2017)
8. Holey, E.A., Feeley, J.L., Dixon, J., Whittaker, V.J.: An exploration of the use of simple statistics to measure consensus and stability in Delphi studies. BMC Med. Res. Methodol. **7**(1) (2007). Article number: 52. https://doi.org/10.1186/1471-2288-7-52
9. International Organization for Standardization: ISO/IEC 25010 - systems and software engineering - systems and software quality requirements and evaluation (SQuaRE) - system and software quality models (2011)
10. Landis, J.R., Koch, G.G.: The measurement of observer agreement for categorical data. Biometrics **33**(1), 159 (1977)
11. Lilja, K.K., Laakso, K., Palomki, J.: Using the Delphi method. In: PICMET: Proceedings of the Portland International Center for Management of Engineering and Technology, Portland, OR, USA. IEEE (2011)
12. Fowler, M.: Richardson Maturity Model (2010). https://martinfowler.com/articles/richardsonMaturityModel.html. Accessed 26 Mar 2021
13. Masse, M.: REST API Design Rulebook, 1st edn. O'Reilly Media Inc., Sebastopol (2011)
14. Neumann, A., Laranjeiro, N., Bernardino, J.: An analysis of public REST web service APIs. IEEE Trans. Serv. Comput. **PP**(c), 1 (2018)
15. Okoli, C., Pawlowski, S.D.: The Delphi method as a research tool: an example, design considerations and applications. Inf. Manag. **42**(1), 15–29 (2004)

16. Palma, F., Dubois, J., Moha, N., Guéhéneuc, Y.-G.: Detection of REST patterns and antipatterns: a heuristics-based approach. In: Franch, X., Ghose, A.K., Lewis, G.A., Bhiri, S. (eds.) ICSOC 2014. LNCS, vol. 8831, pp. 230–244. Springer, Heidelberg (2014). https://doi.org/10.1007/978-3-662-45391-9_16

17. Palma, F., Gonzalez-Huerta, J., Founi, M., Moha, N., Tremblay, G., Guéhéneuc, Y.G.: Semantic analysis of RESTful APIs for the detection of linguistic patterns and antipatterns. Int. J. Coop. Inf. Syst. **26**(02), 1742001 (2017)

18. Palma, F., Gonzalez-Huerta, J., Moha, N., Guéhéneuc, Y.-G., Tremblay, G.: Are RESTful APIs well-designed? Detection of their linguistic (anti)patterns. In: Barros, A., Grigori, D., Narendra, N.C., Dam, H.K. (eds.) ICSOC 2015. LNCS, vol. 9435, pp. 171–187. Springer, Heidelberg (2015). https://doi.org/10.1007/978-3-662-48616-0_11

19. Pautasso, C.: RESTful web services: principles, patterns, emerging technologies. In: Bouguettaya, A., Sheng, Q., Daniel, F. (eds.) Web Services Foundations, pp. 31–51. Springer, New York (2014). https://doi.org/10.1007/978-1-4614-7518-7_2

20. Petrillo, F., Merle, P., Moha, N., Guéhéneuc, Y.-G.: Are REST APIs for cloud computing well-designed? An exploratory study. In: Sheng, Q.Z., Stroulia, E., Tata, S., Bhiri, S. (eds.) ICSOC 2016. LNCS, vol. 9936, pp. 157–170. Springer, Cham (2016). https://doi.org/10.1007/978-3-319-46295-0_10

21. Renzel, D., Schlebusch, P., Klamma, R.: Today's top "RESTful" services and why they are not RESTful. In: Wang, X.S., Cruz, I., Delis, A., Huang, G. (eds.) WISE 2012. LNCS, vol. 7651, pp. 354–367. Springer, Heidelberg (2012). https://doi.org/10.1007/978-3-642-35063-4_26

22. Richardson, L., Ruby, S.: RESTful Web Services, 1st edn. O'Reilly Media Inc., Sebastopol (2007)

23. Rodríguez, C., et al.: REST APIs: a large-scale analysis of compliance with principles and best practices. In: Bozzon, A., Cudre-Maroux, P., Pautasso, C. (eds.) ICWE 2016. LNCS, vol. 9671, pp. 21–39. Springer, Cham (2016). https://doi.org/10.1007/978-3-319-38791-8_2

24. Schermann, G., Cito, J., Leitner, P.: All the services large and micro: revisiting industrial practice in services computing. In: Norta, A., Gaaloul, W., Gangadharan, G.R., Dam, H.K. (eds.) ICSOC 2015. LNCS, vol. 9586, pp. 36–47. Springer, Heidelberg (2016). https://doi.org/10.1007/978-3-662-50539-7_4

25. Vernon, W.: The Delphi technique: a review. Int. J. Ther. Rehabil. **16**(2), 69–76 (2009)

26. Webber, J., Parastatidis, S., Robinson, I.: REST in Practice: Hypermedia and Systems Architecture, 1st edn. O'Reilly Media Inc., Sebastopol (2010)

27. Wohlin, C., Höst, M., Henningsson, K.: Empirical research methods in software engineering. In: Conradi, R., Wang, A.I. (eds.) Empirical Methods and Studies in Software Engineering. LNCS, vol. 2765, pp. 7–23. Springer, Heidelberg (2003). https://doi.org/10.1007/978-3-540-45143-3_2

From Code Refactoring to API Refactoring: Agile Service Design and Evolution

Mirko Stocker$^{(\boxtimes)}$ and Olaf Zimmermann

University of Applied Sciences of Eastern Switzerland (OST), Oberseestrasse 10,
8640 Rapperswil, Switzerland
{mirko.stocker,olaf.zimmermann}@ost.ch

Abstract. Refactoring is an essential agile practice; microservices are a currently trending implementation approach for service-oriented architectures. While program-internal code refactoring is well established, refactoring components on the architectural level has been researched but not adopted widely in practice yet. Hence, refactoring service Application Programming Interfaces (APIs) is not understood well to date. As a consequence, practitioners struggle with the evolution of APIs exposed by microservices. To overcome this problem, we propose to switch the refactoring perspective from implementation to integration and study how refactorings can be applied to the problem domain of agile service API design and evolution. We start with an empirical analysis and assessment of the state of the art and the practice. The contributions of this paper then are: 1) presentation of results from a practitioner survey on API change and evolution, 2) definitions for a future practice of API refactoring and 3) a candidate catalog of such API refactorings. We discuss these contributions and propose a research action plan as well.

Keywords: Agile practices · Application programming interfaces · Design patterns · Microservice architectures · Refactoring · Service evolution

1 Introduction

Message-based remote Application Programming Interfaces (APIs) have become an important feature of modern distributed software systems [32]. Software functionality is increasingly provided not just through end-user facing applications, but also via APIs. These allow mobile clients, Web applications, and third parties to integrate API capabilities into their own applications and to combine different APIs to address new use cases. Such API-based integration approaches impact the software architectures and how these are developed and deployed: a growing number of distributed services must work together and communicate [8,18]. Independent of the technologies and protocols used, messages travel through one

© Springer Nature Switzerland AG 2021
J. Barzen (Ed.): SummerSOC 2021, CCIS 1429, pp. 174–193, 2021.
https://doi.org/10.1007/978-3-030-87568-8_11

or several APIs, placing high demands on quality aspects of the API implementation – in many application scenarios, API implementations have to be highly available, reliable, responsive and scalable.

During the first phases of developing a new API, especially in agile development, the focus is on implementing features (or even just a Minimum Viable Product[1], Walking Skeleton [7] or proof of concept). Questions about reliability, performance and scalability might not have a high priority yet; information on how the API will be used by clients is missing but required to make informed decisions. One could just guess and try to anticipate how potential clients will use the API, but that would not be prudent and violate agile values. For instance, one related lean principle is to make decisions at the most responsible moment[2]. Even if quality aspects of an API were to be highly ranked in the development team's priorities, the API implementation is likely to be created before any real client is using it; so even if the developers wanted to, there would still be no way to measure the actual usage and resulting quality characteristics.

Once the API is in production and receives real-world request traffic, quality issues start to surface. An API that has been published and is used by clients should not be changed ad hoc without carefully considering the positive and/or negative implications. Different strategies exist to mitigate these risks; many of these have been documented as design patterns [15]. For example, an API can use *Semantic Versioning*, so clients can compare versions of an API. The *Two in Production* pattern shows how multiple versions of an API can be provided so that clients can gradually switch to a new version.

Refactoring is a technique for improving the structure of a software system without changing its external/observable behavior [6] – typical concerns are maintainability and readability of the source code. The purpose of a refactoring can also be the alignment of the software with a design pattern [10]. Architectural refactorings [21] aim at improving the future evolvability of the software on the architecture level. Such coarser-grained refactorings "improve at least one quality attribute without changing the scope and functionality of the system" [28].

In this context, this paper presents the results of a practitioner survey that aims at understanding the reasons that force software architects and API developers to change an API and also the consequences of such changes. The survey addresses the following knowledge questions:

- *Q1: What causes API changes?*
- *Q2: How often are quality issues the cause of an API change?*
- *Q3: How do architects and developers mitigate the found issues?*

Taking the survey results into account, our second contribution is to propose a new form of refactoring – *API Refactoring* – to evolve APIs towards patterns:

---

[1] http://www.syncdev.com/minimum-viable-product/.
[2] http://wirfs-brock.com/blog/2011/01/18/agile-architecture-myths-2-architecture-decisions-should-be-made-at-the-last-responsible-moment/.

Improve quality aspects of message-based remote APIs by offering refactoring and continuous API evolution practices, including actionable step-by-step instructions to help API architects and developers mitigate quality issues and evolve their APIs rapidly and reliably.

The remainder of the paper is structured as follows. Section 2 introduces fundamental concepts and discusses the state of the art and the practice in API refactoring. Section 3 describes the survey design, Sect. 4 its results. Section 5 then proposes a definition of API refactoring and outlines a catalog of candidate refactorings, targeting the survey participants' wants and needs. Section 6 critically reviews our approach and presents an action plan for further research. Section 7 summarizes the paper and gives an outlook to future work.

2   Background/Context and Related Work

Microservice and API Domain Terminology. In a *message-based remote API*, a message is sent to a receiver, which must then serve it (e.g., dispatch to an object running inside it, or pass the message on to another receiver). The dispatch/delegation policy and its implementation is hidden from the sender, who can not make any assumptions about the receiver-side programming model and service instance lifecycles. In contrast, remote procedure calls do not only model remote service invocations, but also bind server-side subprogram runs to the service instances they are invoked on; such instances (e.g., remote objects) are visible across the network. While we deal with remote calls, we do not assume that these remote calls are remote *procedure* calls. Message-based remoting services can be realized in multiple technologies and platforms including RESTful HTTP, Web services (WSDL/SOAP), WebSockets, and even gRPC (despite its name). API calls come as HTTP *methods* operating on *resources* identified by URIs and appearing in messages as resource *representations*. A service is a component with a remote interface according to M. Fowler[3]; it exposes one or more API endpoints (for instance, resources in RESTful HTTP APIs) which bundle one or more operations (for instance, HTTP POST and GET operations) [32].

Gray Literature on API, Cloud Application and Service Design. Platform-specific design heuristics for designing highly available and reliable applications include the Amazon Web Services (AWS) Well-Architected Framework[4] or the Microsoft Azure Well-Architected Framework[5]. Such heuristics and guidelines focus on architectural aspects that lead to applications that are well suited to run in the respective clouds of these providers, but not on API implementation-design aspects. They also do not cover the refactoring of existing applications.

Combining refactorings and patterns is discussed in [10], which defines *refactoring to patterns* as "[..] the marriage of refactoring [..] with patterns, the classic

---

[3] https://martinfowler.com/articles/injection.html.

[4] https://aws.amazon.com/architecture/well-architected.

[5] https://docs.microsoft.com/en-us/azure/architecture/framework.

solutions to recurring design problems. [..] We improve designs with patterns by applying sequences of low-level design transformations, known as refactorings." In our context, APIs can be refactored to align more closely with specific patterns, or to switch between pattern alternatives that have similar forces but different consequences.

Academic Publications on API Design and Evolution. API design and evolution concern rather different stakeholders; therefore, we find related work in different research communities, including enterprise computing, software architecture, software evolution and maintenance, and service-oriented computing.

It has been researched how Web service API evolution affects clients; the challenges to be overcome include dealing with newly added rate limits [22] or changes in authentication and authorization rules [14]. This study classifies change patterns as refactorings and non-refactorings and that "web API evolves in limited patterns" and concludes that "a tool addressing all these patterns could potentially automate the migration of clients". Similarly, [24] identified and categorized API changes and how developers react to these changes by analyzing discussions on StackOverflow[6], a Q&A website for developers.

The refactoring of local, program-internal APIs and the role of such refactorings during software evolution and maintenance has been well researched empirically [3–5,12]; to the best of our knowledge, the refactoring and evolution of remote APIs, however, has not been investigated much yet. Design principles, architectural smells and refactorings for microservices are covered in a multifocal review [17]. Another publication show how applications can be split into services and how local interfaces can be transferred into remote ones [13].

Quality of service aspects of services has been the focus of several studies [16,20,26]. Other research has focused on operational qualities [1]. For instance, we presented a decision model for guiding architectural decisions on quality aspects in microservice APIs in our previous work [25].

3   Research Method

We initiated our empirical research with a survey among software engineering professionals involved in the design, implementation and maintenance of APIs to understand the reasons for API changes and the approaches chosen during API evolution. In this section, we summarize the survey design; our findings will then be discussed in Sect. 4.

Figure 1 shows the workflow during survey design. We chose Microsoft Forms as our survey tool because it provides suitable types of questions (multiple-choice with choices in random order; free-text; Likert scale) and privacy policy[7].

The questionnaire comprises 17 questions, organized into two parts. The first part contains questions about the context of the API and the technologies

---

[6] https://stackoverflow.com/.

[7] https://www.microsoft.com/en-us/servicesagreement/default.aspx.

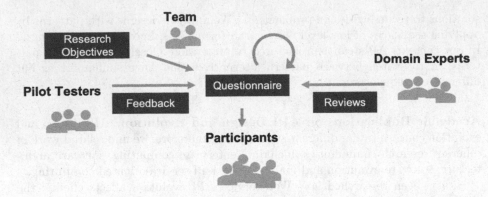

Fig. 1. We designed the questionnaire iteratively: a team-internal brainstorming led to an initial set of questions, which we discussed and refined internally. The first draft of the questionnaire was then sent to several domain experts acting as external reviewers, which provided feedback on the wording of the questions and answering options. A pilot among selected members of the target audience provided further feedback.

used; we asked participants that are involved in several projects to consider their overall experience when answering the questions. The second part of the survey focuses on the forces that drive API changes. We use different types of questions: single- and multiple-choice questions, with a free-form *other* option for additional answers where it makes sense. For questions where there was no natural ordering of the answers, the answers appeared in a random order. For rating questions we used a five-point Likert scale (Never, Rarely, Sometimes, Often, Very Often).

Figure 2 lists the survey questions. We distributed the questionnaire through social media (Twitter, LinkedIn) and via e-mail to our personal networks of professional contacts, asking these contacts to fill out the survey themselves, but also to further distribute the questionnaire within their own networks.

4   Findings

At the time of this writing, we have received 64 completed questionnaires. In this section, we will first look at the usage context and used technologies of the APIs and then begin to answer our research questions with the responses to the second part of the survey.

API Usage Context and Technologies. The first part of the questionnaire aims at understanding the context in which the respondents' APIs are employed and the technologies used. While these responses do not directly contribute to answering our research questions, we can incorporate the articulated

Part 1	Questions about the context and the technologies used:
Q1	Are the users of your API internal in your organization or do external third-parties use the API?
Q2	How many individual end users (e.g., in other teams or companies) access your API via client applications?
Q3	What is the relationship between the API provider (you) and the API client developers?
Q4	How large is the total provider-side code base in terms of lines of code approximately?
Q5	Do you develop the API specification first (e.g. using OpenAPI or Swagger), or do you write the code first and then let tools or frameworks create the specification?
Q6	Which specification or interface definition languages, if any, are you using?
Q7	Which of the following message exchange technologies do you use?
Part 2	**Questions about the forces that drive API changes:**
Q8	What were causes for API changes on your current/past projects?
Q9	Were there other causes for API changes in addition to those listed above? Please also indicate how often these occurred (Never, Rarely, Sometimes, Often, Very Often).
Q10	How often were quality issues the reason for an API change, as opposed to functional changes?
Q11	Which quality attributes were lacking and led to an API change?
Q12	Were there other quality-related problems that led to an API change? Please also indicate how often these occurred (Never, Rarely, Sometimes, Often, Very Often).
Q13	Have you ever decided against changing an API even though there were quality issues? If so, why?
Q14	Which of the following activities do you perform when making changes to an API?
Q15	How do you handle backwards compatibility?
Q16	If you version your API, where do you put the version identifier?
Q17	What do you find the most difficult challenge in API design and evolution?

Fig. 2. The survey questionnaire comprises 17 questions, organized into two parts. See https://forms.office.com/r/R0UjvPHALE for the complete questionnaire.

programming- or specification languages and other preferences when crafting solutions, examples, etc., as discussed in Sect. 6. Of our respondents, 64% have both internal and external clients, 31% have only internal and a mere 4% have just external clients. The numbers of users accessing the API are surprisingly large, with 54% of respondents stating that the API has more than 100 individual end users. The respondents' code bases vary between less than 10k lines of source code up to more than a million lines, with the majority in the 10k to 100k range. Asked about the relationship between the API provider and the API client developers, 57% work together with the clients when changing the API.

We also asked participants about their usage of specification (interface definition) languages and message exchange technologies. The most used specification language is *OpenAPI/Swagger* (see Fig. 3). OpenAPI specification can either be written first and code then generated from it; alternatively, the specification can be generated from annotated program code. Both approaches are common among our respondents, as Fig. 4 shows. The last question in this part of the questionnaire asked about the technologies that are used to exchange messages. As can be seen in Fig. 5, both RESTful and plain HTTP are in the lead, which fits the top response for specification languages.

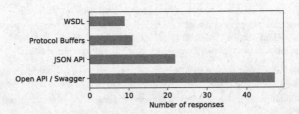

Fig. 3. Which specification or interface definition languages, if any, are you using? – Individually mentioned were Apollo, AsyncAPI, GraphQL, RAML, Apache Avro, XMI/UML, Markdown and "plain text documents without a structured format". Not surprisingly, *OpenAPI/Swagger* came out on top, but older languages such as *WSDL* are still in use as well.

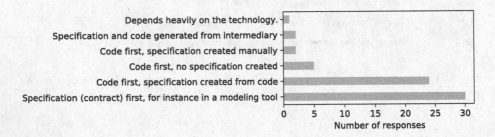

Fig. 4. Do you develop the API specification first, or do you write the code first and then let tools or frameworks create the specification? Overall, the two approaches appear to be equally common.

API Change Drivers. The second part of the questionnaire focuses on the forces that drive API changes and the mitigation tactics applied. To answer our first research question – *What causes API changes?* – we asked participants

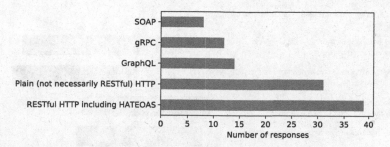

Fig. 5. Which of the following message exchange technologies do you use? – Singular responses were RabbitMQ, Server-Sent Events, Kafka and Java RMI. We were surprised by the high number of "RESTful HTTP including HATEOAS" responses, which seem to contradict earlier empirical observations [19].

about the causes leading to an API change. As shown in Fig. 6, modifications to APIs are most often caused by changed functional requirements, driven by the client or the provider (represented by the first two entries in the figure), whereas non-functional issues were occasionally the cause for a change as well.

The answers to our next question confirms this, as can be seen in Fig. 7. Although functional changes are the main driver behind API changes, quality issues do occur and also result in API changes. Asked about which quality attributes were lacking (Fig. 8), two of them stand out: *usability* and *maintainability*, followed by *performance* and *scalability*.

Change and Mitigation Tactics. When asked to select all actions they perform when changing an API, the top two answers were – unsurprisingly – "update specification or code" and "update API documentation" (see Fig. 9). 59% of the respondents also said that they adjust the API version number, and almost half (43%) also adjust the API clients. These are two important findings for our next steps in designing API refactorings. Backwards compatibility seems to be an important consideration, as can be seen in the answers to our question about the handling of backwards compatibility shown in Fig. 10.

As we saw above, quality issues in APIs do lead to changes, but lack of resources and other priorities also cause developers not to go through with a change. Figure 11 shows the main reasons for deciding against fixing quality issues. With the results from our survey, we can now attempt to find an answer to our initial questions:

- *Q1: What causes API changes?* The main reason for API changes is the introduction of new features, i.e., the provider drives the change. Client-driven changes are also common, but slightly less so.
- *Q2: How often are quality issues the cause of an API change?* Quality issues are common, but not the main driver of API changes. *Usability*, *performance*, and *maintainability* are the most common causes that led to API changes.

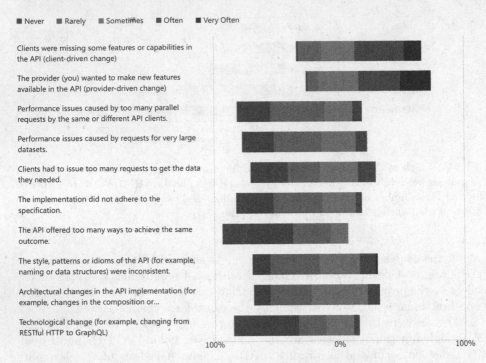

Fig. 6. What were causes for API changes on your current/past projects? The first two scales show that changed functional requirements are most often the cause that lead to API changes.

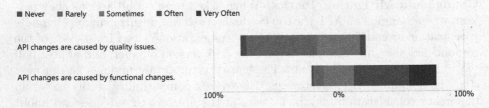

Fig. 7. How often were quality issues the reason for an API change, as opposed to functional changes? The answers reveal a very similar picture to the previous question reported in Fig. 6.

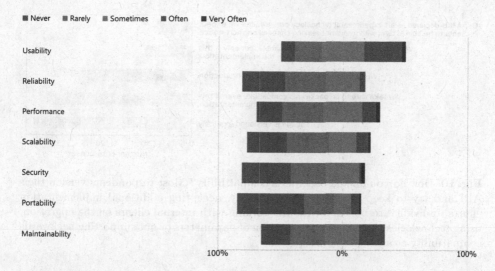

Fig. 8. Which quality attributes were lacking and led to an API change? *Usability* and *maintainability* stand out, followed by *performance* and *scalability*.

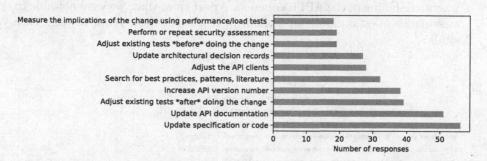

Fig. 9. Which of the following activities do you perform when making changes to an API? The approach to testing seems to differ among respondents: most update their tests after performing a change, suggesting that test-driven development is not used.

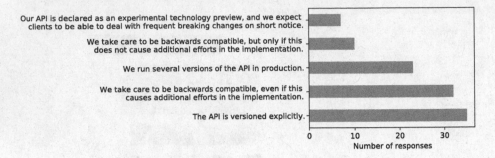

Fig. 10. How do you handle backwards compatibility? Most respondents version their API and try to keep backwards compatibility, accepting additional implementation efforts. Individual responses mentioned working with internal clients on the migration, using technologies that support deprecation of parameters or not supporting backwards compatibility at all.

– *Q3: How do architects and developers mitigate the found issues?* We gained some insights into the steps taken, especially on backwards compatibility, where versioning of the API is common. Apart from that, we were not able to answer this question in detail. Follow-up research will be required (e.g., case studies).

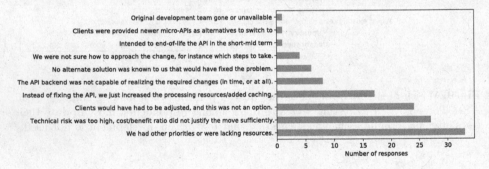

Fig. 11. Have you ever decided against changing an API even though there were quality issues? If so, why? Differing priorities and lack of resources were mentioned as common reasons for not changing an API, followed by the inability to also adjust clients.

The answers to Question 3 deliver candidate refactorings, the answers to Questions 1 and 2 the corresponding smells. Grounding our upcoming research in the survey results – also regarding the respondents' usage of specification languages and message exchange technologies – will increase the chances of getting accepted by developers in practice.

5 Towards API Refactoring

Our survey shows that quality issues in APIs do occur and lead to API changes. One technique to improve non-functional aspects of a software system is refactoring. In this section, we will first review existing types of refactoring and then propose a definition of API refactoring. A draft catalog of candidate API refactorings with scope and smell-resolution pairs derived from the survey results as well as additional input concludes the section.

Definition of Code Refactoring. Fowler defines refactoring as "a change made to the internal structure of software to make it easier to understand and cheaper to modify without changing its observable behavior" [6]. An example of an everyday refactoring is the renaming of a local variable to improve the readability of the code. Not all code cleanup, such as formatting, falls under the umbrella of refactoring, and neither do changes to the software that add new features or fix bugs.

A refactoring is performed as a series of small steps that always keeps the software in a functioning state, and should be accompanied by a comprehensive suite of tests. For example, when moving a method between classes, a forwarding method that delegates calls from the original to the new class can be kept so that callers of the method can be migrated individually.

Refactoring is an essential agile practice: it is one of the extreme programming [2] practices, but also essential in test-driven development as part of the Red-Green-Refactor[8] cycle of development.

Definition of Architecture/Architectural Refactoring. The principles of refactoring can not only be applied to code-level software changes, but also on an architectural level. For instance, Stal defines software architecture refactoring that "improves the architectural structure of a system without changing its intended semantics" [21]. By only ruling out changes to intended semantics, and not the more strict observable behavior, an architectural refactoring allows more radical changes to a software. Zimmermann views Architecture Refactoring as "a coordinated set of deliberate architectural activities that remove a particular architectural smell and improve at least one quality attribute without changing the system's scope and functionality" [27].

An example of an architectural refactoring is the splitting of a monolithic system into several (micro-) services [29]. For example, an e-commerce software could be split into distinct product discovery and order checkout systems. The intended semantics of the overall software stays the same, but the new architecture might allow the individual development teams greater velocity[9].

---

[8] http://www.jamesshore.com/v2/blog/2005/red-green-refactor.

[9] One might argue that this violates the original definition of refactoring because the observable behavior is clearly and deliberately changed. In the refactoring example given earlier, a local variable is renamed, making it unlikely that the observable behavior of the software changes. But refactorings involving multiple classes, for example moving a method from one class to another, change the interfaces of

Proposed Definition of API Refactoring. Due to its hybrid character, we can define API refactoring starting from the above two definitions:

An API refactoring evolves the remote interface of a system without changing its feature set and semantics to improve at least one quality attribute.

API refactoring can be seen as a variant of architectural refactoring – interfaces and their implementations in components are architectural elements – with a focus on controlled evolution. In contrast to code refactorings, an API refactoring can affect the API behavior as observed by clients. The semantics of a specific operation might be changed in a refactoring, but not the overall feature set and semantics of the API. Operating on the boundaries of a system, API providers require an explicit evolution strategy to communicate API changes to clients and manage their expectations. Finally, the goal of an API refactoring is the improvement of at least one quality attribute (e.g., as mentioned in the survey: usability, performance, maintainability) and not to be able to introduce new features or fix bugs more efficiently. Figure 12 compares the different refactoring styles.

	Code Refactoring	API Refactoring	Architectural Refactoring
Improves	Internal structure, maintainability	Interface, many quality attributes	Overall structure, many quality attributes
Target	Source code	Specification, source code, API implementation components	Components, (sub)-systems, documentation, architectural decisions
Impact	Internal only	Externally visible, API clients	Potentially large group of stakeholders (3rd parties, other teams, operations), often system-wide or cross-cutting
Drivers	Code smells, test driven development	Changed client- and provider-side quality requirements, API smells	Changed requirements and constraints, architectural smells
Evolution	Not key, observable behavior unchanged	Important, compatibility with existing clients	Depends on visibility of changes
Examples	Rename, Extract Method, Move Class	Split Endpoint, Inline/Extract Information Holder	Migrate from SQL to NoSQL («De-SQL»), Split Subsystem

Fig. 12. Types of refactorings by scope and stakeholder concerns, according to [6,28] and our own analysis.

---

these classes – possibly including public ones – in a backwards-incompatible manner. Whether this constitutes observable behavior depends on the viewpoint and expectations of the observer: an API client developer might notice and be directly affected by the change, but not the end user of the software. It has been shown that behavior-changing modifications still qualify as refactorings [11].

Let us consider a concrete application of an API refactoring in the following scenario (capitalized pattern names are from the Microservices API Patterns language[10]): You are a developer at Lakeside Mutual, a fictitious insurance company, responsible for the *Policy-Management-Backend* microservice. The service offers an HTTP endpoint to read insurance policy data, as shown in Fig. 13. After the API has been put into production, a performance analysis makes evident that the majority of clients first requests data from the policy endpoint, but then also retrieves the corresponding master data from the customer endpoint (see Fig. 14). By inlining the Information Holder Resource and refactoring to the Embedded Entity pattern, the linked data is now available inside the initial

Fig. 13. The endpoint returns a representation of the requested policy. The response contains a reference to a `customerId` Linked Information Holder. See www.microservice-api-patterns.org for more information on the patterns and icons.

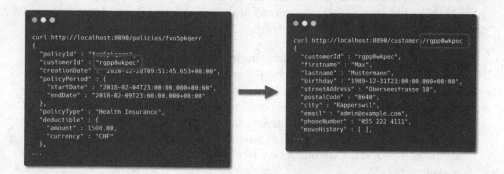

Fig. 14. The customer data can be retrieved by using the `customerId` in a follow-up request to its Master Data Holder endpoint.

---

[10] https://www.microservice-api-patterns.org, also see [15,22,30,31,33].

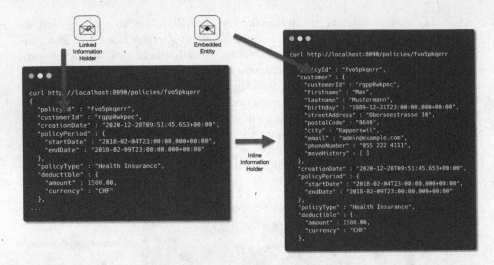

Fig. 15. Applying the Inline Information Holder refactoring, the Linked Information Holder can be replaced with an Embedded Entity.

response message, saving clients the additional request and avoiding underfetching. Figure 15 shows the resulting response structure. While the consequences of applying this refactoring are beneficial for some clients, those not requiring the additional data now face increased message sizes and transfer times. The processing and database retrieval effort in the endpoint increases as well. Alternative patterns that the API can be refactored to are Wish List and Wish Template [32]. These two patterns let the client inform the provider about its data interests.

Draft Catalog of Candidate Refactorings. The survey results unveil a few quality concerns that can be addressed with API refactorings, for instance in the area of performance. Also taking our previous work [17] into account and reflecting on our own industry projects and action research, we have collected the following list of candidate refactorings for further elaboration[11]:

- *Inline Information Holder:* Reduce indirection by directly embedding referenced information holder resources. Figure 16 details this refactoring in a table format adapted from [27].
- *Extract Information Holder:* Decrease message size by replacing embedded entities with linked information holders.
- *Introduce Payload Feature Toggle:* Lessen the mismatch between client expectations and provider capabilities by letting the client decide on the response message content.
- *Introduce Pagination:* Reduce response data set size by dividing large data sets into chunks.

---

[11] At https://interface-refactoring.github.io we have started to publish these refactorings; names and content of the refactoring are subject to change.

- *Collapse Operations:* Enhance discoverability by reducing the number of distinct operations.
- *Move Operation:* Improve cohesion by shifting an operation from one endpoint to another.
- *Rename Endpoint:* Increase developer usability by making the name of an endpoint more expressive and accurate.
- *Split Endpoint:* Move one or more operations to a new endpoint so that coupling between the operations in an endpoint is reduced.
- *Merge Endpoints:* Collapse two endpoints that are tightly coupled.

Note that we articulate the candidate refactorings in the API design vocabulary we established in previous work [32]. This wording differs substantially form that used in the survey reported on in the Sects. 3 and 4 of this paper. We avoided our own pattern terminology as much as possible in the survey to avoid or reduce bias; more specifically, we did not want to steer participants towards desired responses.

When answering research Question 2 in the survey in Sect. 4, usability, performance, scalability and maintainability were reported as the most common causes that led to API changes (see Fig. 8). Inline Information Holder and Rename Endpoint can improve usability, while Extract Information Holder aims at improving performance and scalability. Introduce Payload Feature Toggle and Introduce Pagination also aim at improving these two qualities, but can have a negative impact on maintainability. The remaining candidates address high cohesion and low coupling, general API design principles that did not come out of the survey (it is worth noting that we did not ask about them explicitly). See Fig. 17 for a mapping of causes of API changes to suggested refactorings.

6   Discussion of Preliminary Results and Action Plan

Pros and Cons. API refactoring is a new (some might say yet another) practice. It picks up another, commonly applied one to reduce the learning effort. A related risk is that a different intuitive understanding, that of code refactoring, might cause undesired irritation. The community might argue about the criteria for inclusion/exclusion of refactorings in the catalog: does it claim to be complete? To mitigate this effect we started from the survey results and applied the "rule of three" from the patterns community[12]. Just like code refactoring requires unit testing, API refactoring requires automated API testing so that it can be practiced safely. Tests should ensure that an API refactoring does not accidentally change the request- or response message structures, endpoints or other API elements. Such tests likely have to cover multiple API calls that jointly deliver a particular integration functionality or API feature.

---

[12] Only include a pattern if there are at least three known uses. Not to be confused with the "rule of three" of refactoring [6] duplicated pieces of code, where it refers to the number of duplicates starting from which a refactoring is recommended.

Refactoring	Inline Information Holder
Motivation	Reduce indirection by directly embedding referenced information holder resources.
Smell	Clients have to issue follow-up requests to get the information they need.
Preconditions	The resource to be inlined should be part of the same service implementing the endpoint. Otherwise, the refactoring might introduce undesired dependencies between services.
Steps	1. Add additional attributes to the data transfer object (DTO; code first) or models (design/contract first). 2. From the implementation of the the linked information holder endpoint, copy the code to retrieve the additional entity or value. 3. Paste the code into the endpoint implementation and add the entity/value to the DTO. 4. Remove the link to the inlined resource. 5. Run tests to observe the changed responses; adjust tests to the new response structure. 6. Clean up the implementation code if necessary (observe the *Rule of Three* of refactoring [7]), for example, by moving duplicated code to a common implementation. 7. If under your control, adjust API clients to remove the unneeded API calls. 8. Adjust API description, sample code, tutorials, etc. where needed.
Evolution Strategy	If the refactoring only adds additional information to the response message, the refactoring is backwards compatible. Otherwise, consider applying a *MAP Evolution* pattern: *Experimental Preview, Semantic Versioning, Two in Production* or *Limited Lifetime Guarantee.*
Inverse	Extract Information Holder

Fig. 16. The Inline Information Holder refactoring reduces indirection by directly embedding an entity instead of indirectly referencing it with a link.

Causes for API Changes	Suggested API Refactoring
Clients were missing some features or capabilities in the API (client-driven change)	N/A
The provider (you) wanted to make new features available in the API (provider-driven change)	N/A
Performance issues caused by too many parallel requests by the same or different API clients.	Extract Information Holder
Performance issues caused by requests for very large datasets.	Introduce Payload Feature Toggle, Introduce Pagination
Clients had to issue too many requests to get the data they needed.	Inline Information Holder
The implementation did not adhere to the specification.	Move Operation, Rename Endpoint
The API offered too many ways to achieve the same outcome.	Merge Endpoint, Collapse Operations
The style, patterns or idioms of the API (for example, naming or data structures) were inconsistent.	Split, Merge or Rename Endpoint
Architectural changes in the API implementation (for example, changes in composition or responsibilities of backend services)	Split, Merge or Rename Endpoint and Operations
Technological change (for example, changing from RESTful HTTP to GraphQL)	N/A (Architectural Refactoring)

Fig. 17. Suggested refactorings for different causes of API changes. Causes for which refactoring is not the right technique – i.e., those where features are added – are marked with N/A. For technological changes, an architectural refactoring might be applicable.

Threats to Validity (of Research Results). When designing the questionnaire, conducting the survey, and analyzing the results, we applied general guidelines for survey design [9]. Several threats to the validity of our results remain. The questionnaire was distributed by e-mail and social media, which is not representative of the overall population. While we did state in the invitation to the survey and also in the introduction of the questionnaire that we target "software architects, engineers and technical product owners that specify, implement and maintain message-based remote APIs", we cannot rule out that some participants did not fulfill these requirements. Moreover, targeting a particular industry or domain could lead to different responses, especially regarding technologies used. Nevertheless, the results show that an API refactoring practice would be valuable to practitioners.

Action Plan. The next step in this research are a) gather even more and deeper practitioner knowledge by continuing the analysis, b) describe all refactorings already identified and backed by the survey results in a template similar to that behind Fig. 16, c) implement tool support for selected ones in editors for API description languages (motivated by the survey results in Figs. 3 and 4), and d) validate the usability and usefulness of refactoring catalog and tools empirically (via action research, case studies, and controlled experiments).

The website interface-refactoring.github.io features our emerging API refactoring catalog (i.e., the results of action plan item b).

7   Summary and Outlook

Refactorings offer step-by-step instructions on how to evolve a software system systematically. Combining the agile practice of refactoring with API patterns can help to adapt (micro-)service APIs to changing client demands and quality requirements. Our practitioner survey on API change and evolution motivated the potential use of such a refactoring practice. Taking additional feedback into account, we plan to complete and extend our emerging refactoring catalog and have started to implement tool support for selected high-value refactorings.

A related open research problem is how architectural principles, both general ones such as loose coupling and interface-specific ones such as POINT[13] relate to refactoring. On the one hand, frequent refactoring of continuously evolving architectures can be seen as a principle in itself. On the other hand, violations of other principles may yield API smells suggesting refactorings as well, similar to code/design smells [23]; for instance, if two API operations violate the *I*solated principle in POINT, it might make sense to merge them into one.

Another idea for future work is that of *smart proxies* that mediate between old and new versions of an API in case backward compatibility cannot be assured. Finally, the relation between API refactoring and API testing has to be studied and strengthened.

---

[13] www.ozimmer.ch/practices/2021/03/05/POINTPrinciplesForAPIDesign.html.

Acknowledgments. We would like to thank all reviewers and participants of the survey. The work of Mirko Stocker and Olaf Zimmermann is supported by the Hasler Foundation through grant nr. 21004.

References

1. Balalaie, A., Heydarnoori, A., Jamshidi, P.: Microservices architecture enables DevOps: migration to a cloud-native architecture. IEEE Softw. **33**(3), 42–52 (2016)
2. Beck, K., Andres, C.: Extreme Programming Explained: Embrace Change, 2nd edn. Addison-Wesley Professional, Boston (2004)
3. Cossette, B.E., Walker, R.J.: Seeking the ground truth: a retroactive study on the evolution and migration of software libraries. In: Proceedings of the ACM SIG-SOFT 20th International Symposium on the Foundations of Software Engineering. FSE 2012. Association for Computing Machinery, New York (2012)
4. Dig, D., Johnson, R.: The role of refactorings in API evolution. In: 21st IEEE International Conference on Software Maintenance (ICSM 2005), pp. 389–398 (2005)
5. Dig, D., Johnson, R.: How do APIs evolve? A story of refactoring: research articles. J. Softw. Maint. Evol. **18**(2), 83–107 (2006)
6. Fowler, M.: Refactoring. Addison-Wesley Signature Series (Fowler). Addison-Wesley, Boston. 2 edn. (2018)
7. Hunt, A., Thomas, D.: The Pragmatic Programmer: From Journeyman to Master. Addison-Wesley, Boston (2000)
8. Jamshidi, P., Pahl, C., Mendonca, N.C., Lewis, J., Tilkov, S.: Microservices: the journey so far and challenges ahead. IEEE Softw. **35**(03), 24–35 (2018)
9. Kasunic, M.: Designing an Effective Survey. Software Engineering Institute (2005)
10. Kerievsky, J.: Refactoring to Patterns. Pearson Higher Education (2004)
11. Kim, M., Zimmermann, T., Nagappan, N.: A field study of refactoring challenges and benefits. In: Proceedings of the ACM SIGSOFT 20th International Symposium on the Foundations of Software Engineering. FSE 2012, Association for Computing Machinery, New York (2012)
12. Kula, R.G., Ouni, A., German, D.M., Inoue, K.: An empirical study on the impact of refactoring activities on evolving client-used APIs. Inf. Softw. Technol. **93**, 186–199 (2018)
13. Kwon, Y.W., Tilevich, E.: Cloud refactoring: automated transitioning to cloud-based services. Autom. Softw. Eng. **21**(3), 345–372 (2014)
14. Li, J., Xiong, Y., Liu, X., Zhang, L.: How does web service API evolution affect clients? In: 2013 IEEE 20th International Conference on Web Services, pp. 300–307 (2013)
15. Lübke, D., Zimmermann, O., Stocker, M., Pautasso, C., Zdun, U.: Interface evolution patterns - balancing compatibility and extensibility across service life cycles. In: Proceedings of the 24th EuroPLoP conference. EuroPLoP 2019 (2019)
16. Menascé, D.A.: QoS issues in web services. IEEE Internet Comput. **6**(6), 72–75 (2002)
17. Neri, D., Soldani, J., Zimmermann, O., Brogi, A.: Design principles, architectural smells and refactorings for microservices: a multivocal review. SICS Softw. Intensive Cyber Phys. Syst. **35**(1), 3–15 (2020)
18. Pautasso, C., Zimmermann, O., Amundsen, M., Lewis, J., Josuttis, N.M.: Microservices in practice, part 2: service integration and sustainability. IEEE Softw. **34**(2), 97–104 (2017)

19. Rodríguez, C., et al.: REST APIs: a large-scale analysis of compliance with principles and best practices. In: Bozzon, A., Cudre-Maroux, P., Pautasso, C. (eds.) ICWE 2016. LNCS, vol. 9671, pp. 21–39. Springer, Cham (2016). https://doi.org/10.1007/978-3-319-38791-8_2

20. Rosenberg, F., Celikovic, P., Michlmayr, A., Leitner, P., Dustdar, S.: An end-to-end approach for QoS-aware service composition. In: IEEE International Conference on Enterprise Distributed Object Computing Conference (EDOC 2009), pp. 151–160. IEEE (2009)

21. Stal, M.: Agile Software Architecture. Morgan Kaufmann (12 2013)

22. Stocker, M., Zimmermann, O., Lübke, D., Zdun, U., Pautasso, C.: Interface quality patterns - communicating and improving the quality of microservices APIs. In: Proceedings of the 23nd EuroPLoP conference. EuroPLoP 2018 (2018)

23. Suryanarayana, G., Sharma, T., Samarthyam, G.: Software process versus design quality: tug of war? IEEE Softw. $32(4)$, 7–11 (2015)

24. Wang, S., Keivanloo, I., Zou, Y.: How do developers react to RESTful API evolution? In: Franch, X., Ghose, A.K., Lewis, G.A., Bhiri, S. (eds.) ICSOC 2014. LNCS, vol. 8831, pp. 245–259. Springer, Heidelberg (2014). https://doi.org/10.1007/978-3-662-45391-9_17

25. Zdun, U., Stocker, M., Zimmermann, O., Pautasso, C., Lübke, D.: Guiding architectural decision making on quality aspects in microservice APIs. In: 16th International Conference on Service-Oriented Computing ICSOC 2018, pp. 78–89, November 2018

26. Zeng, L., Benatallah, B., Dumas, M., Kalagnanam, J., Sheng, Q.Z.: Quality driven web services composition. In: Proceedings of the 12th International Conference on World Wide Web, pp. 411–421. ACM (2003)

27. Zimmermann, O.: Architectural refactoring: a task-centric view on software evolution. IEEE Softw. $32(2)$, 26–29 (2015)

28. Zimmermann, O.: Architectural refactoring for the cloud: decision-centric view on cloud migration. Computing $99(2)$, 129–145 (2017)

29. Zimmermann, O.: Microservices tenets. Comput. Sci. $32(3\text{–}4)$, 301–310 (2017)

30. Zimmermann, O., Lübke, D., Zdun, U., Pautasso, C., Stocker, M.: Interface responsibility patterns: processing resources and operation responsibilities. In: Proceedings of the 25th EuroPLoP conference. EuroPLoP 2020 (2020)

31. Zimmermann, O., Pautasso, Cesare Lübke, D., Zdun, U., Stocker, M.: Data-oriented interface responsibility patterns: types of information holder resources. In: Proceedings of the 25th EuroPLoP conference. EuroPLoP 2020 (2020)

32. Zimmermann, O., Stocker, M., Lübke, D., Pautasso, C., Zdun, U.: Introduction to microservice API patterns (MAP). In: Cruz-Filipe, L., Giallorenzo, S., Montesi, F., Peressotti, M., Rademacher, F., Sachweh, S. (eds.) Joint Post-proceedings of the First and Second International Conference on Microservices (Microservices 2017/2019), vol. 78, pp. 4:1–4:17 (2020)

33. Zimmermann, O., Stocker, M., Lübke, D., Zdun, U.: Interface representation patterns: crafting and consuming message-based remote APIs. In: Proceedings of the 22nd EuroPLop, EuroPLoP 2017, pp. 27:1–27:36. ACM (2017)

Author Index

Printed in the United States
by Baker & Taylor Publisher Services

Printed in the United States
by Baker & Taylor Publisher Services